PRAISE FOR **I** (**T**

T0282121

"*(I Think) I Want Out* is a   e for
couples questioning whether to stay together. It shows ... ... how
to be discerning about their relationship in collaborative, conscientious, and caring ways. The many illustrative stories, as well as Dr. Whetstone's openness about her own personal journey, make this a compelling and immediately practical read. This book won't necessarily save all marriages, but it will help couples make wise loving decisions about their future as well as care well together for their children's future. I wish I had had this book to hand to many of the couples that I have treated over the years."

—**David Treadway, PhD,** couple therapist and author of *Treating Couples Well: A Practical Guide to Collaborative Couples Therapy*

"I wish I'd had this book years ago for myself, for my staff, and for my patients because it would have made everyone's life easier when dealing with the pain and chaos of marital crisis. Dr. Becky Whetstone has given us what we've always needed: a clear and simple explanation of the possible causes of a marital crisis, what to do about it, and how to heal from it. Dr. Whetstone doesn't pull any punches. She writes in raw, vivid language about her own experiences and those of others, compelling the reader to ask for more. Dr. Whetstone's method—based on years of research, writing, painful self-observation, and professional work—will provide comfort and direction to millions as they navigate a distressing and painful time in their lives. I applaud Dr. Whetstone for her courage in presenting this helpful and important book."

—**Bick Wanck, MD,** author of *Mind Easing: The 3-Layered Healing Plan for Anxiety and Depression,* founding member of American Academy of Addiction Psychiatry, assistant professor of Clinical Psychiatry at Albany Medical School, and founder and owner of Bick Wanck MD & Associates

I (Think)
I Want
Out

WHAT TO
DO WHEN ONE
OF YOU WANTS
TO END YOUR
MARRIAGE

Becky Whetstone, PhD

Health Communications, Inc.
Boca Raton, Florida
www.hcibooks.com

While the relationships and stories depicted in this work are true, names, cities, ages, and other information that might identify clients mentioned in these pages have been changed.

Library of Congress Cataloging-in-Publication Data
is available through the Library of Congress.

Publisher: Health Communications, Inc.
          301 Crawford Boulevard, Suite 200
          Boca Raton, FL 33432-3762

Cover, interior design, and formatting by Larissa Hise Henoch

For my children,
Benjamin and Casey Marie

Contents

Preface

How does one become interested in the subject of marriage crisis and what to do about it? Probably like you, I never gave one thought to this until I went through one of the most mind-boggling and confusing times of my life: the end stages of a deteriorating marriage and the resulting seismic-level family crisis, a family crisis that decades later has continued aftershocks, affecting more people than I ever thought it could.

My stress reached a crescendo when I told myself, "I can't do this anymore," referring to my marriage. I had sweet-talked, cajoled, complained, bitched, begged, and groaned to my husband of seven years about the state of our marriage for at least five years. "We need to get help," I said, pressing more firmly every time I said it.

We'd go to a marriage counselor, they would give us assignments, we wouldn't do them, and nothing ever changed. The more my marriage didn't change, the more resentful I got. I went from thinking about it a few times a week to a few times a day and then a few times every hour. And then my husband did something so mean-spirited toward me that I hit that moment of distress when my head and heart aligned as if to say, *I can't be around someone who would do something like this.* I felt as if I was under threat, and I felt like one more second in my husband's presence would cause me to implode, run screaming out of the house, or worse.

Very soon after that moment, I told him by phone that we had to talk when he came home from work. He knew something was up. He came in and sat in our newly redone master bedroom while I stood in front of him and said, "We need to separate. I can't take it anymore."

He was completely closed to the idea of separation, and I felt I'd have to jump off a building if he stayed, so we went back to the marriage counselor to find out what course of action to take. The counselor said, "Becky, you have zero motivation to work on this marriage right now; there is nothing I can do. Come back if that changes." Then he looked at my husband and said, "And yes, you need to move out for a while."

We left and began to manage a family crisis in the most disastrous way—with no rhyme, reason, or timeline. After years of his overachieving workaholism, neglect, and no romance, plus numerous angry explosions every time I brought up his lack of interest in our marriage, I was angry as hell, in an entitled state of mind, and I stupidly began dating, creating unnecessary complications. We separated, and like a car driven by a cat, we swerved around, hurt each other, made mistakes, and eventually drove off the cliff. Our two children, Benjamin, age six, and Casey Marie, age three, picked up the tab because of our inability to understand what was going on and how best to handle it. Decisions we made then affected all of us for decades and not in the best way. How I wish I could go back and handle things differently.

The craziest thing of all was, why couldn't a marriage therapist help us? That question got to me more than anything. What on earth are therapists learning in school? I would find out years later when I went to graduate school to study marriage and family therapy. I learned they don't teach much about the subject; it's something you have to take a special interest in, and a lot of therapists like to avoid high-stress crisis situations.

In the years since then, I've had a lot of time to think and reflect. I've thought and reflected so much that I decided the answer is that marriage therapists need to be required to understand and specialize in marital crisis, separation, and helping couples with the decision to divorce, but there also needs to be high-quality, research-based information available to the public about what to do. Do a quick Google search, and you'll find there is almost no mainstream information available for people from therapists and others who actually know what they're talking about.

With more American adults having at least one divorce under their belts, you'd think that there'd be plenty of information available. In the last ten years, I have noticed laypeople creating websites and sharing different ideas they have about getting your partner back. I've also noticed some well-meaning marriage therapists have developed extremely short-term therapy meant to propel couples out of indecision to take action one way or the other, but there still aren't that many therapists who are thoroughly versed in managing the many months of time a marriage crisis is likely to endure. The lack of this is a blight on our profession, in my opinion.

My divorce experience was so traumatic that it ended up lighting a bonfire in my belly, affecting me so strongly that I decided to make it a life mission to learn what could be done to help people through

the darkness and confusion of a marital crisis. My interest in relationship dynamics didn't just pop up when my marriage imploded; I
had always wanted to be an advice columnist like Ann Landers, Dear
Abby, or Dr. Joyce Brothers, and I'd read about relationships from
them and other experts in newspapers and self-help books since I
was a young teen. But my marriage crisis turned me in the direction
of wanting to understand what was going on in a marriage crisis and
what to do about it.

I began seeking answers. Once I was a single mom, I became a
journalist who wrote and talked about relationships in the local San
Antonio newspaper and on television and radio. It was sort of like a
Sex and the City and Carrie Bradshaw sort of thing before that even
existed. I wrote about dating, being a single mom, raising kids, and
how to be healthy in relationships. That was great, such a powerful
venue, and the column was undeniably popular, but it wasn't enough.
I could offer advice, sure, but I couldn't help people one-on-one, and
quite frankly, I needed more knowledge and understanding than I
got from the pile of mainstream books I was reading and the therapists I was interviewing. At that time, I'd seen a few statistics, but I'd
never read any research on the subject and had never read a "serious"
book or seen a presentation by academics who had done research
and analysis regarding relationships, marriage, and divorce.

Finally, I got more serious about learning, and in 2001, I started
graduate school to get a master's and doctorate in marriage and
family therapy. For the next five years, I focused on marital deterioration and studied every aspect of relationships I could find, from
how people meet and decide to marry to then going from feeling all
that love and hopefulness to wanting to end it altogether. My own
dissertation research was about the decision-making process that

leads to divorce in long-term marriages of ten years or more. It was during this one year of intensive study that I came to understand fully how marriages end and how some of them that end could have been saved.

And although I wish couples would bring their marriages into therapists early before so much damage has been done, I have come to realize through experience and working with couples why so many don't. I also learned how a separation, if done properly with a structure and plan, can be a crucial step in the dance to save a marriage. The problem I have seen, however, is that there are couples who separate who should *not* and others who do not separate who *should*. Most of the ones who do separate do it with no rhyme or reason, just like I did years ago, and either way, these people have no idea what they're doing and end up making a mess of their lives when they might have had a better outcome. To me, ending up divorced unnecessarily or prematurely, with children in the mix, is one of life's great preventable tragedies.

Once I finished my education and got licensed, I hung out my shingle to see adults, couples, and families in private practice in San Antonio, Texas. I used my knowledge about the marriage crisis to help people through the fog they were feeling, but when it came time to consider separation, there was no formalized way to do that in Texas.

Legal separation is not recognized in Texas, and a person has to file for divorce even if that is not what they want because it's the only way a couple can ensure that one person leaves the household and financial and custody agreements can be enforced. To most of my clients, this was completely overkill and unnecessary. Just the idea of filing for divorce to be able to separate with a plan terrified my clients, so I went home from work one night and wrote down a separation agreement and plan that my clients could use. I called it a managed separation agreement, using the word *managed* because part of it was that a therapist or trusted source had to oversee and make clients accountable to the process and to make sure that couples were moving forward and not becoming stagnant. Stagnation in separation leads to separation limbo, which is a bit like feeling ambivalent toward the end of a marriage, but it is now ambivalence about making a decision while separated. This is exactly the type of situation that this agreement sought to avoid.

When I separated, I estimated that I'd need a year to even be able to consider working things out with my husband. Now, I know that this was too long. Unwilling to wait that long, or any length of time at all, my husband rushed and pressured me into making a decision quickly, giving me all of two weeks to decide—another huge mistake. When I manage separations now for couples, we make sure the time frame is not too short or long, and we keep tabs on how each person is faring to see if anything needs to be adjusted.

To make it available to more people, I created a website called Marriage Crisis Manager (www.MarriageCrisisManager.com), where people can read about the basic dynamics of a marriage crisis and download a separation agreement for a fee if they feel it would be helpful. Since then, hundreds of people have downloaded it and used it to save their marriages.

You can manage your marriage crisis on your own or with the guidance, wisdom, and compassion of your therapist, which I recommend. If you do end up deciding to divorce, it's my hope that you will have the peace of mind that you have done all you can to save your marriage and have concluded that ending the marriage, although sad, is the wisest and best decision for you and your spouse.

In this book, I have provided something that I wish had been available in 1992 when I was facing my marriage crisis. It is my sincere hope that this fills the gap that remains and provides you with some peace of mind during a very difficult time. You will get through this, and I'm here to help, support, and encourage you throughout.

A Note to the Reader

If you are reading these words, chances are your marriage or relationship is in deep trouble, and you are agonizing about what to do about it. If you had all the answers and understood exactly what's going on, you wouldn't be looking here now, and I know that.

Please don't beat yourself up for feeling uncertain and confused. It's perfectly normal to not know what to do. No average person should know or understand what's going on and what is the best thing to do when a relationship reaches the crossroad of the decision, "Do I stay or go?" The answer to that question is almost never clear-cut and can be wildly complicated. Add to that the terror of possibly making a choice that you'll regret, and most often a person stands miserably in his or her own indecision and chooses not to choose. The fact that so many people are confused or anxious during a marriage crisis is why I have written this book. I want to guide you out of the fog, help you find a direction, keep you moving forward, and help you end up with an outcome that was well-thought-out and in the higher interest of all.

Leaning In or Leaning Out?

A marriage crisis is preceded by one person carrying a secret, and the secret is that they are seriously and unceasingly unhappy in the marriage. The person who will initiate the marriage crisis, the Decider, has been having an internal conversation about what to do about their discontentment, never fully sharing their secret with their spouse. They have been sitting in a chronically unhappy state of not knowing whether to go or stay while having no idea that the limbo in which they are suspended won't last. Without realizing it, they are in a deterioration process that will lead to a moment of stress so intense that all of a sudden, everything they have been telling themselves about why they must stay ceases to matter, and the urge to run becomes overwhelming. That might be where you or your spouse are right now. It is when the secret is revealed, and the announcement of marital unhappiness or the suggestion of divorce is made, that a couple is propelled into a marriage crisis.

Even after a person announces, "I am unhappy," or "I think I want a divorce," and a marriage crisis begins, the marital ambivalence is likely to continue, and that is where I come in with strategies designed to delicately push a person out of indecision. The Decider, who has revealed their unhappiness, is often on the fence, fearful about making a decision they'll regret. The Leaning-In partner is in full panic mode, frantically seeking and trying ways to get the Decider to change their mind.

This book is about educating the Decider and the Leaning-In partner about what is going on; how to slow down the process enough that positive and thoughtful decision-making and action can take place; how to minimize the chances of the marriage getting stuck in the marriage crisis limbo; and how to do everything we can to prevent premature, unwise decision-making that so often takes place during a marriage crisis. We care passionately about assisting you in making the best decision for you and your family.

Ending a marriage or going through the effort to work things out is one of life's most crucial choices. Whether you are the one who wants to leave or the one who wants the marriage to survive, the information here will tell you what to expect and the wisest things to do in the middle of the confusion of a family hurricane. What I'll be asking of you will be difficult and require more self-control than you have ever had to muster, but it will be worth it.

I understand all this, of course. I've actually been on both sides of the equation. I have left a husband (1992), and a husband has left me (2002). Marital partings are rarely mutual decisions as depicted in books or movies. Instead, one person initiates the crisis, which will wake up their spouse from their usual state of marital apathy and cause them to begin a fierce quest to save the marriage. For both parties, it is a confusing and frightening time. Survival instinct kicks in, the Decider will go into flight mode while a Leaning-In partner will go into the fight response, and mistakes will be made. My goal is to prevent as much of that as possible by educating and coaching you about the crisis dynamic and best strategies and decisions to address it and also to inspire you to do the individual mind, body, and spirit self-care your soul has undoubtedly been longing for. Why? Because your individual health has everything to do with your relational health.

Everything within these pages is designed for you and your spouse to make the wisest, most thought-out decision you possibly can about your relationship. The one thing every person who has been through this says to me is that no matter what happens, they want the peace of mind that comes with knowing they have done all they could to save their marriage, and this is true even when marriages don't make it. If you follow my direction, you will have that.

Although there can be peace in your future, I know you are distressed right now. The first chapter in the book will describe what a marriage crisis is like in detail and will offer advice and wisdom about what to do and what not to do. If you are the Leaning-In partner, you will learn why you must fight your instinct to woo and pursue your spouse during this phase of the crisis. If you are the Decider, you will be coached not to do anything impulsive and to slow yourself down so you can make wise decisions. A marriage crisis begins as a house on fire, and learning how to minimize damage at this stage, to not make things worse than they have to be, will be all-important.

The second chapter will diagnose your marriage and explore how you got to this point in the first place. Burying discontentment along the way or not responding appropriately when your partner told you they were struggling or refusing to go to couples therapy when asked is one part of the problem that will have to be corrected moving forward whether you stay together or not. As you examine the dynamics of diagnosing your marriage, you will look at the stages of a deteriorating marriage and understand the stages your own marriage went through. I'll help you come to understand how important it is to see your part in the breakdown between two people who at one time chose each other and signed up to spend their lifetimes together.

Your marriage crisis has you facing one of the biggest decisions of your life, and Chapter 3 will explore your options. You have several choices between keeping things as they are, doing intensive marriage therapy to try to repair the relationship, separation with and without intensive relationship therapy, or going straight to the divorce decision. We will look at each choice individually, discuss the pros and cons, and lead you toward a well-thought-out plan of action.

Everyone knows the heavy price children pay for their parents' decision to divorce, and Chapter 4 explores how to best handle your crisis and move forward when it comes to the children. Divorce is painful for children no matter how old they are, but there are things we must do to ensure that our younger ones suffer the least and come out on the other side of the family crisis in the best possible shape. With adult children, there are also things you can do that will minimize bad feelings and guilt often felt by adult children of divorce. Whatever you decide about your marriage, your children most likely would rather see you happy together. If your decision is to be happy apart, then you will learn how crucial it is for your children to come first in your lives until they enter the life stage when friends become more important than family. Knowing this will and should affect your decision-making process, as putting your children first after a divorce requires personal sacrifice for the one who didn't ask to be in this position.

All too often, infidelity plays a role in marital crisis, and Chapter 5 discusses why people cheat, the types of infidelity (including the emotional affair), management of an affair once it is revealed, and what your options are and the ways to approach them. This will be a subject where those black-and-white thinkers out there will have to face the gray, and your knowledge about it will have to expand for you to make an informed and intelligent decision about what to do. Both the person having the affair and the scorned spouse will be spoken about compassionately and with understanding as we discuss why an affair happens, how to heal from it, and how to prevent it moving forward.

We're pretty sure your decision to marry in the first place wasn't thoroughly explored, so in Chapter 6, we'll take a bird's-eye view of what got you into this situation in the first place. Most people who choose to marry are not extremely mindful about choosing their mate, and we will look at who you chose to marry and why, the red flags you ignored, things about yourself you may have neglected, and understanding which things are fixable and which are not. What about expectations in marriage? What is reasonable; what's asking too much? If your marriage can be repaired, what is the best situation you can hope for?

While deciding what to do when your marriage hangs in the balance, there are a few things that should be considered. Chapter 7 will offer an overview of things to keep in mind such as physical, mental, and emotional health. You'll learn about the three marital felonies; see the range of marital crimes; and take an honest look at the beliefs, values, friendship, compatibility, and more held by you and your spouse. We'll consider the amount of work it truly takes to have a thriving marriage and whether you are willing to put that effort into it, as well as gain understanding of the most that anyone can expect in a lifelong, committed relationship.

Managing yourself during a marriage crisis is one of the most important things you can do to come out of it with resilience and the ability to thrive moving forward. If you're the Leaning-In partner, you should not ignore the importance of your own mind, body, and spirit health as your partner considers whether to stay married or not. Even when it appears they don't care at all, I can assure you they will be looking over their shoulder to see how you fare during this distressing time, and there are things you can do to help them become doubtful that divorce is the best option and to improve the possibility of a reconciliation. In Chapter 8, we will explore all this and how to handle social media, friends, family, and coworkers. There are things you must and must not do, including knowing whom to share your problems with and whom to be wary of.

Should we separate? The decision to separate is an enormous one, and if you are considering this option, Chapter 9 looks at when it's wise, how to choose a purpose for the separation, and understanding how to implement it. We'll take a look at the managed separation agreement and discuss every point and clause, why each one is there, and why changing any of it decreases its chance of success. I'll explain why I think having a marriage and family therapist to help you manage your separation is a great decision for your family. Having that caring person in the middle during a crazy emotional time could make all the difference in whether our interventions are successful.

Reconciliation: when and how to come back together. Sounds simple, right? But too many separated couples panic and run back together too soon, before any root causes of their troubles have been addressed. This often results in a failed reconciliation and divorce, and research clearly backs this up. In Chapter 8, we look at a smooth reconciliation in the same way we look at landing a plane. We need to know when it is safe to reconcile, how to do it, and what will make it last. Knowing if you are ready to try again is one of the most important things you need to understand in the marriage crisis dynamic. The way I look at this is that a reconciliation must be earned, and I will thoroughly explain what that means and how to get there.

After taking your time and considering all your options, some will decide to end their marriages. Chapter 7 discusses the healthy way to end a meaningful relationship, as well as hiring lawyers, mediation, the choice to not be adversarial, and what to expect. Divorce is always painful and sad, but it can be the doorway to a new and brighter beginning for all involved. If divorce is your choice, we'll guide you to the healthiest way to approach it.

Things will get better following a divorce. In all the years I have talked to people who are divorced, most tell me that the end of their marriage was sad and painful but for the best. There will be lessons learned, compassion and wisdom gained. Most people who end up in divorce never want to experience it again, so in Chapter 8, we will talk about becoming a better partner, dating, and considering remarriage. If you haven't learned from your mistakes, then what's the point, right? We'll also discuss the importance of understanding the future when you share children and consider bringing stepparents and stepsiblings into their lives.

CHAPTER ONE

What Is a Marriage Crisis?

A marriage crisis begins when one spouse makes a pronouncement that they are unhappy in the marriage and are thinking of, or wanting, separation or divorce. Within thirty seconds, with just a few words, everything will change for the two, and life will never be the same. A period of time will ensue known as a marriage crisis, though for some, it feels more like temporary insanity. Like mammals under threat, running or fighting for their lives, two life partners feel that same feeling: One fears losing their sanity, the other, their marriage. Like any nervous system that is activated, the pulse races, rational thinking disappears, digestion stops, and desperate acts begin with one person anxiously trying to dispense with the status quo while the other scrapes and scratches to hang on to it.

The couple has no way of knowing they are in a relationship process that has been going on for years in predictable stages, which ultimately culminates in the life-changing thirty seconds that will cause them to desperately seek answers to what is going on. This chapter will shed light on that process and what happens to every couple whose marriage hits rock bottom, a phenomenon that happens across every culture and socioeconomic reality.

Right now, you want to know what's going on, how long it will last, and when will the spouse who is the Decider come to their senses. Previously unmotivated partners are now all ears and willing to do whatever it takes to save their marriage.

What's Going On with the Decider?

Telling your spouse you think you want out of the marriage takes every ounce of courage you could possibly muster. Unsure of your partner's reaction, you tread carefully. Of course, some Deciders announce it during a fight or other intense moment, and if they do, this time, they won't walk it back. They're dead serious. For them, pressure has been building to this moment; they've waited and watched for the right time, and when their serious intention to possibly end the marriage is finally expressed, it is like the bursting of a volcano. The pressure inside leads finally to a point when the burning lava shoots out, then runs down the hill. The town is in danger, but the volcano itself may feel better post-eruption.

Some Deciders will tell you that prior to the announcement, they thought their spouse might welcome the news. Paul, a forty-four-year-old professional, insisted his wife had been as unhappy as he was prior to the evening he dropped the emotional bomb of wanting out of their eighteen-year marriage.

"We've both been going through the motions, making no effort," he said. "In fact, I thought my wife might beat me to the announcement that she wanted out. She never acts like I'm important to her, ever. She just wants to be with her friends or the kids, so I say, let her."

Paul was astonished and caught off guard that his wife, Mary Kate, who seemingly didn't care about the marriage at all, protested firmly and loudly in the moment, as if awakening from a deep sleep to a multialarm emergency.

"Over my dead body!" she screamed. "We can't divorce. What about our vows, our friends, the house under construction, the kids? No, no! You will not divorce me! I'm not going anywhere, and neither are you. Get your act together, Paul! What the hell is wrong with you?"

Having found his courage, Paul was not backing down, at least not on the idea of getting away for a while. As happens with most Deciders, once Pandora's box is opened, one way or the other, things won't be the same. Paul was going to leave, but he had no idea what to do next. Should he tell anyone? Should he call a lawyer? Where should he go? When? Does he sleep in the bed with her tonight? Do they still have sex? He was confused about everything in his life and knew only one certainty: He had to get away from Mary Kate so he could sort out his feelings and decide what to do. Life could never, ever go back to the way it was.

What's Going On with the Leaning-In Partner?

Mary Kate sat on my couch, tapping her feet and looking around as if she was looking for any reason to get up and leave. The forty-two-year-old blonde hadn't eaten for days after her husband, Paul, had said he wanted to move out. She looked frantic and drained at the same time.

"I feel like I need to smoke," she said, "and I've never smoked in my life."

Mary Kate was perplexed by Paul's sudden announcement that he was unhappy and might want out. She could not peg why he was so miserable. Nothing about his behavior made any sense.

"Seems like he's lost his mind all of a sudden," she said. "We hardly ever fight. We have a good life. The kids. Maybe I've put too much focus on them. We've been building a house, and some of that we disagree on, but I haven't done anything that deserves this. I just need you to figure out what's wrong with him and get him to settle down. This is ridiculous. He's acting like a fool."

Just like a lot of Leaning-In partners, Mary Kate was in a state of shock and denial. She was probably in cruise control mode with the marriage, thought it could be better, but never thought it was in trouble. She described a day-after-day routine of work, kids, chores, TV, and, ultimately, snoozing on the couch.

"Life is hard; we're busy and tired all the time," she said. "Maybe he and I just need to go on a long vacation alone together. That's it. We need some quality time together."

So many Leaning-In partners express shock and amazement that their spouse is seriously thinking of leaving the marriage. Like Mary Kate, they're so shocked that they just won't believe it, and they often assume a quick fix will make it all go away. But believe it they must, as the threat is real.

It is at this point in the marriage crisis that mistakes can be made that could make it impossible to repair, and that is why I wrote this book.

People in Mary Kate's predicament will have to be coached and cajoled to go against instinct when it comes to how they interact with and approach the Decider. Both spouses will need wise counsel during a very delicate and fragile time. Though I know you will reach out to friends and family to seek advice and explore options, you should be highly skeptical of what they say and turn instead to a marriage and family therapist who will be able to provide valuable information and context and likely save you from yourself. The first thing a Leaning-In partner needs to do is see the crisis as real and potentially marriage ending, and the second thing they need to do is stop telling anyone who will listen that their husband or wife has lost their mind because to their spouse, and maybe even to their spouse's therapist, they may feel they are finding themselves at long last.

Coming Out of Denial

So, yes, any marriage in crisis is in serious trouble. One reason Leaning-In partners are so shocked at the beginning of a marriage crisis is because they didn't realize how much work is involved in maintaining a healthy marriage. That "marriage is work" is a worn-out cliché, but the evidence and my personal and professional experience show that people really don't know what true work in a relationship is. While it involves a lot of time and thought, it is most certainly a huge personal sacrifice to get it right. I'll be explaining more about that in Chapter 6, but for now, I just want you to know that couples *must* monitor the health of their marriage just like the health of their bodies.

In this age of health and wellness and living longer, most adults are aware that they need to monitor the health of their bodies. Thanks to the enormous amount of easily available information, you know a lot about how to do it. You know the nourishment your body needs and what your body doesn't need, such as greasy French fries, Ding Dongs, HoHos, and my personal temptation, hot cinnamon twists from Shipley's Do-Nuts! You know that smoking and too much alcohol hurt your health, that your body needs exercise, and that you need to keep your heart working. You know your teeth need to be regularly cleaned and maintained so they can last a lifetime.

In addition to knowing what it takes to be healthy, you are aware of the signs of serious illnesses that can threaten your life. Katie Couric brought attention to the importance of colonoscopies, and the media blares information about diabetes, cancer, stroke, and heart disease symptoms. Women know they have to get mammograms and perform monthly breast self-exams, and men over fifty know about the necessity of prostate screenings. The point is that most of you know there is a positive payoff to maintaining and guarding your health.

The benefit of this knowledge is that if you experience warning signs, such as severe chest pain, shortness of breath, or sudden bleeding, you know you need immediate medical attention and that if you ignore your body's warning signals, you might die prematurely.

Being aware of your marriage's health is just as important. Your marriage is in trouble and most likely well into a process of deterioration that could ultimately lead to its death. You can ignore your body's health, and you can ignore the health of your marriage, but if you do, be warned that it's extremely risky. If you want your marriage to be healthy and to last, you must monitor, nourish, exercise, and maintain it. Unhealthy habits and behaviors threaten your marriage's health and lead to warning signs that something's not right. When you notice those signs, you must take action.

In 1969, Elisabeth Kübler-Ross wrote the groundbreaking book *On Death and Dying,* in which she described the five stages of grief. Today, those stages are universally accepted as what follows the loss of a loved one: denial, anger, bargaining, depression, and acceptance. Experiencing those stages of grief—in some order—is as inevitable as the sunrise and sunset.

With exactly the same inevitability, when a marriage dies, it goes through five distinctive stages. They are as predictable and unavoidable as the five stages of grief. Unlike the stages of grief, however, the stages of a dying marriage occur in order. It is the speed at which the marriage goes through each stage that differs. Understanding these stages is as important to your marriage's longevity as understanding the warning signs of a heart attack is to your longevity. Since your relationship is already in trouble, you will want to explore this list to find out where your relationship fits. Do note that your perspective may put your view of the marriage at a different level of deterioration than how your spouse sees it, and an important part of this process is for you to recognize where you are and to accept your partner's viewpoint, for better or worse, which may be different from yours.

Five Stages of Marital Deterioration

Marital deterioration begins with disillusionment: The idea that what you once thought was a pretty good or great thing isn't after all. I liken it to a stock drop. You bought the stock high, and now its value is low. As the couple falls into the marital deterioration process, at least one spouse notices the esteem in which they once held their partner has diminished and continues to fall. Enter Stage One of the dying marriage.

STAGE ONE: Low-Grade Marital Fever

You become aware of discomfort in the marriage. The feeling lingers. You have more than likely had this thought: *Uh oh, this isn't working,* or *I think I'm unhappy in this relationship.* The next thought is *I hope the feeling passes. I know marriages have ups and downs, so maybe this is just a down period.* You decide to watch the situation to see if it improves.

STAGE TWO: Medium-Grade Marital Fever

Your feelings haven't improved, and you now recognize that your concerns are serious and not going away. Your awareness of the discomfort in the relationship has increased, so you are thinking about it more often. A process of marital erosion has begun. In your understanding of how serious this is, you briefly consider divorce and quickly dismiss the idea. You've gone over all or many of the considerations that influence you strongly to stay in the marriage, such as finances, children, fear of the unknown, and more. You keep your unhappiness in the marriage a secret, but it shows in passive-aggressive actions toward your spouse, such as snide remarks and a refusal to cooperate.

STAGE THREE: High-Grade Marital Fever

Your unhappiness increases, and your ability to tolerate it decreases. You may feel trapped, and you fantasize about being single. Some may tell themselves, "You know what. If he or she would just die, it would make my life so much easier." You emotionally detach yourself from the relationship and begin major activities outside the home that do not include your spouse—schools, hobbies, friends, travel, work—telling yourself, "If I can just find some level of enjoyment over here for myself, then I think I can keep going along in the marriage." You may seek an affair as a replacement or potential stepping stone out of the marriage or at least have become vulnerable to the possibility. You exhibit public displays of disrespect toward your spouse, no longer willing to act like your marriage is wonderful when it is not. You may bring up things that aren't working, ask to go to marriage therapy, issue warnings and ultimatums. Whatever happens at this point, your spouse isn't responsive enough to make permanent changes, and you sit back and wait for the marriage to die. Discord between you and your spouse may take place in front of others.

STAGE FOUR: The Point of No Return

A situation or event—a minor infraction, huge violation, or something in between—becomes the straw that breaks the marriage's back, and the Decider's stress reaches a climax, activating their sympathetic nervous system and propelling them into a fight, flight, or freeze mode, usually flight. The Decider realizes they cannot be married to a person who would do/ say/behave in that way. Suddenly, you are clear that you no longer want to be in the marriage, or at least devoted to the marriage. Most or all previous fears about leaving cease to matter. You may have heard a person in this place say, "I don't care if I am out on the streets and have to be homeless or lose all my money. I don't care what my family will say, I cannot stay in this marriage." Whether the couple separate or divorce at this point is uncertain, but an emotional divorce will take place. The Decider will no longer put themselves out or make an effort for the marriage and focuses solely on finding happiness for themselves.

STAGE FIVE: The Death of the Marriage

The Decider believes that the marriage is dead and cannot be revived and may also feel an overwhelming sense that if they don't get away from the Leaning-In spouse, something catastrophic may happen. They make plans to leave, and when things are in order, they tell their spouse, initiating the marriage crisis.

Knowing the characteristics of each of the five stages allows you to diagnose the state of your own marriage. One of the reasons people aren't aware of the process is because of how individuals go through the process in secret, as previously described. It is only after becoming certain that the discontentment is real and likely will not change that a person steps forward to reveal the truth—and many times, this is too late.

What ultimately needs to change in our culture is the secretiveness of the process. Individuals need to feel safe to discuss with their spouse what they are thinking and feeling, even if it will be unwelcome news. This is the fundamental ingredient that must be present in every marriage that hopes to be healthy, and I can tell you that 100 percent of the couples who come to my office for marriage counseling are not doing this.

Let's take a look at the stages of a deteriorating marriage that ultimately lead to the thirty-second revelation through the eyes of Celine, a client whose spouse called asking for help.

Celine is forty-one, an attractive woman, intelligent, friendly, and funny. Men were always drawn to her, but at thirty-one, she reported still patiently waiting to meet an extraordinary man and settle down. Admittedly, Celine was tired of the dating scene, the flakes, the less-than-emotionally-available men, but she wanted to stay in the game to find the man she referred to as "the One."

After one especially unpleasant relationship ended, Celine spent a long, hot August on her couch wearing cotton pajamas, drinking wine, and snuggling with her dogs. Finally, her sister in Albuquerque invited her to fly over for the weekend, promising dates with sexy, eligible men.

"This will cheer you up," said her sister. "I promise."

On her first evening in Albuquerque, Celine met Jack, an intriguing heart surgeon in his last year of residency. He was short but handsome, with brown curly hair, a nice smile, and a deep tan. He was well-dressed, from his beautiful olive sport coat down to his lizard-skin loafers. His small, wire-rimmed glasses made him look eccentric and didn't match his strong features.

Ugh, I hate those glasses, Celine thought to herself.

By the end of the weekend, Celine had dismissed the other two men she had met in favor of Jack. Clearly, he enjoyed the finer things in life. He had taken her to fine restaurants and ordered wine like he knew what he was doing. Before she left on Sunday, she visited him in the quaint cabin he rented near the medical center. They had sex surrounded by a stack of rifles, mounted deer heads, and rusty traps hanging from the wall.

Those things can't be his, she thought. *They're disgusting, and he's too sophisticated.*

And so began a whirlwind, long-distance romance. Jack worked long hours as a chief resident at the Health Science Center, so Celine did most of the commuting to see him. By December, they agreed that she would quit her job and move into the cabin.

"Can I bring my dogs?" she asked.

"No," he said. "No dogs. You can get new dogs another time."

Devastated but not willing to rock the boat, Celine drove her dogs to a new family she'd found. She felt nauseated as she dropped them off.

"Why am I doing this?" she asked herself, her heart pounding. She dropped her forehead to the steering wheel and wept.

Jack helped her move to Albuquerque. During the trip, she asked about his childhood.

"I don't want to talk about that."

Later, when she asked him about his former relationships, he again snapped, "I don't want to talk about that," and changed the subject.

Okay, thought Celine. *It doesn't matter. I guess he's just a private person. He loves me so much that nothing else matters anyway.*

What Jack would talk about was heart surgery. He had dreams of being the best. He told Celine he would have to work long hours, but to make up for that, he agreed to live anywhere in the country that she wanted when he finished his training.

"I'd love to live in Aspen or New York City," she responded.

"Great. Find me a job and we're there!"

First, though, Jack wanted to spend a year overseas in a medical fellowship. Celine didn't want to go, but she knew the experience would be good for him, so she cheerfully agreed.

Celine and Jack got married in a small ceremony a few days before his graduation, eight months after they had met. They left for England a week later.

Once there, Celine often found herself lonely and depressed. Not allowed to work, she learned to cook to pass the time. One night, a fish she'd bought that day from the local market turned out to be spoiled. Celine watched in horror as Jack's face turned angry; he got up from the table, grabbed the frying pan, and drove to the shop to threaten the man who had sold her the fish. She told herself Jack was tired and overworked. And anyway, he was so attractive and smart, she couldn't believe how lucky she was to be with him.

Celine thought her marriage was good at first, and she counted her blessings. But not long into the marriage, her enthusiasm to greet Jack after work was often met by his dark, distant moods. She also noticed a downward turn in his desire to have sex. When she initiated sex these days, he almost always turned her down. When she asked him about it, he'd mumble that it was his problem, not hers, and wouldn't talk about it.

"Can we do something about it? Do you need counseling?"

"Yes, counseling. I will do it when I'm not so busy," he replied.

When they returned to the United States, Celine began searching medical journals for job listings for heart surgeons in New York or Colorado. In the meantime, Jack set up a practice in Albuquerque. Celine sent Jack's CV out, but whenever he was invited for an interview, he found a reason he couldn't go or why that job wouldn't work. For Jack, the time or opportunity to go somewhere else was never right. Months, then years passed, and Celine realized he never intended to leave Albuquerque.

Bitterly disappointed, Celine began having migraines, low-back pain, and anxiety attacks. After numerous tests showed that nothing was medically wrong, her doctor suggested she see a psychiatrist.

What Celine didn't know is that from the moment she first felt disillusionment in her relationship with Jack, her marriage became ill. It had started a process of deterioration that would spiral downward through predictable stages that, if unstopped, would end in the death of the marriage.

Three years into the marriage, Celine had their first child, and they bought a house. Jack hung the rusty traps on the wall even though Celine protested. As a father, Jack had always wanted a son and doted over the boy. After the birth of their second child, a girl, Celine noted that Jack showed no enthusiasm at all for his daughter. He said he didn't want their son to feel left out, but Celine wondered if it might have to do with her gender.

When their daughter was two, Celine realized the last time they'd had sex was when their daughter was conceived, and not only that, her husband had never initiated sex with her at all, not even when they were dating. *What the hell?* she thought. She decided to wait and see if he ever would, and the day never came.

Frightened for her marriage, she told Jack, "We've got to do something about our marriage soon. I don't know how long I can hang on. Our sex life is nonexistent, you work all the time, you leave the house before the kids and I get up, and you come home just in time to eat and go to bed."

Jack continued to promise that he would get help, but he always said, "After that big October event is over." Then it would be "after the holidays," and on and on. Celine began to realize that, just like moving to another state, the day he would be proactive about getting help would never come.

They were now nine years into the marriage, and Celine began to feel as though her world was closing in on her. Jack still wouldn't talk about anything personal. He wasn't nearly as cultured and intellectual as she had thought; although he wined and dined her when they dated, he now preferred to spend his free time hunting and chopping down trees on a piece of property they had bought. When she mustered the courage to talk about any of their issues, he would explode and storm off, sometimes leaving her stranded in public locations. She began to think, *There's no hope for us if we can't talk.* Enveloped by a feeling of being trapped in the marriage, she began to treat Jack with disrespect, throwing out snide remarks and comments about his dysfunctional and critical family, whom she thought was responsible for him being so shut down. He threatened to divorce her if she didn't stop the verbal attacks.

She went to individual therapy to try to understand, and her therapist told her that not wanting to have sex, not being open, and having rage attacks when she wanted to talk about their issues wasn't normal or healthy.

Besides her children, the one bright light in Celine's life was volunteering for an animal rescue group. It gave her life purpose, and she began to think she could make a career of it. Jack, the man who loved to kill animals, hated her involvement there, declaring her to be a "libtard." To punish her, he cut her allowance, explaining that she wasn't working toward her potential or contributing to the family as much as she should.

"You don't even cook me a hot meal anymore," he said.

"You aren't home to eat it," she said. "You're joking about the allowance, I hope. You aren't going to cut my allowance when we are making more money than we've ever made, are you?"

"I am not joking," said Jack, who was making over $500,000 a year, with large increases every year.

Celine felt overwhelming loathing for her husband at that moment. *That's the last straw,* she thought. *How could he be so meanspirited? I am making a promise to myself that I am going to divorce him before the year is out. I can't be married to someone who would do something like that.*

Celine began working on a plan to leave. She'd survive somehow, some way. One night two months later, Celine was waiting for Jack when he came home from work.

"You have to move out," she said. "It's over. I want out, at least for now. I don't know what I want, but I know I need to get away from you."

Jack and Celine's marriage had completed the marital illness stages, passing through each of the five stages because no serious attempts were made to stop the downward slide. Celine made pleas along the way and sent off warning shots, but Jack didn't respond with action. To her, he was all talk: "Yes, we will move; yes, I will work less; yes, I will get help."

The death of the relationship was apparent with Celine's sense that she did not have one more ounce of anything to give to the relationship. She lost hope that he would ever change. Her feelings about Jack and the marriage had flatlined. Not only did she want to leave the marriage, but she felt like she *had* to leave it to survive.

What's sad is that if Celine or Jack had known the stages of a dying marriage, the symptoms might have been a wake-up call for them to do something. But each of them assumed there was time left to work on the marriage. They didn't know that when a marriage is in trouble, the decline is absolute if not tended to and that it leads to a tragic end. The end is predictable. Only the timing of the end isn't.

Celine told me she could not believe how her marriage had turned out. At one time, she had loved Jack passionately and with all her heart. How on earth, she pleaded, could her feelings have changed so much?

Now let's look at how Celine went through the stages.

Signs of Celine's marriage's low-grade fever: Celine ignored (or attempted to suppress anger about) several signs of lingering discomfort—giving her dogs away, Jack's refusal to talk to her about his life, moving overseas when she didn't want to, Jack's temper, his workaholism, and his sexual rejection.

Signs of Celine's marriage's medium-grade fever: Celine's discontentment intensified when Jack didn't keep his promise to move out of New Mexico. She resented that he never directly told her he would not move, that she had to figure it out. She began to look at the relationship in a new light, a more realistic light, she felt. She began to feel she had been duped by him, that he knew she wanted a more sophisticated lifestyle and led her to believe that is what he offered, that he never intended to leave New Mexico, that he wasn't going to get help or really take action on anything that she requested. He had become an expert at putting her off. This resulted in a loss of respect, and she began to occasionally make snide remarks that revealed her disappointment and resentment. With each new disappointment, Celine considered divorce but quickly dismissed the idea.

Signs of Celine's high-grade marital fever: Celine began to see her situation in the marriage as hopeless and focused more frequently on how unhappy she was. She found work with a local nonprofit to find happiness and fulfillment. Celine warned Jack that they had to do something about the marriage because she didn't know how long she could hang on. Her stress was nearing an unbearable peak.

Signs of Celine's point of no return: The breaking point came when Jack cut Celine's allowance. Celine refused to be married to a man who would do something like that. She saw it as mean and controlling. At that moment, all previous concerns that kept her in the marriage ceased to matter, and she made the decision to leave.

Signs of the death of Celine's marriage: Celine lost all desire to work on the marriage; she felt she wouldn't survive if they stayed together. Without telling Jack, she calmly made plans to leave him. When she was prepared, she told Jack to leave. From Celine's perspective during this time, she felt that nothing he did at this point would turn the marriage around. She was not ready for divorce, but she needed time apart and lots of it. Not surprisingly, Jack was now ready to do any and everything to prevent a divorce, or so he said. His anguished pleas for her to give him a chance fell on deaf ears.

Although a marriage crisis often seems to come out of the blue for the Leaning-In spouse, the stages of a deteriorating marriage show us that marriages die slowly, over a long time, in predictable stages. If only couples were aware of the stages, they could get help in Stage Two before numerous incidents have occurred that lowered the stock of the relationship. Since first doing my own research on how marriages die, which backed up what sociologist Diane Vaughan wrote about in her book *Uncoupling: Turning Points in Intimate*

Relationships, I've come to realize that the stages really apply to any relationship that ends, whether it is with a family member or friend.

Now that you know where your marriage stands within this dynamic, we will move on to more diagnostic tools to check our math about the state of your relationship. This will be especially helpful to the Leaning-In spouse who may be in denial about just how serious their situation is. Accepting what is true in your relationship today is going to be very helpful in the days, weeks, and months to come.

Now is your chance to figure out when you went through the stages of marital deterioration yourself. Although this primarily applies to the Decider, I would like for the Leaning-In spouse to also do the exercise from their point of view and again from what they think their partner would say.

Whether the Leaning-In or Leaning-Out (Decider) spouse, I want you to use the following exercise to go through each stage and describe when you feel you first entered it. For example,

- **Stage One—Disillusionment:** "I first noticed I was unhappy in the marriage when my husband/wife kept accusing me of doing or saying things I never did or said."

- **Stage Two—Erosion:** "I knew it was serious when I would point out that I was not doing the things accused of, and it kept happening, and they didn't believe me no matter what I did or said. It even happened more frequently, and I knew they were wrong. I felt helpless."

I understand that you may not have made it all the way through every stage, so just go as far as you can so you can see how the feelings toward your relationship spiraled downward into the predictable stages.

Okay, got it? Now it's your turn. . . .

Stages of Marital Deterioration

Based on an unhappiness scale of 0–10
0 = Not Happy   10 = Very Unhappy

Stage One	Stage Two	Stage Three	Stage Four	Stage Five
Disillusionment*	Erosion	Detachment**	The Straw**	Death of the Relationship**
Stage One: A partner becomes aware of discontentment and says to self, "Uh-oh, I think I'm unhappy." This is followed by, "I know relationships have ups and downs, so I'll just wait and see if it's serious."	Stage Two: The partner concludes the situation is serious and could lead to divorce, though the idea of divorce is quickly dismissed due to many factors such as children, finances, fear of failure, religion, etc.	Stage Three: As the level of discontentment increases, the partner makes a bargain with self: "I can stay married if I put focus on things away from the marriage, such as going back to school, hobbies, working out, or an affair."	Stage Four: In one cathartic moment the disgruntled partner experiences a crescendo of stress followed by clarity that they can no longer remain with a person who would say or do whatever it is the person just did. All other considerations against divorce cease to matter and a decision to disconnect is made.	Stage Five: The partner now feels apathy and disconnect. A divorce decision may be made at this point, or the partner will stay physically but exist in a state of emotional divorce.
The person in Stage One usually feels a level 2–3 on the scale of unhappiness.	*The person in Stage Two is usually a level 4–5 in the scale of unhappiness.*	*The person in Stage Three is usually a level 6–7 on the scale of unhappiness, and the number will increase.*	*The person in Stage Four is a level 10 on the scale of unhappiness.*	*This person has no motivation to work on the relationship or marriage.*

Important Note:
Once a partner enters Stage One, deterioration of the marriage will continue if action is not taken. When a person reaches Stage Two, this is the ideal time to act by:
1. Revealing your unhappiness to your partner and
2. Making an appointment for marriage counseling.

* Where most relationships begin: with positive regard for each other and functioning well.

** Disillusionment, Erosion, Detachment, The Straw, Death of the Relationship: The relationship is in a state of disconnect and apathy.

Exercise: Consider the Stages of Your Marital Disillusionment

Stage One: Disillusionment, or "Uh oh, I think I'm unhappy in this marriage."

I first entered into Stage One when . . .

_____

_____

_____

_____

Stage Two: Erosion, or "Oh no, my unhappiness is serious and not going away. This could lead to divorce—oh no, I will not get a divorce!"

I entered into Stage Two when . . .

_____

_____

_____

_____

Stage Three: Detachment, or "I am very unhappy in this relationship, but I am not divorcing. I can stay if I find something else to distract myself that I'll do on my own away from my spouse like [fill in the blank]."

I entered Stage Three when . . .

_____

_____

_____

_____

Stage Four: The Straw, or something your partner said or did, caused you to hit the peak of stress—a level that propelled you to realize you cannot tolerate the relationship anymore and you must take immediate action to plan an end to the relationship or to get away.

I entered Stage Four when . . .

_____

_____

_____

_____

Stage Five: Death of a Marriage, or "I really can't imagine ever being close to romance with my partner again. I just want them out of my life."

I entered Stage Five when . . .

_____

_____

_____

_____

When working with couples on the brink, I also use this next tool to help them visually understand what is going on in a marriage crisis. As simple as it is, it is a very powerful presentation that especially helps the Leaning-In spouse see why they must stop pursuing and wooing the Decider for the time being.

The Relationship Circle Exercise Created for Couples in Crisis

In my practice, I love to use diagrams and often draw pictures on a whiteboard for couples as we move through their therapy process. I like the idea of making difficult concepts simple to understand, and I love it when clients take out their cell phones to take a picture of what I am showing them so that they can remember it. When couples come into the office in crisis, one of the most effective and helpful graphics I use to help them diagnose their marriage and to know if separation is an option is what I call the "Circle Exercise." After reading about the exercise, I want you to complete your own.

At https://youtu.be/6_LiTAkgbuo?si=5LI4nE7zDZLMaP2I, you can watch me draw the circles as I do in my office, which may help you understand the concept a little better.

Circle one. A healthy marriage. Outside the circle represents freedom and being single. Inside the healthy marriage are two small circles. The circle on the left represents Person A, and the circle on the right represents Person B. In a healthy marriage, the partners are firmly inside the circle, facing each other. Each person is focused on the other.

Circle Representing a Healthy Marriage

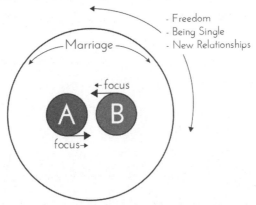

Circle two. Deterioration has begun. The second circle (page 24) represents the marriage of an unhappy couple, or at least one unhappy partner. In this example, Person A is firmly inside the circle, focused on their partner, or maybe not paying much attention to the marriage but is not contemplating leaving. Person B has started drifting away and has pulled close to the edge of the circle. The Decider is experiencing increasing disillusionment and is looking back and forth between their spouse and the possibility of leaving the circle, representing the infamous ambivalence that often accompanies a marriage crisis—the internal conversation of *Do I stay, or do I go?* and sometimes equally wanting both at the same time.

Circle Representing the Deteriorating Marriage

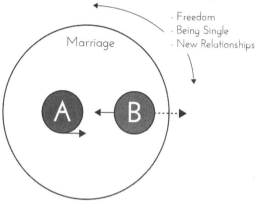

Circle three. A marriage crisis is imminent. In the third circle (below), Person B has stepped to the line of the circle and has probably made, or will soon make, the announcement that they are unhappy and either thinking of leaving or planning to leave the marriage. Person A has noticed the drifting by now and senses something is happening. Like a dog that hears a sound in the hall, they watch and listen to see if there is a true or imagined threat. This marriage is in imminent danger of Person B leaving the relationship.

Marriage Crisis Is Imminent

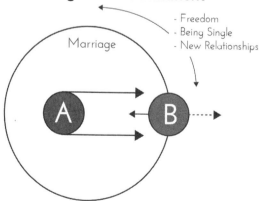

The Line of Uncertainty.

Circle four. Marriage crisis begins. In the fourth circle (page 26), Person B has made an announcement that initiates the marriage crisis. Person A is firmly inside the circle, hyper focused on their spouse, strongly defending the marriage and resisting any idea of separation or divorce. Person B is outside the circle with their back turned on the marriage and looking out toward freedom and being single. When Person A realizes they are losing their spouse, that this is not a spat or idle threat and the marriage is in serious danger of ending, attachment panic is triggered. Attachment panic is when the Leaning-In spouse's sympathetic nervous system is triggered, and they go into fight mode while their partner's nervous system is in flight. Person A's instinct is to chase after the Decider and do everything possible to pull them back into the circle. This heavy pursuit by Person A usually involves being on their best behavior, doing things they usually did not do, such as writing love notes and sending flowers, calling and obsessing over mistakes made, making up for mistakes, and meeting Person B's needs. The problem is that Person B's back is to the marriage, and they are not receptive to the frantic pursuit and are mostly repelled and annoyed by it.

In my experience, the harder the Leaning-In spouse pursues the Decider, the farther outside the circle the Decider will go. This is why I implore Leaning-In spouses to give the Decider space and room to breathe and to end the pursuit so they may have a chance at calming their nervous system enough to come out of activation and back to a calm state, where wise decision-making can take place.

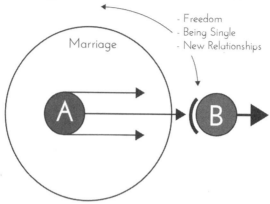

Marriage Reaches a Climax of Stress

- Freedom
- Being Single
- New Relationships

Marriage

A   B

Spouse B steps outside the circle.

Whose Story Is This?

In a marriage crisis, we all tell our version of a story about what is going on, and in the story, whoever is telling it will most often like to play hero, with their spouse playing the role of villain. Human beings embellish and exaggerate their marriage stories, rewrite history, and throw in some bends and turns all to avoid being negatively judged. Typically, the Decider far prefers to be seen as a downtrodden and emotionally abused spouse who has had to seek shelter away from their family to find peace.

The admission of an affair, if there is one, will change the marriage crisis dynamic completely. The Decider outside the circle has leverage to get their spouse to change, grow, and become a better person. The Decider who is in a full-blown emotional and physical affair will likely lose that leverage, and it will be the Leaning-In partner who now has a seat at the head of the table with demands of their own. It is plain to see why the Decider has every motivation in the world to lie about what they are up to. I will be discussing infidelity more thoroughly in Chapter 5. For now, I want the Leaning-In partner to be very skeptical of the Decider who isn't willing to come to the table to discuss possibly working things out. Be awake, be aware, and know that people with integrity who normally do not lie will, almost always, lie about infidelity.

Now it's your turn. . . .

Exercise: Draw Your Own Marriage Circles

Below is a circle, and that circle represents *your* relationship. Anywhere inside your relationship circle, draw a small circle that represents where *you* are today. This could be firmly inside the circle, near the edge, on the line (half in/half out), or all the way out. If possible, ask your partner to draw where their position is within or outside the circle. If your partner is not available, draw where you believe them to be within or outside the circle. Next, draw an arrow showing which way your focus is directed. Is it directed toward your partner? Is it directed outside the circle to freedom and being single . . . or toward someone else? Have your partner draw their arrow or you draw where you believe their focus is directed.

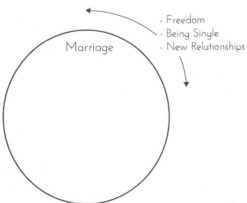

The information you just gained from doing that exercise is very valuable as we work to diagnose your marriage. We still have a bit more to do in our diagnostic process, so I don't want you to be jumping to any conclusions just yet about what it all means. Just keep reading and learning all you can about this and know that we will eventually be able to make a very accurate assessment, and we can then prescribe the best plan for you and your family.

CHAPTER TWO

What to Expect During Your Marriage Crisis

If you are part of a couple in a marriage crisis, it is vital to understand a few things: You both are afraid and confused, your nervous systems are activated and in threat mode, you have little or no idea about what to do, and you're incapable of thinking and acting rationally. Couples in crisis will likely do things that look absolutely crazy to the outside world. This book is dedicated to minimizing the crazy, making sense of it for both the Decider and the Leaning-In partner, calming down their nervous systems, and creating a space for intelligent and rational decision-making.

I first want to explain the sympathetic nervous system in as simple a way as I can because doing so will help you understand at least 75 percent of the *why this* and *why that* questions you might have.

Your Nervous System's Reactions

Every animal has a nervous system except for blob-like organisms like sponges, jellyfish, coral, and other microscopic things that most of us can't pronounce. The physical parts of the nervous system are the brain, spinal cord, and all the nerves that branch out throughout the body from there. The purpose of the nervous system is to keep living things functioning and alive. The brain is always on alert and ready to get us out of danger; it scans for survival threats four times a second.

When we are calm, our parasympathetic nervous system is in operation. If you think of a stoplight, this is when the light is on green—moving through the intersection with ease while listening to easy-listening radio. That's when we do most things required of daily life, like eat, sleep, digest, think, shop, learn, and more. But when mammals like human beings sense a threat, our sympathetic nervous system fires—activates—like a rocket on a NASA launch pad. With animals like dogs and tigers, the sympathetic nervous system fires when things they hear or see appear to be potential threats. An example you'll recognize from the animal kingdom is a dog who hears something out in the yard, stiffens, and listens to gauge if there is a threat or not, and if it is, it's off to the races. We've all seen a film where one animal is chasing another. The animal being chased is experiencing a true threat and is running for its life. You can be sure its sympathetic nervous system is on all systems go.

The Sympathetic Nervous System and Your Marriage Crisis

Thirty seconds before the announcement of unhappiness, the Leaning-In partner is in full parasympathetic mode, perhaps even relaxed on the couch, looking at their phone with no immediate care in the world. Green light. The Decider comes in, makes the announcement, and now the Leaning-In partner gets activated and goes into a fight response. Red light. The Leaning-In partner's impulse is to fight for the marriage with all they've got and capture the Decider in an imaginary net and pull them back into the marriage; I call this *attachment panic*. The Decider is in flight mode. Both the Decider and Leaning-In partner are activated and have entered very dangerous territory where mistakes are made. Neither one's brain is calm enough for common sense or rational thought. Both are now prone to act on impulse.

When the sympathetic nervous system is in full throttle (which I call *being activated*), things are said that aren't meant; people lash out, threaten, and harm one another. I often use a nonfactual example to explain to clients what happens when activated, saying, "Think about it as if both partners' IQs just lowered by twenty points." When my friends and family speak of someone going through a marriage crisis, they may say that the person has *lost their marbles* or *is acting crazy*, and I respond, "Forgive them, for they know not what they do," and I mean it. They really aren't themselves when activated; no one is.

We need to minimize damage at this point. Think of your marriage as a body that is on the floor and bleeding badly. We want the bleeding to stop so we can see if the person can be saved. If we don't stop the bleeding, the person won't make it. If we can get the bleeding under control, we can see what's going on, how bad it is, and what we need to do, including what's possible.

Calming Down to Assess the Situation

This is why it is so important for you to do all you can to come out of activation, to become calm, and to do everything I suggest along the way. Controlling yourself during these days will be the

hardest thing you've ever done, but you must do it. Everything both
of you want depends on it. I will be helping you with suggestions for
how to do this, but for now, use every piece of self-control you have
to will yourself to take action from the best part of your personality.
Remember, a lot is at stake, and you simply have to do it.

Things you can do to help yourself come out of activation:

- Splash cold water on your face
- Take a cold shower
- Use an icepack on your face and forehead
- Sleep on your right side
- Exercise or engage in physical exertion
- Spend time in nature
- Meditate—visualize calming resources that always make you
  feel better
- Slow down breathing to ten to twelve breaths per minute or
  less
- Stay away from negative people, places, and things
- Use vibration noises such as voooo, owmm, or gargling noises
- Spend time with a child or pet
- Engage in a favorite hobby
- Use touch. Your nervous system responds positively to
  calming touch, so do this to soothe yourself. If your chest or
  heart aches, put your hand there, keep it there for a while, and
  notice if the feeling changes. Put your left hand under your
  armpit and your right hand on your left shoulder in a self-hug.
  Also, try holding the back of your head, like a mother might
  hold an infant's head. When I do these things, I listen to my
  gut or intuition about what needs tending to. Learning to
  listen to yourself by checking in with your body is a good exercise to start; where do you feel energy forming? The energy

in your body is how your nervous system speaks to you. Get a sense of what you need and what sort of touch will make you feel better.

My Favorite Self-Soothing Ritual

Young children have self-soothing techniques to reduce stress—they have lovies, pacifiers, blankies, and whatnot that will do the job of calming them down when needed. Now is a good time to take a cue from them; just because we grew up doesn't mean we don't still need self-soothing rituals. I have one that works for me every time, and here it is:

Step one: Use physical exertion to release negative energy. I like to get sweaty and dirty, so I may go for a power walk or bike ride in nature, work in the yard pulling up weeds or trimming trees and bushes, or detail my car. Before I begin this, I tell my brain, "I am upset about X, and what I'm about to do is to help me release the negative energy I feel about that." Then I do it. If I don't have that kind of time, I have a three-foot-long piece of water hose that is about two or three inches in diameter that I beat against a pillow or mattress. I whack, whack, and whack while focused on my emotional pain. Pretty soon, my brain tells me I have completed what I was doing it for, and I stop.

Step two: Following step one, I go home to take a shower or bath, then create a soothing atmosphere—music, candles, maybe a glass of wine. I put on something warm and comforting, get in bed with some books or magazines, or watch a favorite spirit-lifting movie. Then I fall asleep. My wounded inner child feels totally taken care of and nurtured in these moments.

I suggest you create a similar ritual that fits you. Think of what a compassionate mother or father might do for their child, and then do that for yourself. You will need this ritual quite a bit during the coming days, weeks, and months, and I urge you to embrace it.

Understanding the Parts of Our Personality

I keep talking about controlling your behavior during a marriage crisis and how difficult it can be when your sympathetic nervous system is firing. I want to explain more clearly what I'm talking about.

I'm a trauma therapist who has worked with thousands of clients over the years, and I have never met anyone who doesn't have childhood developmental trauma. Pia Mellody published a book in 1989 titled *Facing Codependence* that showed the world what childhood trauma is and how it happens. I trained with her over a period of three years (starting in 2010) and use her powerful theory in my work today. I sincerely believe there is nothing else like it for helping people recover, grow up, and be their best selves.

Mellody's definition of a trauma-causing event is "anything that happened in childhood that was less than nurturing." What comes from it is the development of *toxic shame*, the idea that we aren't good enough, don't fit in, are defective, and can't measure up to the world's expectations. When people ask me what the number-one cause of divorce is, I say, "Toxic shame." Why? Because no one can have a healthy relationship with anyone if they are full of toxic shame and view the world through the lens of *I'm not good enough*. In addition to putting inaccurate and negative meanings on things, the toxic shame–filled person beats themselves up regularly and processes every interaction from *I'm less than* or *inferior* viewpoints. People loaded up with life's wounds and toxic shame tend to take things personally, have numerous activations when there is a perceived slight, and likely have either an emotional bucket that doesn't ever seem to get filled up enough by friends and family or have turned off needing and wanting altogether. If you don't think this applies to you, think again. Even those I've met who have a *better than* or *superior* stance have toxic shame lurking underneath. Feeling better than or superior to most others is also a result of childhood trauma. Neither one is conducive to healthy relationships.

Example: Bree's self-esteem is less than or inferior. Deep inside, she feels her husband, José, is too good for her. She tells herself that he doesn't love her and wishes he could leave her, none of which is true. She loves to have lunch with him as often as possible, and when she gets home from work one day, she slams cabinet doors and pouts. José asks what's wrong. "You couldn't even make time to have lunch with me. You'd rather be doing anything else!" José is astonished. "What? I had a meeting, sweetheart. I had a lunch meeting with my sales manager. It had nothing to do with you."

Bree created problems where there were none because of her toxic shame. Over time, these sorts of interactions wear down husbands like José, and it's all so unnecessary.

The Sympathetic Nervous System in Action

The following graphic shows the three parts of the personality of any person who took on toxic shame in their childhood, including the Wounded Child (WC), the Adaptive Child (AC), and the Functional Adult (FA).

The WC is the part of us where all our childhood wounds are stored—the time you weren't invited to the birthday party, your parent said something cruel, your dad forgot to pick you up. Anytime something happens and we feel intense emotions like hurt, shame, anger, pain, or fear, that is our WC reacting. For example, if my husband says he didn't like the meal I cooked, there's a good chance it will hurt my feelings, and my WC will feel the hurt, reminiscent of other times I was hurt long ago when I disappointed someone else and felt toxic shame, the feeling of not being good enough. The themes of the past return in these moments, along with the stored-up negative emotion, when someone says or does something, or doesn't say or do something, that mirrors a wound from our past.

I tell clients the best way to know your WC part has arrived is that they will feel intense emotion. If you step on my toe, I will feel a normal level of anger because the feeling is about physical pain and is something new happening right now. If you tell me I failed to please you, I may feel rage, just like I did when my dad pointed out things I did that weren't good enough. This part of a person's personality is related to the limbic part of the brain, which is primal and about survival. A young child expresses survival threats through intense emotions. When a person's nervous system is calm, green light, the WC is not around, but if something happens that the WC perceives as a threat, it wakes up and fires the sympathetic nervous system. Red light.

The AC is an older child and is the part of us that reacts when the WC feels emotionally injured and senses a threat. It helps to think of it as a protector of the WC, but the problem with the AC is that its responses are immature, as it is somewhere between nine and fourteen years old emotionally.

If you were ever a snarky teenager yourself, or happen to know one, you know what it looks, sounds, and acts like. Ironically, this is also the voice that bullies the WC when it feels it has fallen short.

"You blew it; everyone saw what a fool you were" might be something it would say when it doesn't like something its younger counterpart does, so I suppose you could say the AC thinks it's perfectly fine for it to abuse the WC, but it won't tolerate anyone else doing it.

When the sympathetic nervous system fires because the WC perceives a threat, the AC readies itself with the fight, flight, or freeze response. It will fight by being defensive, retaliatory, or saying something immature, or it will go into flight and run away or shut down and freeze.

These two parts are where most of the damage is done in relationships, and they will definitely be around for the Decider and Leaning-In partner during a marriage crisis. It is vital that you understand this and learn to control the AC's role as the reactor.

Luckily, we have a third part that can better handle the threat the WC is sensing, the FA. This is the healthy, better self all of us have. If I met someone I admired this afternoon, it would be my FA they would encounter. For example, I once read an article on a world-famous celebrity who said that people they meet always show them their best selves and are extremely generous and kind. *Yep,* I thought, *people turn on the bright light they are capable of when it matters.*

Everything a human needs personality-wise is found in the FA part of their personality. The marriage you long for is found there. Unfortunately, our wounded selves in the form of the WC and AC are the baggage most of us drag around, and until we do the healing work we need to do, that is how it will be.

What I will be asking you to do for now is when your nervous system becomes activated, slow yourself down before you react. Wait a few seconds. You will hear the voice of the AC giving you terrible advice about what you should do. Whatever that is, don't do it. Instead, seek your better self, the FA, and respond from there.

A Model of Codependency:
Three Parts of the Codependent Personality

How We Start Out	Common Influencers	1 Wounded Child (WC) Unhealthy and dysfunctional	2 Adult Adaptive Child (AC) Unhealthy and dysfunctional; the AC is also known as the "Rebellious teenager."	3 Functional Adult (FA) Healthy and functional
As babies, we are blank slates except for our DNA and personality.	The fundamental truths will soon shift from the child's perspective due to external influences like . . .	We take on shame and start beating ourselves up at a very early age.	**Characteristics:** Arrogant Aggressive Addict Protective Hellraiser Super mature Attacks Defends Shuts down Walks away Unfazed Punished Uncooperative Pouts	**Characteristics:** Loving Reasonable Authentic self Curious Confident Courageous Compassionate to self and others.

As babies, we are blank slates except for our DNA and personality.

The fundamental truths about us at birth are that we are . . .
Valuable
Vulnerable
Imperfect
Dependent
Spontaneous

The fundamental truths will soon shift from the child's perspective due to external influences like . . .
Religion
Family
Culture
Education
Media
Peers
. . . and many more

This is part one of the codependent personality.
The WC is the container for all our shame-filled thoughts and feelings.

We take on shame and start beating ourselves up at a very early age.

The Shame Core

Container of Wounds
Our shame has a voice and tells us:
"I'm not good enough."
"I'm not smart enough."
"I'm defective."
"I don't fit in."
Our body stores up and contains all the hurts and wounds of our life where we felt not good enough.

Because we don't like ourselves, we create a false persona— "This is who I *think* I should be."
Pleasers, perfectionists, overachievers, caretakers, knights in shining armor

Characteristics:
Arrogant
Aggressive
Addict
Protective
Hellraiser
Super mature
Attacks
Defends
Shuts down
Walks away
Unfazed
Punished
Uncooperative
Pouts

This is part two of the codependent personality.
When you have a shame attack, the response is from the AC and is called a **TRAUMA REACTION.**

Characteristics:
Loving
Reasonable
Authentic self
Curious
Confident
Courageous
Compassionate to self and others.

Emotional intimacy and connection are only found here.

This is part three of the codependent personality.
The initial definition of recovery is in how you react to shame attacks.
The goal is to bypass the AC and respond 51% of the time out of the FA.

Wounded child (WC). All of us have an inner WC who is hurt, frightened, angry, or in some state of emotional pain. Much of the time, this part sits at our side quietly, though it stands ready to activate anytime someone says or does something that it perceives as a threat. This part of us resides in the limbic part of our brain, where emotions and survival reside. There is no reasoning done here, only experiencing extreme emotions. Bree's WC was provoked, and she became activated when José told her he couldn't have lunch. She wrongly assumed it was because he didn't want to spend time with her.

During a marriage crisis, a person's WC will be activated again and again. Both the Leaning-In partner and the Decider feel the emotional pain of becoming activated to the core. What happens during activation, when one or both partners are feeling a threat, is where I am asking both partners to learn to control themselves.

Immediately after the WC is activated, most of us fall into the response of fight, flight, or freeze, where a terrible trap awaits. If you fall into it, you damage your relationship. In this second phase, the WC allows the AC to protect it but through self- or relationship-sabotaging behaviors.

Adaptive child (AC). We have an older child self that is the reactor to the emotions that arise in the WC. As stated before, this is the WC's protector. When the announcement of marital unhappiness is declared, the WC rises in fear or fury, and in individuals who don't know better, the AC unleashes its unedited, uncontrolled response of fight, flight, or freeze. Deciders notoriously flee, while Leaning-In spouses fight to keep the Decider from leaving. It is right here, in these responses, where damage is done. Why? Because the AC is emotionally immature, fourteen or fifteen years old, and responds to emotional hurts in an immature fashion.

When Bree slammed cabinets and pouted, she allowed her AC to take control of her personality. She let José know (in a passive-aggressive manner) that he had screwed up. Since José was falsely accused, he became frustrated and wanted to disregard her pain, which activated Bree even more.

The AC is immature, punitive, obsessive, and vindictive. Here are things I've seen the AC part of the personality do in response to perceived hurt during a marriage crisis:

- Become verbally, emotionally, and/or physically abusive
- Take money out of bank accounts or close credit cards
- Threaten to take children away
- Talk smack about the other person to friends and family members
- Call the partner's boss or visit their workplace to cause a scene
- Stalk the other partner
- Burn their partner's possessions
- File for divorce
- Put the house up for sale
- Give away a beloved pet
- Threaten suicide or harm to the other partner
- Refuse to respect their partner's boundaries

Listen for the FA Voice

If I could get your WC to stop feeling the emotional pain it no doubt is feeling right now, I would. That pain comes from piles of wounds from many decades of life's difficulties that the brain has stored in its hard drive. A trauma therapist can help reduce the emotional pain associated with those wounds, but right now, you still have them, and they are going to fire up the limbic brain numerous times during this crisis and send you into survival mode. What I am asking you to do is *not* to let your AC be the responder. Sure, the first voice you will hear is the AC telling you what to say or do, to run away, shut down, or do something nasty. Wait a second or two longer and gain access to the FA, located in a different part of your brain, the frontal cortex, where a more adultlike and reasonable suggestion can be found. Learning to do this can mean the difference between saving and losing your marriage.

What about the pain and fear the WC is feeling so intensely? We must tend to it. When mine is feeling that way, I pull up the self-soothing ritual I wrote about earlier. This is my FA reaching around and nurturing and taking care of my WC. It works, and it heals. Allow your FA to compassionately parent you while you are feeling vulnerable and lost. It will go a long way toward bringing you out of activation and into making wise decisions. Don't hesitate to ask yourself, "What would make me feel better right now?" Needless to say, the answer cannot be self- or other-person destructive and needs to be something you can provide for yourself, as we can't always count on others to be there for us. Use this tool as often as you need, as people like me in trauma recovery do day in and day out. Learning to nurture yourself is one of the best medicines available, so use it.

Accessibility, Responsiveness, and Engagement

Marriages have been studied for decades by many intelligent people. Almost anything you can think of has been looked into, from what ingredients tend to produce long-term, happy marriages to what behaviors predict divorce, and every marriage and family therapist knows what they are (Gottman, 1994).

I can pretty much predict which behaviors you and your partner have been engaging in to get you into the fix you are now in, but when you are in a marital crisis, we won't be able to spend much time talking about who did what; that will come later. In the moment, we need to get both partners out of activation, where the sympathetic nervous and threat response settle, the parasympathetic nervous system takes over, and relative calm returns—the haven for healthy action and decision-making. When activated, people who think they don't love their spouse anymore might just file for divorce and end up single prematurely, only to come out of activation and later find they made a huge mistake. It's my job to make sure no major decisions or actions with permanent ramifications take place during this time and that as little damage as possible is done between the two parties that might prevent reconciliation. We are seeking stabilization, and when we get it, we can get a more accurate view of how motivated you are to work on the marriage.

Also, know that part of what makes it exceedingly difficult is that I need *two* motivated people, not just one. Often, getting both on the same page at the same time is like trying to catch feral cats. We will need luck and precise timing for all things to fall into place for there to be reconciliation potential. No matter how adamant the Decider is about being done with the marriage, I still know that their mind could change. I know this because I have experienced it myself and seen it numerous times with couples I've worked with.

In the meantime, whoever *is* motivated—and almost always, that is the Leaning-In partner—can begin self-improvement and growth for themselves. Doing this is so important that it can absolutely make or break the final outcome of the marriage crisis. You may have heard that if one person changes in a marriage, it will change the family. This is what we are taught to understand in graduate school as marriage and family therapists who work with the entire family system, whether individually or together. Families are like systems, and if a broken part is repaired, it changes the machine.

The couples and individuals I see are like you, confused about what to do and desperate to hear what I have to say. I take this very seriously because I know their lives and futures are hanging in the balance. Their marriage is red hot, cold as ice, or the battery has died, and at least one person is about to walk. The questions of two anxious and emotional people are "Should we separate? Divorce? Do marriage therapy? Is there hope? No hope? What's going on? What should we do?"

I've seen it, experienced it myself, and I get it. Once we go through the questions, I will give you the answers you're looking for—and couples cannot believe that someone has so accurately pinpointed them and how they are feeling. That is not because I am psychic; it is because human beings are predictable, how a marriage gets sick and deteriorates is predictable, and how couples react and respond during and after "the point of no return" is predictable. The marriage crisis dynamic has been studied, and the way most couples react during a potential split is very similar (Gottman, 1994).

The Sugar, Flour, and Eggs Needed for a Healthy Marriage Cake

If creating a healthy marriage is like baking a cake, it is next to impossible to do marriage therapy with two people who do not possess the sugar, flour, and eggs that a marriage needs. Therefore, I also use the Accessibility, Responsiveness, and Engagement (ARE) diagnostic tool created by the late Dr. Sue Johnson (2008), the amazing marriage and British family therapist in Canada, to pinpoint more about where a couple is in their relationship and what can be done.

1. **Accessibility:** Can I reach you? Staying open to your partner even when you have doubts and feel insecure. Wall-free.
2. **Responsiveness:** Can I rely on you to respond to me emotionally? If your partner asks for you to connect or be there, you do it.
3. **Engagement:** Do I know that you will value me and stay close? This means you are into your partner and show it with your actions (Johnson, 2008, pp. 49–50).

Johnson created Emotionally Focused Family Therapy, which posits that the key aspect to having a healthy relationship has to do with having a healthy and strong attachment with your partner (Johnson, 2008). This means you feel a rock-solid sense of security in the relationship and that your partner is there for you. What hurts a relationship at its foundation is if one or both partners are either avoidant of connection or anxiously insecure in seeking connection. The theory has strategies for couples to move past the walls they may have up, learn to feel secure and relaxed in their relationship, and develop a strong sense of feeling open and secure with each other.

I use ARE to assess whether or not marriage therapy to repair the marriage while the partners stay together is a viable option, at least at the present time. I use the words *at the present time* because another thing that is also predictable about couples in crisis is that their feelings and emotions about whether they want to stay, go, separate, work on it, or end it for good will flip back and forth and up and down and are an ever-changing crazy cornucopia of uncertainty.

While Peter may want a divorce today and Julia absolutely does not, they may switch places several times during the entire process.

To me, ARE is a litmus test for whether you are open-minded to dropping your defenses and doing what it takes to connect with your partner. If a couple has lost these components and a person tells me they can't imagine doing any of those with their partner, that tells me one person has zero motivation to work on the marriage *today*. Remember, it could change later this afternoon or tomorrow because the process of a marriage crisis, with the sympathetic nervous system firing throughout, creates a state of chaos and constant change and uncertainty. People are so freaked out that they often pivot between extremes of "I want to stay" and "I want to go." It's just telling us that at *this* moment, a two-way conversation about give-and-take, negotiations, and compromise cannot take place successfully.

If a person's words "I am done" were solid and irrevocable, and we absolutely knew the Decider would never come back, this book would end now. But because the Decider so often changes their mind, and the nature of the marriage crisis beast is volatile, flaky, confused, and uncertain, I work to keep the union intact for as long as possible to see if we can hit that magic moment when both partners are all-in and want to work on the relationship.

The "I Want to Work on My Marriage" Scale

Here is what should be an obvious question, which I call the *Big Question*: **Do both you and your partner want very much to save your relationship, and are you both ready and willing to do the work right now to save it?**

When looking at a couple's motivation to begin marriage therapy, many marriage and family therapists present a scale like

the one below. This one I call the "I Want to Work on My Marriage"
scale:

Exercise: What Is Your Level of Motivation?

Circle the level of motivation you have for working on your
marriage today:

I do not want to = 0

I absolutely will do anything and everything to work on my
marriage today = 10

0   1   2   3   4   5   6   7   8   9   10

Now, ask your partner to do the same on the scale below.
(If your partner is unwilling or not available, just put in what
you think they would say.)

0   1   2   3   4   5   6   7   8   9   10

Of course, ten is the number every therapist hopes to find
from both partners. With that, we can get a lot done toward
helping your marriage, and separation would be off the
table. However, if one or both of you is a five or below, that
means there probably is not enough motivation to navigate
through the work we will need to do to get you back on
course. If one person is a zero, making a decision to separate
as a way to create a shift in someone who has almost no
motivation is a distinct possibility. Think of it this way: Some
people think they will love getting away, that perhaps a separation is the answer to their problems, but not everyone
enjoys separation as much as they think they will. More on
that later in the chapter.

While I know the mention of separation terrifies many Leaning-
In partners, I am asking you to believe what I am saying and take
the risk of trusting me. I do not want marriages to end that can and
should be saved; that is my mission in life.

One of our goals, if ARE is not present today, is to build enough desire to create ARE so that committed marriage therapy can begin. Motivation to work on the marriage is what we need and are looking for, but without that, there are still a few more things to try before throwing in the towel on your marriage. Yes, even though things may seem really bad now, there is still hope ahead.

Note to Leaning-In Partners

I have done this work enough to know that you are white-knuckling it while reading what I have written so far. It looks bleak, and you don't want me to look at it that way; you don't want me to talk about time apart, endings, giving your partner space, and while you think I may be your enemy right now, I am, in truth, the friend you need. I am your voice of reason, and I know what I am doing. I can't guarantee reconciliation, but if that is what you want, I will be doing everything I can to facilitate that. Still, the reality is that your marriage is in big trouble right now, and the odds are against you. Accepting that will go a long way toward helping yourself during this process. I have seen marriages turn around that I thought certain wouldn't make it. I have witnessed miracles. If there is one to be had for you, I will try to find it. I am trying to help marriages that otherwise could not have been saved, prevent unnecessary or premature divorce, and help people make the right decision for them. I ask that you please trust that I have your best interest at heart.

Diagnosing Your Marriage

Okay, now, like a math equation, it's time to put the things we just discussed together and see what we have, starting with the stage of marriage crisis you perceive yourself to be in.

Part One Exercise: The Stages of Marital Deterioration

Mark the one that fits where you are best:

STAGE ONE. Low-Grade Marital Fever. You've had the "Uh oh, I think I'm unhappy" moment and are now watching to see if your situation is serious or just a phase.

STAGE TWO. Medium-Grade Marital Fever. You have concluded that your negative feelings are serious, and the thought that this could lead to divorce quickly crossed your mind and was just as quickly dismissed for a wide variety of reasons.

STAGE THREE. High-Grade Marital Fever. As unhappy as you are, you have decided to remain in the relationship, and the way you've decided to cope is by pulling away some- what and finding enjoyable things to do away from your partner, such as going back to school or work, beginning a fitness routine, or having an affair. After a time, you notice the level of your discontentment increasing, and you think about divorce more and more.

STAGE FOUR. The Point of No Return. Your negative feelings come to a head in a dramatic decision-making moment. Your partner says or does something one day—it could be big or small—that gives you clarity that you cannot remain with a person who would say or do that thing. You make the decision to end the relationship right away or in the near future.

STAGE FIVE. The Death of the Marriage. The relationship appears to be at its end, though this could change. The Leaning-In partner is usually informed of the Decider's unhappiness or desire to leave, and details or potential for uncoupling may be discussed. All is not lost at this point, and anything could happen. This is where my coaching for the Leaning-In partner must be followed so that the Decider's decision to leave does not become an easy one.

The rejected partner almost always vehemently resists the end of the relationship. Although this is called the "death of relationship," it really is the death of the way the relationship *was*. Whether the couple is able to reconcile, or they divorce, the way their relationship *was* will cease to exist, and a new beginning—or end—will reveal itself. Now the real work begins as to whether this marriage can be saved.

If there was a Stage Six, I would call it the "fragile period" because things must be handled and done a certain way during this time to make sure you do no more damage than you have already done to your relationship, ensure you don't make any quick or snap decisions that may be difficult to undo before it is absolutely the right time, and make sure those decisions are made intelligently and for the right reasons. This is a period when a couple must tread delicately with each other while their instincts may be telling them to create drama or cause a scene. Although the Decider has likely now expressed they want out of the marriage, or at least expressed doubt about whether they want to stay or go, I know that we are a long way from being certain one way or the other.

Part Two Exercise: The Marriage Circles Exercise

When it comes to the Marriage Circles, we'd be optimistic for a positive outcome if the Decider is still in the circle, on the line, or outside the circle and looking back and forth. And to have the motivation to do marriage therapy and repair, we need to have ARE or the willingness to develop it.

With that said and based on your understanding of the Marriage Circles Exercise, where do you believe the Decider is now?

Do you believe your marriage has ARE currently?

☐ Yes   ☐ No

Do you believe both partners in your marriage are now ready to attain ARE through dedicated marriage therapy?

☐ Yes   ☐ No

If either partner is outside the circle, you are in a marriage crisis and may need a managed separation intervention, and if there is no motivation to do marriage therapy now or to attain ARE, the same is true.

As far as the Big Question, both partners need to be willing to work on their marriage, and on the motivation scale, we need a six or above from both partners.

Now you should know and understand the situation more clearly. No matter where you or your partner are in this process, let's make sure to put our focus on stabilizing things and not making matters worse.

This means controlling your response behaviors and learning all the helpful information available to help you and your family make the wisest possible decisions. Because you were drawn to this book in the first place, I am guessing things are really bad right now, and you have concluded that your marriage is indeed in crisis and could end in divorce. That means the situation is fragile and must be handled very carefully. Again, I strongly recommend that you have a marriage crisis manager like me to coach you or a marriage and family therapist with experience to help you every step of the way.

Wrapping It All Up: An Overview

Taking everything together, let's look again at how serious your marriage issues are.

Best-Case Scenario

- No affair. In Stages One, Two, or Three of marital deterioration, no one's back is turned on the marriage, but the Decider is leaning outward and is ready to leave if there is no change.
- The Decider wants to stay in the marriage if repair, change, and growth occur on both sides.
- The Leaning-In partner is willing to repair, grow, and change.
- Both are at six or above in willingness to work as indicated on the "I Want to Work on My Marriage" scale (see page 45).

Worst-Case Scenario

- One of the partners is in an ongoing, emotionally involved love affair.
- The relationship is in Stage Four or Five of the marital deterioration process.
- Outside the circle, the Decider's back is turned away from the marriage.
- The Decider has no interest in marriage therapy or repair.

With a heavy interest in working things out and a motivation level of six or above, we can get a lot done toward repairing your marriage, and separation would be a highly premature idea. But if the Decider's motivation level is at zero, separation is often the best option because it gives them room and time to return their nervous system to the parasympathetic. Once they are no longer in a reactive state, we may see what remains and hopefully motivate them to return to working on the marriage in a way it has never been worked on before. And remember, even though a person is at a motivation level of zero today, it does not mean it will always be a zero. The nature of a marriage crisis is such that anything can happen, and for the Leaning-In partner, this is very good news.

Other marital interventions for couples in crisis can also be explored, such as discernment counseling, which is an intervention of five sessions or less to move couples out of ambivalence. In those few sessions, a discernment counselor guides a deliberate conversation meant to assist couples in exploring their roles in the marriage's issues and what they have done to see if it could be saved. The three choices presented to the couple are (1) decide whether to stay married and keep the marriage as it is, (2) separate and immediately divorce, or (3) dedicate an intense six-month effort to working on the marriage followed by a decision to stay together or divorce. I will explain discernment counseling more fully in Chapter 6.

It is my hope that what was confusing is now becoming clearer. You are starting to understand that the marriage crisis is real; it is a serious threat to a marriage; the Decider has not lost their mind, but their sympathetic nervous system is firing, and they are in flight mode; things can be orchestrated to give a couple the best chance for reconciliation (if that is their first choice); and there are ways to manage the situation when a person has no interest, at least today, for reconciliation. A marriage crisis is volatile, and anything can happen, and how both parties conduct themselves in the coming days, weeks, and months will determine what happens in the end.

CHAPTER THREE

How Did This Happen?

When we meet the person we fall in love with, a chemical reaction that is as intoxicating as some of the world's best-known mind-altering drugs usually kicks in. Just like heroin and cocaine, being near our love interest causes high levels of dopamine, serotonin, and norepinephrine to be released in our brains, which send us into a giddy-goo-goo euphoric mood zone where appetite and ability to concentrate are altered, sleep feels unneeded, and we end up in the place that has inspired thousands of love stories and songs. It is during this period, known alternatively as the *attraction, romantic chemistry, cathexis, limerence,* or *seduction stage,* that people who are probably not functional enough for a healthy relationship may appear to us as marvelous mate material.

What do I mean by functional enough? A person who has their self-esteem, boundaries, perception, interdependence, and moderation skills solidly in place. Someone who conducts themselves as an emotional grown-up. They have integrity and do what they say they will. The problem is that almost anyone can fake being solid and thoughtful for a certain period of time. That is why it's easy to fall for people who aren't healthy for you.

In this mesmerizing state of new love, our idealized perception contorts reality so much that we can make a gerbil appear to be Mr. or Ms. Universe, or at least "the One." When this happened to me years ago, I called it "falling in love." Years later, when I searched for answers about relationship and marital mistakes, I came to consider this feeling a warning sign. Why? The chemicals gave me a love high, putting me under a spell where I made important life decisions under the influence. These were decisions that led me to do misguided things, things that I would ultimately pay a painful price for.

I came to understand that my reasoning power was compromised in this love-struck state. When I felt the stirring of the chemicals, I'd dive right into the shallow water headfirst when I should have been leaving the pool. As I researched, read everything I could, and considered the evidence (Peck, 1987; see also Mellody, Miller, A., & Miller K., 1989; Mellody, 2003), I learned that mature love doesn't feel like a fireworks show (Powell, 2018). Instead, it's easy and comfortable, like an old leather shoe that has molded to hug the foot in the most gentle and supportive way. After major chemistry has long drifted away, our love remains driven by the cuddle hormone oxytocin (Schneiderman et al., 2012). Oxytocin helps maintain bonds, and it is that, and not wild and crazy love, that keeps couples together over the long term (Gravotta, 2013).

In an article in the *Harvard Gazette* (Powell, 2018), Richard Schwartz, associate professor of psychiatry at Harvard Medical School, explains the chemicals at play in love and bonding. He says the state we describe as love raises cortisol, a stress hormone, and turns on the neurotransmitter dopamine, which turns on the brain's pleasure centers. That gets coupled with a drop in serotonin, which causes obsession, and that is the crazy chemical concoction that causes us to forgo rational decision-making. This state of feeling like we have been stung by a bee usually lasts about a year, he says. Once that settles down, it is replaced by oxytocin. It is that warm and fuzzy calm feeling that cements bonds and keeps couples together over the lifespan, Schwartz explains. That's the feeling that I describe as the comfortable old shoe; it just feels so nice when you're wearing it.

I still believe that love relationships don't need to begin as a fireworks show and can—and maybe should—start off as a warm and fuzzy feeling instead. My experience is that when we are dating, if we feel the warm and fuzzy feelings and not the intense chemicals, we tend to write off a potentially wonderful partner. I like the idea of giving the more understated feelings a shot because you are able to keep your brain online and make rational decisions.

Do couples go through this chemical state and end up successfully married? Of course. It's most likely to happen when the courting period lasts at least two to three years and each partner has plenty of experiences together to see if they're compatible. But when individuals decide to saddle up for marriage early in the process, before learning who their partner really is, it's a game of marriage roulette, and the odds aren't in the couple's favor.

You can call the intensity of initial chemistry and romantic attraction "love" if you choose, but whatever it is, it influences us to do crazy things. Prior to the chemical attraction, we usually walk around in our daily lives with some sort of protective wall or veneer that safeguards us while we work, go to school, and are productive. When someone attractive to us appears and a mutual connection is made, we get zapped between the eyeballs with Cupid's dangerous arrow. Seemingly punch-drunk or under a spell, like cartoon characters who've been hit over the head with a love hammer, seeing stars and hearing cuckoo clock noises, our protective walls come down, and we become our most vulnerable selves with our newfound love. It's easy to become vulnerable when the spell is mutually shared because the person we're falling for presents themselves as safe. They receive whatever information we impart in the most accepting, positive, and loving way, like a therapist does in many ways. We have found our person, we tell ourselves; life is wonderful and worthwhile at last.

In reality, when we are under a love spell, we're in such a narcissistic trance that we conclude our love is different from the rest. We fantasize about a future together, in love, helping each other through the trials and tribulations of life. Sharing dreams and secrets with someone safe and validating is one of the best experiences emotional intimacy has to offer if it lasts.

If it lasts? I've had a handful of couples say they still have it after ten or twenty years, but I'm skeptical that we're talking about the same thing. Schwartz estimates that it lasts about a year, and though the length of this chemical-high period varies, dizzying love chemicals typically flow for about eighteen months to three years (Tennov, 1984). The way the love trance ends can often be abrupt and one-sided. For most of us, while we're floating on a cloud of intoxicating love, the day comes when we reach for our lover, and we notice something has changed. A criticism may arrive, we might be abused over a private matter we shared and have it thrown back in our face, annoyance or impatience may be shown, or we may be pushed away when reaching for affection. Alas, the walls have returned, and though we may stay together, our springtime love fest is over.

What happened?

Getting Zinged

I've described this phenomenon to friends and clients as the day we get *zinged*—the day we find out that something's wrong in our own little love paradise, thinking at first that perhaps our love is not feeling well or we did something to cause a temporary chill, and surely their warmth will soon return. Hundreds of my clients over the years have said, "If he or she would just go back to the way things were in the beginning, we'd be great."

Sadly, most often, it never does, as the relationship has come out of the seduction and chemical-high phases and entered a new stage where we return to real life. Our partner's best, most diplomatic self has left, and their dysfunctional relationship patterns begin to appear. They may become more critical and scrutinizing, want space and distance, or become needy and want more and more. They may now want us to be accountable for where we go and whom we see. They may resume their activities with friends as if there are no responsibilities at home. They may shift from sex on demand to sex on occasion or "by the way, let me tell you about the kinky things I've been thinking about." The possibilities are endless, but one thing is certain: a different part of them has arrived, and often, we don't like it very much.

As best behaviors fade away and we turn to more of the average, everyday us, whatever that is for each person—harried, disorganized, clean freak, controlling, ambitious, or no ambition at all—the idealization of our partner fades, leaving us to now see who they really are. Things overlooked or brushed aside are now clearly seen. Our ability to reframe or overlook the things our partner does that cause us to bristle is not as forgiving. The truth of who they really are in relationship is unfolding, and we ask, "What have I done by choosing this person?"

Cindy was forty-one and completely confused about what happened to her marriage. "When I married Sydney, I thought I had won first prize," she said. "But now I feel stuck with the booby prize. What am I going to do?"

Thankfully, many will be able to work through reality as they now see it and conclude that with flaws and all, their partner still has enough of what they need and want in a lifelong relationship to move through the romantic relationship levels to where good marriages end up, the mature marriage. Some can even successfully request a few tweaks from their partner and get the relationship working again. Marriages that function well are where power struggles are worked out and couples continue to grow and evolve and proceed through life's stages with minimal conflict. But others ponder whether a mistake has been made.

The Work of Marriage

As I have said, some people believe that the chemistry and seduction phase is love, but in my opinion, it is not. In the book *The Road Less Traveled* (1978), author Scott Peck, MD, says the possibility for love can't happen until after the intoxication period ends, for then, to love another becomes a choice. What does he mean?

If love is a verb, an action word, it means that *to love* is to do things for our love that make them feel loved. When we first fall under the influence of the seduction chemical cocktail and begin to obsess about our partner, doing things for them happens naturally. Once the chemicals simmer down, doing things for them becomes work. The work of loving someone is for adults who have the self-discipline and presence of mind to keep wooing their partner in the ways they appreciate and enjoy. In my experience, this is when the *will-we-remain-content-together-in-the-long-term* factor is decided. When I tell struggling couples that every night when I go over my calendar, I consider when I'll have time to work on my marriage, they appear surprised, but that's what it takes.

What I know from experience is that generally, both men and women want to be a priority in each other's lives, to be treated as if they matter. Women report they especially want to be wooed and treated like a girlfriend, and men tell me they want to be gushed over and petted like a puppy. No man or woman has ever denied this in a marriage therapy session when asked. So why don't we do it?

One of the bestselling books for couples, with over 20 million copies sold, *The Five Love Languages*, was written by Gary Chapman (2010). Chapman was a marriage therapist for thirty years when he realized that couples' complaints ran along five different areas: physical touch, words of affirmation, quality time, acts of service, and gifts. Note that each of these categories is focused on loving *actions*. If your partner's love language is *acts of service* and you rarely help them out, I'm guessing you hear about it. What most individuals don't realize is that when you don't do the things that make your partner feel loved, they will eventually lose their romantic feelings. The huge tank of love fuel you started off with is not hooked to an endless pipeline, and it must continually be refilled and topped off. If your spouse's love needs and wants are ignored or not done enough, the tank will eventually go on reserve and then become empty. When a tank is empty, you can feel it. I can see a spouse who is resentment filled, checked out, and stubbornly waiting for a miracle that, if nothing changes, will likely never arrive. When I see this, I know I'm looking at an empty love tank.

If I were the person issuing marriage licenses to couples across the land (and how I wish I were), I would want to tell them how much time and work are involved in maintaining a good marriage. I would explain that such a commitment is serious and for adults only. Girls and boys who want to do what they want to do without regard for others are not marriage material. I would also say that by getting married, you are agreeing to join a team, and what your partner wants is as important as what you want, and you have to be willing to negotiate outcomes that benefit the whole. Only after a mutually agreed decision is made between the two is it ever appropriate to have expectations of the other.

Your Part in the Marriage Crisis

Thousands of factors can take down a marriage. Incompatibility, different personalities, different levels of maturity, desires, dreams. What I am interested in is what you believe your part in it to be. The most powerful thing you can do for yourself right now, whether you are the *Decider or the Leaning-In partner, is to figure out why you dropped the ball in your marriage.*

Exercise: What Is My Part in the Failing Marriage?

Here are some questions to ponder:

When my partner wanted to talk about issues, I was receptive and open.   ☐ T   ☐ F

If you answered false, describe how you responded to the requests.

_____

_____

_____

_____

When I had issues with my partner, I was able to go to them and calmly and respectfully talk to them.
☐ T   ☐ F

If you answered false, describe if and how you let them know you were struggling in the relationship.

_____

_____

_____

_____

If my partner asked to go to marriage therapy, I was more than willing.   ☐ T   ☐ F

If you answered false, describe why you were reluctant to get counseling.

_____

_____

_____

_____

Did you put enough focus on keeping your relationship alive through the years?   ☐ Yes   ☐ No

If you answered no, what kept you from doing so?

_____

_____

_____

_____

Were you flexible and "go with the flow" in your daily life, or were you more rigid and controlling?
☐ Flexible   ☐ Rigid and controlling

If you were more rigid and controlling, what was your reason for that?

_____

_____

_____

Thinking back on your fighting and arguing style, was it effective in getting you what you wanted and needed?

☐ Yes   ☐ No

If not, how could you have approached your partner differently?

_____

_____

_____

_____

Did you encourage and support your partner's hopes and dreams?

☐ Yes   ☐ No

If not, what was your reasoning for not doing so?

_____

_____

_____

_____

Do you feel you have done everything you could to work things out in your marriage?   ☐ Yes   ☐ No

If you answered no, what things could you have done, and perhaps could still do, to work things out?

_____

_____

_____

_____

And finally, what do you think the purpose of marriage is?

_____

_____

_____

_____

The Loss of Hope

When a partner gives up hope of having their needs met, the formula is in place to create an eventual marriage crisis. Typically, an unhappy partner may begin expressing themselves in a passive-aggressive manner about things they're not happy about; then they become more aggressive and move on to an angry plea; and then finally, they make an anguished plea. If the anguished plea doesn't get results, the Decider concludes they have run out of options and they sit back and wait for the marriage to die. This exhibits the loss of hope for change.

Dialing the clock back to the beginning, many of the couples I see had promised to love, honor, and cherish in their wedding vows, which is quite a serious promise. Whoever thought up the vows originally must have known something about what it takes to keep a marriage alive. What does each one mean?

- **Love.** Practice the love languages and the loving actions that make your partner feel loved. If they need to be touched, touch them. To refuse to do so or make excuses for not doing it is a refusal to love.
- **Honor.** This is respect: keeping the level of conversation on the high road, never hitting below the belt; speaking to each other on equal footing, never talking down to the other; being influenced by your partner's wishes, hopes, and dreams.
- **Cherish.** Value your partner through words, actions, and deeds, showing them that they are precious to you.

Most of the couples I've worked with said the wedding vows but never sat down and gave much thought to what they were promising, and this is a big mistake. If a spouse hasn't considered the seriousness of the vows, they might still be aware of the five love languages being something that marriages need, but are they practicing any of it? No, and the excuses are all the same: We are busy with work, children, aging parents, going back to school, you name it. Too many people in our culture have allowed themselves to become human pack mules, carrying too heavy a load to be able to enjoy the lighter, fun side of life and the joys of a connected, intimate relationship. Relationships are something you make time for.

Setting solid boundaries and saying no to things that could tilt us into a state of overwhelm is the daily tweaking a relationally minded person does. When I was married to my children's father, he never explained to me that his goal was not only to be the best doctor of his kind in our region but to be one who was super involved in the community. I started seeing it unfold, and to me, he was already busy enough working crazy hours as a doctor, but he kept piling on responsibilities. He'd become president of an organization, then become the doctor for a university or high school sports department and be required to attend their games. Rather than including me in his dream of making a true difference in people's lives, he kept it a secret. I had no idea why he was doing all these extracurricular activities, and all I could see was that every time he added something else to his agenda, it meant he wasn't going to be with the children and me, and guess what? Resentment piled high.

When we'd go to one of the many community events he attended, people used to brag to me about how selfless he was, and all I could think was that the adoring public enabled him, and three people were paying a high price for that. I think he didn't explain what was happening out of fear of my reaction, but had he included me in his dream, let me be a part of it, I think I'd have been all in.

Excuses and Justifications for Not Giving a Marriage What It Needs

I tell friends that someday I'd like to write an article about all the excuses and justifications I have heard in my career for why a person won't do the obvious right thing for their family and relationships. The excuses and justifications for not making time for marriage and children are hope killers, and it is the loss of hope that leads a Decider down the marital deterioration tunnel and straight into the marriage crisis. Some of the things said that kill hope are:

- "This is just the way I am. Deal with it."
- "You're the one who needs to go to therapy, not me."
- "I will stop [fill in the blank . . . drinking, smoking, chewing . . .] after [fill in the blank . . . the holidays, next month, after the project at work, after our summer vacation . . ."]
- "It's my birthday [or whatever commemorative day] month."
- "What I'm doing [or not doing] is not that bad!"
- "You want me to be perfect, and I'll never be perfect!"
- "I don't know how."
- "No one in my family ever expected that."
- "Why can't you be like my parents? They never complained."
- "Your friends [or family] have got you thinking there's something wrong with me! They're the problem, not me!"
- "I do not have a drinking problem! I can quit anytime I like!"
- "Pot is safe and never killed anyone!"
- "You're being [a nag, an asshole, mean]!"
- "You've got it so good; I can't believe you have the nerve to complain."
- "You just can't be happy."

Yes, people are busy, but those who want to have a thriving marriage will eliminate the unnecessary things and create balance in their lives, enough to give their partner what they need or, if their partner would be amenable to it, find a way to include them as part of the team. The key word is *enough*. Most of us do not expect a utopia of love and romance over the decades, but by golly, can't you put your focus on me enough to let me know that you are happy to have me in your life and that I am special to you? If you haven't done your part, wake up. You may get a chance for a do-over with the person you're married to now, but if you don't and want to meet someone new, make sure you are ready and willing to put in the time and focus that it takes to have a good marriage; otherwise, the same pattern will likely repeat itself.

Is Anyone Happily Married?

Beyond the basic pattern of how a once-loving partnership shifts into a deteriorating process as just described, there are so many factors that can take a marriage down that sometimes I think it's a wonder some marriages remain happy over the long term, though we know they do.

Professor and researcher John Gottman has provided prolific insight into every aspect of marriage and divorce, and his research is a reference point for virtually all marriage therapists like me. In *The Seven Principles for Making Marriage Work*, Gottman and coauthor Nan Silver write that around 60 percent of couples report being happy (1999), though my gut, experience, and personal observation tell me it's not that high. The report really does beg the question, "What is it to be happy?"

Gottman has provided insight into what predicts divorce, and his

Four Horses of the Apocalypse (Gottman & Silver 1999) divorce predictors are legend to marriage therapists. They are:

1. **Criticism.** Direct verbal stabs at who someone is. Examples: "You are [fill in the blank: lazy, an asshole, frigid, a bitch, selfish]" and on and on.

   What to do instead: Understand that sentences beginning with "You . . ." seem to be a trigger for most brains. We hear that word, and our brains say, "You are about to get slammed; brace yourself." If a partner is doing something you don't care for, talk about it from your point of view.

   Old way: "You are so lethargic and lazy; how much TV are you watching anyway?"

   New way: "I'm not romantically attracted to you when I see you devoting so much of your life to watching TV."

2. **Defensiveness.** Denying responsibility for something as opposed to just admitting it or at least validating how the other person sees it. Also includes minimizing, deflection, and other defense mechanisms.

   What to do instead: It's difficult for most of us, and impossible for others, to see ourselves as doing anything wrong, much less admit it. Sure, you didn't intend to do something your partner disliked, but they disliked what you did, so acknowledge it.

   Old way: "I am not always late! Stop saying that. You are late sometimes, too, and anyway, you certainly aren't perfect. Let's talk about when you. . . ." Defending yourself against things your partner knows are at least partially true frustrates them and lets them know that you will keep doing it.

New way: "Yep, I am sometimes late, and I know that irritates you. I promise to work on it." Admitting at least a grain of truth in what the person says will deflate the speaker's ire immediately. Try it.

3. **Contempt.** Coming from a better-than-you stance, a person looks down at another in disgust. I consider this one to be the metastatic cancer that will eventually kill the marriage as it reveals an often irreparable loss of respect. It has to be off-limits.

   What to do instead: Recognize that you are looking down your nose at your partner in disgust like a parent to a naughty child. Remind yourself that nothing good comes from this stance; put yourself on your partner's level and address your needs or wants as an adult.

   Old way: "You think you're perfect, don't you, Ms. Big Britches? Well, that's a laugh. I see now that you are just like your mother, and it's disgusting! I don't know why I didn't see it when we were dating."

   New way: "I feel hurt, and it's a huge turn off when you do things like X."

4. **Stonewalling.** Shutting down, walking away, refusing to cooperate.

   What to do instead: Your partner said something, and you got activated. Freezing comes from the AC, so do not do it. Instead, say something diplomatic from your best self. Lean into your partner. If you are too activated to respond, tell them to give you twenty minutes to cool off, and then return to the conversation from your wise adult self.

   Old way: Benson says something that doesn't sit well with

Martha; she looks at him and goes mute. She then refuses to speak to him for three days.

New way: Benson says something that upsets Martha, and she slows herself down to respond, takes a deep breath, and says, "Benson, I hear that you think I'm always irresponsible, but in my opinion, that's an exaggeration. Can we at least agree that sometimes I am responsible?"

The four behavior patterns above are extremely common and do great damage. I have seen too many couples do all four in fifteen seconds or less, but these are not the only things that inflict damage on a marriage. Here's a list of common scenarios that often weigh heavily on compatibility and the ability to enjoy life together:

- **Power discrepancies.** One partner has more power than the other, whether it's in the form of money, education, age difference, beauty, socioeconomic class, or career.
- **Health issues.** Hypochondria, migraines, chronic illness, depression, and other mental, mood, and brain disorders.
- **Loyalty to and enmeshment with friends or biological family.** At least one partner values or is more influenced by what their friends or biological family want or need over what their spouse wants and needs. Some partners allow their family or friends unfettered access to their family home and personal business.
- **Lack of boundaries.** This can play out in thousands of ways. If boundaries are our protection system, a person without boundaries might talk about things to others their spouse doesn't want talked about; post personal things on social media; allow people to touch, hug, or kiss inappropriately; demean their spouse in front of others; be unable to say no; or engage in the ever-subjective inappropriate dressing.

- **Secret keeping.** Most of us know what rates as headline news in our lives and is worth sharing with our spouse. Those who keep important information—like financial decisions or difficulties, a financial windfall, spending habits and high credit card balances, loss of a job or suspension, bad grades, illness, withdrawal from school, cross-dressing, questioning sexuality, upset and resentment, staying in touch with exes, or gambling—as a secret from our partners will likely deeply regret not letting them know.
- **Finances.** Friction arises over spending, the inability to provide or contribute, irresponsibility, or being too conservative or frugal.
- **Sex.** Whether it's too much, too little, outrageous requests (including open marriage), perversions, or kinks, being on different pages creates problems.
- **Child raising.** Parenting styles collide when one parent is too lenient, too strict, or too attached.
- **The three marital felonies.** Addictions, abuse, and adultery.
- **Activity level.** From too active to sedentary or a shift from one to the other.
- **Household cleanliness and organization.**
- **Religion.**
- **Different ethnic or socioeconomic backgrounds.**
- **Different beliefs and values.**

My cultural pet peeve is how many ridiculous courses are taught in middle and high school, things most of us will never use, like dissecting a cat and the features of the solar system, and though attempts may be made today to teach healthy relationship and social dynamics skills, many people over thirty have never had those classes, and I'm not sure that what they're teaching today is thorough enough to change a culture anyway.

Instead, we learn about relationships through our families and friends, and most of us were raised by dysfunctional people. Even my clients who insist they had a great family and childhood eventually learn that it wasn't as wonderful as they once thought. When I first started going to therapy in my twenties, I was searching for answers to the question, "What is it to be a healthy adult mentally, emotionally, relationally?" I had no idea if I was the problem, if the people in my life were the problem, or if it was a little of both. I wanted someone to tell me what being healthy was, to point me to a book and lay it all out as you would lay out a map and find a route to a destination.

The therapy helped me understand that I was not crazy and that, in fact, I was a very reasonable and accepting person. This was a relief, as I was prepared to hear what my family had been telling me for years: that I was not smart, I was a bubble off-center, I had no ambition or drive, my personality wasn't serious enough, and what a complete mistake-making factory I was. It took me years to unlearn these ideas and begin to see myself as who I really am.

What really propelled me in life to start homing in on my own reality about who I really was and where I needed to head on the map to being healthy and functional was the book I mentioned before, *The Road Less Traveled* by Peck, plus some weekend seminars I attended where they drilled down on people to get real for three twelve-hour days at a time. I walked into the seminars a meek and tentative form of me and walked out ready to take on anything and everything, and that's never changed. Today, resources abound for learning what being healthy and functional is, like books (print, digital, audio), podcasts, YouTube videos, workshops, and seminars. (See Appendix II for my list of recommended seminars, workshops, books, and videos.) I wish every person would seek them out and do all they can to peel away the layers that keep them from being their best self because the best self is who we should be bringing to our relationships, and the question is, have you been bringing that, and if not, why not?

What Makes a Person a Good Spouse?

Most of my clients tell me that their measure of being a good spouse is to be nice, a good person. Traditionally raised Caucasian men often tell me that they were taught by their fathers that a good-enough husband is an ample provider and doesn't abuse or beat his wife. With criteria like this, it's not surprising that so many marriages struggle and end up in the deterioration process.

Since American women successfully rebelled against the male-dominant culture in the last century, with only 12 percent of married women working outside the home in the 1930s, 40 percent by 1970, and 76 percent by the late 1990s (Yellen, 2020), they have required more from their relationships. Women want men who can connect emotionally as well as physically, and they want help with the burdens of life.

Additionally, mass high school education meant more women graduating, new technologies increased demand for clerical workers, and women increasingly filled those jobs, and jobs became cleaner and safer, removing some of the stigma of married women who worked (Yellen, 2020). Of course, more working wives meant more wives became able to support themselves, resulting in kicking out husbands who squandered their power when they had it. Most men got the message back then and understand that women are unwilling to settle for a marriage without emotional intimacy and fair distribution of life's responsibilities. The problem is, thanks to the way American culture is, men still struggle with the emotional intimacy aspects of relationships, and it's no surprise. Maybe they had male influences who preached toxic masculinity, or as teens, their friends teased one another for showing weakness, which, by their definition, is the equivalent of showing emotions and vulnerability. In the end, men can and will try to fit in with men, but when they come home, they have to switch to the Relationship Channel and be what women want and need, which is different and not easy or natural for them.

Good marriages don't just happen. They are deliberate and thoughtful and take a lot of time and effort. Who do you know that practices this? Hundreds of books have been written on how to have a great marriage. Who reads them and then practices what the authors say on a day-in, day-out basis? Almost no one, of course. I'd guess that most people who read them, usually women, get some takeaways they practice for a month or two at the longest. That's not the kind of change that creates what we're talking about. To really change a belief about something, we have to conclude that change is necessary, and the new belief has to make more sense to you than your previous one.

Marilyn was referred to me by her boss, who is a friend of mine. He was very worried about her, saying, "Her husband said he wants a divorce out of the blue, after almost forty years together. She's an absolute basket case. Please help her."

When the sixty-seven-year-old arrived, she looked frail and defeated.

"My husband wants a divorce, and he won't even give me a chance to change or win him back," she said. "I don't know what I'm going to do or how I'm going to survive financially or in any other way. I really can't even afford this visit. I can't believe he's doing this to me. Why didn't he say something?"

Marilyn is a secretary, and her husband is in real estate. She insisted they have lived paycheck to paycheck their entire marriage, though I find that hard to believe. She loves her husband and their life together and fears becoming destitute. Her fears are real.

After hearing her story, it seems to me she knows very little about the family finances, what's going on with her husband, or much of anything else. She's been checked out and couldn't answer most of the questions I had about what got them to this point. I asked if I could reach out to her husband for insight, and she agreed.

Robert is seventy-two and sounds chipper on the phone. He agreed to speak to me one time, saying he wanted me to help Marilyn move on. Firm in his desire to divorce and seemingly happy about it, he said Marilyn had been withdrawn and a nonparticipant in the marriage since the beginning. "She barely functions," he said. "She just goes through the motions with no passions or interests, and she's barely acknowledged me for years. I only have a few more years to live, most likely, and I want to spend it finding some joy for myself, and you can't convince me she has been happy all this time."

I've heard this story many times: a couple who married and do not understand what it takes to keep a marriage alive and thriving. In the beginning, there was chemistry and attraction, so they were attentive to each other. Then, as time goes on, they get busy and stressed and stop making their partner a priority. Daily routines of work, chores, and eating and sleeping with little or no focus on the romantic relationship is a wonderful recipe for killing a marriage.

The next time I saw Marilyn, I gave her a copy of *The Five Love Languages* by Gary Chapman (2010) and asked her to read it so she could better understand what had happened to her marriage. When she returned, the book had numerous highlights, underlines, and dozens of little place markers sticking out the sides.

"I didn't do any of the things they tell you to do in this book," she says. "I didn't know you had to do all this to keep a marriage going. Why didn't anyone tell me? I told Robert we were fools, that I'd do all of it now, but he doesn't want to hear it. He just wants me to accept that we're getting a divorce. Why won't he give me a chance?"

These are the saddest situations. Marilyn was indeed in trouble. She'd put all her eggs in the man-basket, and her future was now uncertain. When she told me how much money she made as a secretary, my heart sank. She didn't make enough from social security or work to pay rent in a decent place, and as far as she was aware, they had no savings. In her marriage, Marilyn admitted to practicing the "no news is good news" philosophy, and Robert kept his rising discontentment to himself. He felt lonely and neglected and eventually became vulnerable to another woman's positive attention. Yes, though he denied it, I felt certain he had a secret relationship that brought not only the smile to his face but the courage to leave Marilyn and stand his ground.

Can such a marriage be saved? Probably not. But there are many lessons and takeaways for Marilyn and all of us to learn and benefit from. The first is practicing stellar self-care—mind, body, and spirit—and every individual who ever contemplates marriage should have a Plan B if their marriage ends prematurely through death or divorce, a plan that prepares them to financially support themselves in a manner whereby they can more than survive. All of us should be doing this at the minimum. For men or women who are in a rocky marriage now, I implore you to start on your Plan B solution without delay. It is never too late to prepare to take care of yourself financially, no matter what happens.

Other Things That Help and Hurt Marriages

Marriage therapists know that certain personalities and upbringings can be predictors of a person's unsuitability for a give-and-take relationship, and the rule is that the more grandiose or better than, rigid, controlling, strict, or closed off someone's upbringing was, the more likely their romantic relationships will falter. This is common sense. Think about it—who on earth would be happy with someone who controls, criticizes, and demands that certain rules be followed? Indeed, the more grandiose or rigid a person is, the more likely their fighting style is nasty and may draw blood. That these qualities don't work well in marriage is an understatement.

On the other end, marriages that tend to be happy involve individuals who are humble, flexible, good-natured, go-with-the-flow, accepting people willing and able to bend and grow as their partner and the marriage itself changes. That two people will change during a marriage is a given, and the better anyone is at having the ability to step aside and allow their partner's life journey to unfold, the more likely their lifetime relationship will experience mostly smooth sailing. The fighting style of these good-humored folks is typically to laugh things off in a gentle, teasing way. When they fight, it barely appears on the surface to be a fight. Never, ever would a person like this hit below the belt.

One of the most common years of a marriage for people to divorce is year twenty-two. Both my brother and sister got divorced during year twenty-two, and I could name dozens of other couples off the top of my head who did, too. Why? Typically, the couple married young. Often, the female grew up during her twenties and changed a lot from the girl she was when she married, becoming more independent, so how does her mate handle her demands to have a seat at the table and have her own opinions and sway in the relationship? If she had children during those years, she likely focused a lot on them and maybe work, too, while culturally, men usually focus more on their careers. If the couple puts little focus on the relationship during these years, then when the kids leave the nest, the couple may find they have nothing in common anymore, and they'll find themselves at a crossroads—do we have enough still to build something greater for phase two of the marriage, or are we so far apart that we'd prefer to chuck it and move on? A lot of couples choose to chuck it, though the decision is usually made by one partner, not both.

John Gottman (1999) writes that happy marriages have seven components:

1. Knowing each other so well that each of you could pass a comprehensive exam about each other's lives, interests, hopes, and dreams.

2. You work together to make life's dreams come true.

3. You both allow yourselves to be influenced by your partner, discuss issues that come up in an adultlike manner, and know how to take care of yourself and possess an ability to soothe yourself.

4. You share fondness and admiration for each other.

5. When you call out for connection, your partner is there for you, and vice versa.

6. You possess positive perspectives about yourself and each other, thinking in terms of we as opposed to me.

7. You create shared meaning, such as rituals you do together, things you both look forward to, traditions, and favorite things and places.

When you look at this list, and as you read through this chapter, I imagine you are starting to see areas where you and your partner weren't doing many of the things it takes to keep love and mutual respect alive. Is it too late to start implementing them?

For now, there is only one thing to do: Get as healthy as you can within yourself, for yourself. While your original rocket fuel for this endeavor may come from wanting to get your marriage back, no matter what the end result is, you can't lose. You will be prepared mentally and emotionally to be a fully healthy adult who has the ability to be relational and do the give-and-take healthy partnerships require, whether it's in your current marriage or future committed relationships.

Advice for the Decider

When my clients come to me in a marriage crisis, I tell Deciders they must earn a divorce if that is the direction they are leaning because too many people regret ending their marriages when they did. Research on the subject containing exact numbers on how many Deciders regret divorce is difficult to come by, but looking back, if you add the idea of seeing how everyone fared, and knowing what you know now, I am convinced that a large number of Deciders wish they had done *more* to try to save their marriages when they had the chance. Though I am happy in my marriage now and wouldn't trade it for anything, I would put myself in the group that wishes they had done more when it comes to my children and their dad. I know for certain that we still loved each other and that where we went wrong was in the way we handled the crisis itself. Our children suffered greatly because of our divorce, the conflicts between their dad and me, and the resentment felt toward the stepparents we brought into the mix. Their dad and I were smart and capable, and we could have done the work it would have required to reset our lives and move forward in a positive way. All I can do as redemption for my errors is help you now, so you don't follow in my footsteps.

You have to ask yourself, "Have I done everything I can to get the marriage I have working for us both? Is it possible I am giving up too soon? Would time spent apart be a worthwhile endeavor so we can both see how we feel in six months or a year?" If you have any doubt whatsoever about proceeding toward divorce, then I am pleading with you to slow yourself down, take your time, let the dust settle, and see where you are in the months ahead. You will not regret it, but you may well regret leaving too soon.

Advice for the Leaning-In Partner

For the Leaning-In partner, this is *not* the time to run to the Decider and tell them you've been taking an inventory and are starting to understand the many facets in which your marriage took a wrong turn and now you're prepared to fix it. Why? Because they will be disgusted that you are taking such an interest now when you did not or were not willing to earlier. They likely have zero interest in working on the marriage right now, though this can and often does change. Bide your time, keep learning and growing. The purpose of this exercise is to help couples in a marriage crisis come out of denial that the marriage was pretty good and the one who wants to leave is crazy. It is meant for you to wake up and have insight into the errors made, learn from them, and keep them in your back pocket for when the Decider is ready to hear what you have to say. Your focus needs to be on getting as healthy as you can as an individual so you will be ready when either the Decider wants to hear what you have to say or your life moves forward.

Can Every Marriage Be Saved?

Not every marriage can or should be saved. Idealists out there will hate reading those words, but hear me out. Emotional immaturity is something that can be repaired, and at the end of the day, a lot of marriages end wrongly because of things that could have been repaired and improved fairly quickly with a couple's trauma therapist—it's their job to help people become emotional adults.

But there are things about people that cannot be changed or are highly unlikely to change. When a person suffers from serious mental disorders such as narcissistic, histrionic, borderline, or antisocial personality disorders, it is what it is—what endless havoc these people wreak in other's lives. The way these people are wired means that they won't accept responsibility for their many wrong actions, and if people won't recognize their own shortcomings and issues, there will not be change. Many abusive individuals have one or more of these or other personality disorders. The odds of someone abusive doing a 180-degree shift to being kind and understanding are very low, and without extreme motivation to change and intensive therapy designed for abusive people, the chances are nil.

Other things that are hard to overcome are the three marital felonies: adultery, abuse, and addiction. Adultery can often be overcome if it is not a chronic sex and love addiction, and if it is, recovery is difficult. All addicted people could go into recovery, but the first hurdle is getting a person to admit they have a problem, and the second is to get them to agree to get help. Without help, the odds are stacked against them because the factors that lead a person to addictive behaviors are so multifaceted, and all the twisted knots of their thinking and woundedness need well-thought-out treatment plans and lifelong commitment. If a person thinks they can stop their addiction by controlling themselves, it tells me how much they don't know. Quit the behavior, yes, but the underlying toxic shame and immature responses to slights will remain. All too often, one addiction will be exchanged for another.

I'll be going into more detail in the next chapter about things a person should take into consideration when pondering whether to divorce, as well as offer more detail about mental health, physical health, and addictions. I want Deciders to understand which types of situations are repairable and which may not be.

CHAPTER FOUR

Other Questions to Consider as You Ponder Whether to Work on Your Marriage

People are amazing and complicated, and understanding whether a marriage can be saved is complicated, too. We talked about motivation, and we simply must have that to do successful marriage therapy, but all the motivation in the world won't help some couples. In a moment, I will go into the things that make me pessimistic about a relationship's future, or at least the ability for it to become healthy, but I first want to say that though many of us make those wedding vows and promise to hang in there through bad and good, I don't think all of us can make it until death and have marriage be a healthy or wise choice at the same time. Whether someone can change, and how much, is the important question in a divorce decision.

I'm glad most of us say those vows and take them seriously. However, they have sometimes become such an obstacle to getting people to make healthy choices for themselves that I began to really think about what the vows mean. Does promising those things really mean we have to put up with anything and everything in a relationship no matter what?

I do not believe so.

The situations most difficult to deal with are the ones where one or both partners have serious mental illness, such as extreme uncontrolled bipolar disorder, personality disorders, addiction, abuse, manipulative and controlling tendencies, rigid black-and-white thinking, serial infidelity, immaturity, issues with telling the truth, extremely low self-esteem, grandiosity, and insecure feelings. In these cases, we simply have to consider how likely a person is to go from being in a place where they do emotional harm to their partner or cannot be a nurturing and life-enhancing partner to becoming a healthy and balanced person. If we conclude that one or both partners probably aren't going to be able to change that much and the negative patterns are likely to continue, you will have an important decision to make.

I had a professor in graduate school, Dr. John Koiner, who taught human growth and development, and while I dreaded the class, thinking it wouldn't be interesting, I could not have been more wrong. Part of the reason I enjoyed it so much was that Dr. Koiner was experienced and seemed to delight in sharing golden nuggets of counseling wisdom that are now imprinted in my brain. I use them often in my practice, and more importantly, in my experience, everything he taught us turned out to be dead-on.

One of those fabulous nuggets was what choices any of us have available to us when we have a problem. There are only three, according to Dr. Koiner:

Accept the situation the way that it is.

Change the situation by asking a person to do something differently, or you can choose to think of the situation differently and then accept it.

Eliminate the situation if you can't accept or change it. That could mean ending a relationship or a job.

Wow. That conversation was so profound for me that I went home and made a little poster on green paper with those three words on it, framed it, and hung it in my office. I am always delighted when a client says, "That's all, only *three* choices?"

Yep, only three. I think these three choices are important to keep in mind as you ponder what course you are going to take in your relationship. For example, you may be able to change, but your spouse not so much, or vice versa. That leaves you with the option of accepting or eliminating. Most clients in terrible marriages and seriously contemplating divorce tell me that accepting the situation *as is* is not an option. But when they see that the word *elimination* is the only one left, they often look nauseated.

Still, I think you need to keep the three choices in mind as we now talk about the issues mentioned before: serious mental illness, addiction, abuse, manipulation, power and control tendencies, rigid black-and-white thinking, serial infidelity, issues with telling the truth, extreme self-esteem issues, and insecure feelings. These are the most difficult things to change, and most people who have extreme sorts of behaviors or beliefs are going to have a very difficult time indeed with turning from those ways to becoming moderate and healthy. It can be done sometimes, though I've only seen it rarely, and they have to want it badly and work their tails off for a long time, even a lifetime, to maintain their newly attained mental health, a journey of continuing maintenance that is not likely to end.

In the following sections, I'll go over what I would ask myself or anyone to consider when they are seriously contemplating divorce.

Why Won't People Change?

Why people will or won't change is a fascinating subject. I use the word *will* purposely as I believe that, with very few exceptions, it's a choice. The first thing to look at is the person's personality. Some personality types are more open-minded and amenable to the idea of learning new information and growing while others are closed to any idea of that, and, of course, there's everything in between. The more willing a person is to look within with a compassionate yet critical eye and accept responsibility for mistakes made, whether intentional or not, the more likely change is possible. The people who do not change much or at all are the ones who feel they have little or no part in the deterioration of the relationship, may be dedicated to being a victim, or are closed off to the possibility of change and growth.

Being a healthy adult mentally and emotionally and having a healthy relationship with others is a learned skill, like snow skiing. No one teaches us about relationship dynamics and self-care in school, and our families are often poor examples, so most people enter adulthood not knowing a thing about it. This includes highly educated people like doctors, lawyers, therapists, and psychiatrists. Believe me when I tell you that even highly trained mental health professionals often don't know much or anything about these topics.

The reason I know about them is because early in life, I was struggling mentally, emotionally, and in relationships and wanted to know what it was to be healthy. As I have said, I was looking for something to shoot for—a place of being, a way to be that was functional. My intense curiosity about the subject led me to see therapists, become a therapist, and study the subject for decades. I am still seeking to learn more all the time, so if you decide to dive in to understand more about who you are, why you're here, and how to be healthy in relationships, know that the journey never ends.

Sometimes I get a couple who has one eager spouse and the other only willing to come in for couples therapy one time. I may see the other spouse alone after that, but it's astonishing to me that anyone would not be willing to explore new possibilities, and it's heartbreaking. The reasons are often that the person will not believe it's partially their fault that their relationship is on the downslide, their thinking is too black-and-white when relationships are all gray, and they are so avoidant of confrontation that they will not face any difficult or uncomfortable conversations with anyone, much less a marriage therapist. Their refusal to work on the marriage as a team when their partner is eager to do the repairs will lead to one thing: the eager partner will lose the ever-important hope for change, the relationship will die, and it's all so unnecessary.

Selfishness

Without self-care, a person cannot thrive and will not be able to bring their best self to their relationships. What do I mean by self-care? I mean taking care of your mind, body, and spirit the best that you can.

Presenting your best self to your family is requirement number one for healthy families and relationships. If a client wants a standing ovation from me in the self-care department, they need to be someone who gets regular medical and dental checkups, exercises, has good nutrition and hygiene, and sees a doctor when there's a concern. Add to that someone who is balanced with their time: They work, play, enjoy downtime, sleep well, and do things they love that make them feel fulfilled—do this and we'll be on our way. Add to that maintaining solid social connections and challenging their brain with new ideas and concepts, and now you have a recipe for a long, healthy physical and emotional life. A person who practices great self-care and is in touch with themself notices when things aren't right and takes stock of what's going on with themself to figure out what's going on and if it needs to be addressed. The last healthy step is taking action to make it right.

Thelma came to see me when her husband of twenty years sat her down and said he was done. She was sixty-four and admitted that she never took care of herself, instead spending any free time she had after work making sure her many grown children were okay. She was in full attachment panic and thinking of every way to get her husband back, but he was adamant that he was done.

"We had a great sex life until we didn't," she said. "Sex became painful for me about six or seven years ago, and I just told him I was done." It never occurred to Thelma that she could take herself to the doctor and seek out solutions to this common problem with post-menopausal women. Instead, she closed the door to something her husband considered vital, and he slinked away, finding other ways to be happy. He took up biking as a hobby and soon met a vibrant and healthy woman in his biking club who was more than interested in a physically healthy man and an active sex life.

All of this was completely preventable, but Thelma thought she was being a great family member by focusing on her kids and offering verbal support to her husband.

The Importance of Self-Care

I've been practicing excellent self-care for decades by making time for it. It's something I feel is necessary, so I plan and clear space for it. When for whatever reason I'm not able to do it for a bit of time, I feel a heaviness and loss of energy all over my body and in my mind.

I have a little red poodle, Penelope, who exhibits joy and enthusiasm for life to the point that neighbors and friends comment on it. She is this way because she gets her mind, body, and spirit needs met. We know what she needs and provide that, and we know what she loves, like love, affection, and running through the woods and weaving in and out of the trees, leaping over logs and chasing after the occasional squirrel or raccoon. We make that happen for her as part of our responsibility as pet owners. People are the same way and have the same sorts of needs, and each adult is responsible for knowing themselves and creating the environment in which they'll thrive.

Interestingly, Thelma and her husband divorced, and she started practicing self-care for the first time in her life. She was having a lot of fun with it, but against my recommendation, she also jumped right onto a dating website. She quickly met someone, went through the seduction stage, moved across the United States to move in with him, and lost her motivation to take care of herself. Within two years, her new beau reconnected with an old high school crush and ended his relationship with her. She reached back out to me and said he told her he lost interest when she stopped her self-care routine, gained weight, and became lethargic. I will never forget her words: "I did everything you told me told me not to. Now my heart is broken a second time, and I live a few thousand miles away from my family and can't afford to move back home."

When I see clients who are depressed, lack energy, can't relax, can't sleep, or are already exhibiting signs of chronic illness, I can pretty much guess they aren't taking care of themselves. Unbelievably, this phenomenon is as common as milk in a grocery store.

What's going on? The majority of people I've met over the years are doing very little to nothing to ensure their health and vibrance and do not give their bodies the fuel they need, and their excuses are many. Here are just a few:

- "I don't have time or the energy."
- "I can't leave the kids."
- "I can't afford it."
- "It's selfish."

It's selfish? Once that word is said, I won't be hearing it again, as I ask clients not to use the s-word moving forward, and yes, I do have a spray bottle and spray them with water if they forget. It always provides a good laugh and ensures they remember the next time.

Although the original meaning of selfish was not negative and was more about self-focus, it has turned into a negative and shaming word by our culture. What I dislike about the word is that it *discourages* self-care, and no one can thrive as an adult or in a relationship without taking really good care of themselves. Have I pounded that idea into the ground? If so, it's because when it comes to relationships, it's that important.

If your marriage is hanging in the balance, you must use whatever energy you have to raise your game from a health point of view. If you don't, the Decider will conclude that the status quo is all that awaits, and they will not go back to what was.

If you're still reluctant to focus on yourself, then you can be sure you have been negatively conditioned by a culture that applauds self-lessness and the concept that one suffers to "deserve" good things to happen to them. A nice house, car, vacation, the things you want but perhaps don't need must be earned through suffering, or people will negatively judge you. I can't count the number of times I've told someone I was going on a nice vacation or bought a new car, and the response was "That's great, Becky, you work so hard, you deserve it." I personally think we all deserve great things all the time and should not have to suffer for that to be okay.

Evie, forty-seven, looked tired and haggard. Her husband had begged her to take care of herself for years, but she didn't, thinking it was selfish. The result was a woman with chronic health issues and depression, a woman who her husband described as "a downer" and was set to discard.

"I was raised to believe that a good woman sacrificed for others," she said. "This was the measure. Selflessness. Better to give than re-ceive. If I put any focus on myself or what I wanted as a child, my parents called me selfish and bad. I wouldn't even know where to begin when it comes to self-care."

Stories like Evie's are tragic. What are the chances she'd start the process of making herself a priority? To her, buying healthy foods, exercising, and meeting her wants and needs would be so guilt-provoking that she dared not try. Her belief system was entrenched in the idea that being generous to yourself is wrong. Yet, if I could get her to understand how it is the opposite of wrong, that it is ab-solutely necessary to make sure you are vital and healthy first so you may then help others if that's what you love, and that being a healthy, well-balanced woman is necessary to save her marriage and herself, we might get somewhere.

One of my favorite examples of getting it right is found on every commercial airline trip when the flight attendant goes over the safety rules: "In case of loss of cabin pressure and you're traveling with children, put an oxygen mask on yourself first, then the children." The message is as clear as it is poignant: if Momma doesn't get oxygen, no one else will, either.

The message of selflessness as a positive attribute is thrown in our faces continually. Religion tells us it is "better to give than receive," and when someone is interviewed on the news about someone who died tragically, it's common to hear, "They were just the most selfless person ever, always putting others first."

I suppose most viewers receive that in an *ooh* and *ahh* sort of way, but I cringe and say, "There you go again, citizens of America and the media, encouraging others not to do things for themselves by highlighting selflessness as a positive trait."

The fact that people are reluctant to take care of themselves makes my job as a marriage crisis manager more difficult than it has to be but hear this: If you want to save your marriage, you're going to have to be as healthy as you can possibly be. If you're a Leaning-In partner, this is where your focus needs to be right now. Spend all the energy you have found to get the Decider back and use it instead to become healthy. If you haven't been doing this, you have to do it now. Your marriage can't go back to the way it was, and you can't go back to the way you were.

Stubborn Pride

Many a marriage has gone down over at least one partner's stubborn pride, a hardened, inflexible heart that refuses to back down. If either the Decider or Leaning-In partner gets stuck in this state, the odds against healthy reconciliation will be high.

Roger, a contractor peering over his truck's steering wheel, and his wife, Amelia, sitting in her living room, did a session via tele-health. Amelia, who had an air of desperation, said she had had a short-term affair three years earlier, something she deeply regretted, but said that Roger's unwillingness to stop bringing it up regularly was driving her crazy.

"I know what I did was horrible, but as far as affairs go, it was minor. I wasn't in love, I was just drawn in by someone who was very kind and gentle with me, and I needed that at the time. Roger can be hard," she said. "It meant nothing, Becky. I have done everything he's asked to make up to him, to tell him how sorry I am, but he brings it up numerous times every day, and I don't have any peace. It has to end. I'm literally losing my mind!"

Roger wasn't having it. "You are disgusting," he said. "The sight of you literally makes me sick."

He was speaking to her with contempt, a never-okay, seething way of talking down to someone in disgust, a predictor of divorce that spreads resentment quickly and kills marriages in short order.

I point out the contempt and tell him it has to stop or his wife will likely leave.

"Why are you still with her?" I ask.

"We have kids," he said. "If we didn't have kids, I'd be out of here."

I tell him we need to have the conversations that will enable him to put her huge misjudgment in the rearview mirror so they can move forward. We have to say all that needs to be said, reach an end-point, and end the conversation about it for good.

Staying hateful will hurt his children and destroy his marriage.

"Yeah, well, I'm the one that has to live with it," he says. "And I'm never going to let her forget about it. She humiliated me."

Roger was stuck energetically on the hard rock station, and he resisted every attempt made to switch him to the soft rock channel where miracles can occur. He reluctantly agreed to another appointment, but Amelia soon texted and said he didn't want to come back. "He just won't stop or let it go," she said. "At least you and I tried. All I can do now is make my plans to leave because I am not going to live this way."

I've come to know that people like Roger feel they must rage at and punish a partner who made a huge mistake to underline the point that the injury was a *big damn deal*. Instead of just saying that, they spew verbal and emotional waste onto their partner for months and sometimes years. It is painful to watch. I believe they are also trying to say "If you make mistakes with me, it won't be pretty."

Roger's wife clearly understood that his relentless badgering caused her to retreat to an emotional foxhole. She wanted to come out of the foxhole and enjoy her family again, but perhaps Roger had concluded that she had lost her right to peace and happiness.

He was wrong.

Humility and grace are what save broken marriages, and to implement them, you have to be willing to take a risk in the interest of love and family. If you've been injured by your spouse's marital violation, you have to drop your sword and shield and hear what the person asking for forgiveness is trying to say. If the Decider or the Leaning-In partner gets stuck in their pride or ego and dedicate themselves to digging in on whatever issue keeps them apart, then the odds for successful reconciliation are against them.

Every person's brain has a gauge for what is fair and reasonable. Amelia's brain has already concluded that the punishment dealt to her has surpassed the crime, and every time Roger pounds her after that will have diminishing returns in the form of anger, fear, and resentment. Their marriage won't make it, and on the death certificate, I would not put infidelity as the cause, I'd say stubborn pride. Roger was unwilling to take a risk and let her back in his closed-off heart, and it was his loss.

Codependence

This is one of the most misunderstood topics that I bring up in therapy sessions, and even if you think this does not apply to you, please do not skip this section. There is something about the word *codependence* that usually gets intense positive or negative reactions, yet I've never met anyone who doesn't have it. I believe the misunderstanding comes from the fact that two authors with similar names and very different approaches have written popular books on the subject, and the two camps have difficulty understanding each other because of their different definitions of what codependence is.

This played out in my own life recently when I was contacted by a major voice and well-known author in the love addiction realm who had read one of my blogs on codependence. She said I was wrong about what I wrote, which was that all addicted people are codependent, but when we talked, we found that each of us followed a different influencer on the subject. Neither of us was wrong; we just used different models. The woman followed the work of Melody Beattie, and I follow Pia Mellody's childhood developmental trauma model.

In 1986, Beattie released *Codependent No More*, and in 1989, Mellody released *Facing Codependence*. In Beattie's model, codependence is about the unhealthy behaviors we take on, such as relying on other's approval, putting others ahead of us, assuming responsibility for other's behavior, and fixing damage they cause, and it originates from alcoholic families or those with serious mental illness. Beattie herself came from a family of drugs and alcohol and followed in their same path until she woke up and started figuring out what was going on. She turned her knowledge into a career of enlightening thousands of readers about codependence. I read this book a long time ago, and it was helpful, but for me, something was missing.

Mellody, a nurse who worked at the Meadows Behavioral Health Center in the 1970s, was trying to help addicted people and their families go into recovery. At that time, addiction was not clearly understood, and there was no solid game plan to help people. Mellody's husband, Pat, was the executive director of the Meadows and asked her to solve the puzzle.

Reluctantly, she did. Over fifteen years, having visited with thousands of patients and families, Mellody found that most people suffer from the same issues that addicts do, only some don't become addicts and others do. The treatment, which she calls post-induction therapy, refers to "after you were traumatized as a child" is the same for you, me, and the addict, no matter whether substance abuse is involved. Her model of "developmental immaturity" became the base for behavioral health and rehabilitation centers around the world and continues to be respected and used today by world-renowned trauma researchers as the place to begin for all who research and understand the subject.

Olympic swimmer Michael Phelps went to the Meadows to undergo post-induction therapy years ago and turned his life around, becoming a spokesperson for healthy mental health. What he studied while there was Mellody's model. Others who have been there are Kevin Spacey, Elton John, Whitney Houston, and Selena Gomez. Post-induction therapy is powerful, and it works.

Because I had a strong interest in learning more about trauma, I happened upon Mellody's model almost fifteen years ago, went to her three trainings for therapists, and dedicated myself to using her model for individuals and couples ever since. I have never seen anything more powerful or effective for my clients, and here is the primary message: We are all struggling in life because of childhood trauma. It doesn't take much for a child to get traumatized, and most of us have thousands upon thousands of trauma wounds that lead us to dysfunctional thinking and behaviors, but in the end, childhood trauma renders us emotionally immature. Emotionally immature humans are incapable of emotional intimacy. I believe the reason your marriage is on the brink right now is explained by Mellody's model, and going into recovery from childhood developmental trauma is the solution.

Earlier, I presented a model showing the three parts of the dysfunctional personality, and it comes from the work of Mellody. The same pattern you are in now, in your marriage crisis, is what Mellody figured out so long ago: When an old trauma wound is hit, we get activated like an animal under threat; we go into fight, flight, or freeze; and our response is from our Adaptive Child, or AC, an immature and toxic part of us that thinks it's protecting us but instead is self- and relationship-destructive. Since people in marriage crisis are activated, if they allow their immature selves, the WC and AC, to make their decisions, terrible, regrettable mistakes will be made. Those two parts are what created your marital mess, and those two parts will take you down. Mellody's model teaches us how to recover from our many childhood wounds, how to lessen the WC's and AC's roles in our lives, and how to handle most of life's issues and dilemmas from our functional adult (FA) selves. Her model teaches us to grow up mentally and emotionally.

Most of the things that drive us crazy in relationships can be traced to various childhood traumas—neediness, emotional unavailability, lack of self-control, too much control, and more. In Appendix II, I list books to read about this as well as places to go where you can begin your own recovery. If I had my way, every person in America would learn Mellody's model and learn how to grow themselves up.

In the end, all codependence is about not practicing self-care and refusing to face problems head-on. These are immature behaviors, and that's what codependence caused by childhood trauma does: it leaves us as emotional children in adult bodies dealing with life in seemingly ridiculous ways.

My, how the world, and marriage, would be different if we all went into recovery from it and worked to grow ourselves up. That is what I am asking of you now.

Serious Mental Illness

Many a book has been written on mental illness, and I am not going to reinvent the wheel here. I just want you to be aware of some of the signs of serious mental illness so you can look further into the matter on your own should you feel that you or your partner may be experiencing it. It is important to talk about because as much as a marriage and family therapist would love to be able to help or save every marriage, some marriages are not able to be helped, nor should they be. Serious mental illness can be one of those obstacles that cannot be overcome. If a person gets to the point where they realize their partner is seriously mentally ill and not likely to recover, a well-thought-out decision must be made about what is best for them for the family moving forward.

One of the most common scenarios I see is a couple in which at least one person has a personality disorder. As a therapist, I can assure you that when we figure out what's going on, we take a deep breath because it's going to be a bumpy therapeutic ride. Why? Because people with personality disorders are not reasonable. Think about it: their personality literally is disordered!

The basic characteristics of all personality disorders are that the person's perspective and reality are not accurate; they see things and bring up issues that a healthier person wouldn't even notice. They are often dramatic and erratic, and doing therapy with a person like this is next to impossible as they almost never take responsibility for anything they have done. Therapists know to watch for those who blame and play the role of the perpetual victim; in marriage therapy, these are the people who come to a session or two and then blame the therapist or their spouse for why their marriage couldn't be helped.

Before Jumping to a Diagnosis . . .

If you know a person who can't admit when they're wrong or who often plays the victim, it does not mean they can be diagnosed with a personality disorder. Before you conclude such a thing, read all about the various disorders and all their characteristics, and seek professional help: http://psychcentral .com/personality/ (Casablanca, 2021).

I have had people with personality disorders fire me, question my education or credentials, threaten to report me to the board, stand over me in an intimidating manner, and call me a quack and other pejoratives, all because I delivered news they didn't want to hear: that they were at least partially at fault in their relationship problems.

For a therapist who is trying to help a couple in which at least one person has a personality disorder, it's never a fun afternoon. One spouse will never humbly admit or take ownership of any shortcoming or flaws in their behavior, and any time you try to explain to them why sometimes they may be wrong, they respond by saying things like "I feel you are attacking me," or "Why are you spending so much time focusing on me? This is all one-sided; my spouse isn't perfect, you know. Let's talk about them."

Bottom line: A person like that is not open to change because of the way they see and perceive things. When a therapist "picks" on them, as they see it, they revolt, take it personally, and never come back. I have worked with people with personality disorders who have been to five or six different therapists, looking for the one who doesn't point the finger at them, a phenomenon called "therapist shopping."

The National Institute of Health funded a study in 2007 to find out how common personality disorders are (Lenzenweger et al., 2007), and they concluded that 9.1 percent of the population presents with one, though other studies raise the number to "at least 10 percent" (Sansome & Sansome, 2011). That is at least one in ten people, people! But therapists in the trenches who know how to recognize personality disorders would probably tell you the number is probably higher. In any event, it's terribly common.

The Big Six Personality Disorders

There are three clusters of personality disorders. Cluster A is known as the odd, bizarre, eccentric category. Cluster B includes dramatic and erratic behaviors, and Cluster C is the anxious and fearful category. Add up all the personality disorders in the three categories and you'll find a total of ten personality disorders contained in the *Diagnostic and Statistical Manual of Mental Disorders*, known commonly as the *DSM-5-TR*, which is published by the American Psychiatric Association. The disorders we see most often are obsessive-compulsive personality disorder (OCPD), narcissism personality disorder (NPD), borderline personality disorder (BPD), paranoid personality disorder (PPD), antisocial personality disorder (APD), and histrionic personality disorder (HPD), in that order, and there is no doubt in my mind that you have encountered all six, and probably many of the others (Sansome & Sansome, 2011).

A person with obsessive-compulsive personality disorder (OCD) experiences a pervasive preoccupation (obsession) with order, perfectionism, and control and insists on a specific way of doing things. People who want things folded a certain way or insist the dishwasher be loaded to their standards are common examples. They may come off as indecisive, unwilling to compromise, and overly focused on other people's flaws (Cleveland Clinic, n.d.). Elite athletes often have OCD, and it's probably the reason they're so successful at what they do. What works in golf, track and field, soccer, and other sports that require consistency and perfection may not work in marriage, however. It's probably easy to see that a person who has to have things a certain way and can't compromise would not be easy to live with.

A narcissist, in a nutshell, has an "overwhelming need for admiration, and usually a complete lack of empathy toward others. People with this disorder (ND) often believe they are of primary importance in everybody's life or to anyone they meet" (Looti, n.d.). These are people who love to use and take advantage of others for their own personal gain and have an "I'm entitled and better than you" attitude.

When I was in Marriage Therapy 101 class in graduate school, our professor told us we would not be able to help the married narcissistic client and that it is impossible to be happily married to one. I have since verified that this professor was correct. Unless you are an amazingly tolerant person and choose to spend lots of time reading about narcissism and learn strategies for how to best live with a narcissist without going crazy, it's probably best to not deal with it at all, whatever that means to you.

Borderline personality disorder (BPD) has characteristics that resemble Dr. Jekyll and Mr. Hyde. So very wonderful, charming, nice, and generous, and then, without warning, a mood switch flips and they become one of the most wicked people you have ever encountered. People with BPD are unable to regulate their emotions, and they feel everything to an exponentially high degree. When they are happy, they are much happier than the average person has ever been, and the same goes for sadness and anger. This is why one of the most famous books written for people living with a borderline loved one is titled *Stop Walking on Eggshells: Taking Your Life Back When Someone You Care About Has Borderline Personality Disorder* (Mason & Kreger, 2021).

Borderlines have a lot of turmoil-filled relationships. Makeups, breakups. Drama, chaos. I've had BPD clients who reported slashing tires, keying cars, stalking, and more. I can never forget a client who dated a BPD male who got angry with her and cut down all the trees in her front yard. The next day, when he came out of his rage, he was ready to make up and came back and stacked the wood neatly in her yard so she could use it as firewood.

Since the primary criteria for BPD is having abandonment issues, the person with BPD can be very needy, insecure, anxious-attached, and afraid to be alone. Their sense of self is so low that they take things personally that the average person wouldn't be bothered by. Remember the movie *Fatal Attraction*? Yep, Glenn Close was no doubt playing an extreme form of a woman with BPD. Same thing with the movie *Mommie Dearest*. After attending graduate school and being able to diagnose mental disorders, I realized the character portrayed as Joan Crawford in that movie was BPD all the way.

Paranoid personality disorder (PPD) is often mistaken for schizophrenia because both have similar features, such as "suspiciousness and paranoid delusion" (Lee, 2017). One of the most neglected personality disorders, its traits include highly neurotic features, disagreeableness, negative emotionality, hypervigilance, rigidity, and an aggressive, hostile disposition. In an era when the Internet allows numerous legitimate and illegitimate or propaganda-minded news and media sources, social media platforms, and online bulletin boards, people believing bizarre, unproven conspiracies flourish, enabling a platform for those with PPD to envelop themselves in believing things that have no basis in fact.

When I think of the antisocial personality (ASPD), also known as a sociopath, a con man or woman comes into mind. This is someone who can marry fifteen women at the same time and bilk them of their money and have absolutely no guilt or remorseful feelings whatsoever. Social media has shown the many *catfish* predators waiting to bilk single people out of their life savings with the promise of everlasting love and fortune. These are people who have absolutely no regard for other people's rights and most often have a disdain for people, especially the ones they take advantage of. I once saw a sociopath interviewed on television who stated that if people were dumb enough to fall for his dirty tricks, they deserved what they got. Infamous people who are thought to have ASPD are Adolf Hitler, Ted Bundy, Jeffrey Dahmer, Bernie Madoff, and many more.

Histrionic personality disorder (HPD) is one I have been seeing more frequently. Characterized by a need to be the center of attention, usually with a sexy and flamboyant image, they often have strong personalities and opinions. Often seen as fake or shallow, they can be easily influenced by others and have rapidly changing moods. The clients I've seen who have this dress in an inappropriately sexy way for whatever situation they may find themselves in. Picture a perfumed-up mommy at a children's birthday party in spike heels, short shorts, and an elastic midriff top while most of the other moms have on nice shorts, T-shirts, and comfortable sneakers, with sweat dripping down their faces.

The clients I've seen like this seem to be saying, "Come have sex with me," though I don't know if that is the message or not. I do know that the ones I have worked with were having affairs and ultimately left their husbands for newfound love. I've also made note over time that many of these women became easily bored after seducing and capturing their latest mate and were soon casting their fishing line elsewhere.

You can see by the general descriptions of six of the most common personality disorders that having an equal and loving partnership with a person like that would be next to impossible. The category of personality disorders stands by itself in the diagnostic manual of mental disorders because they are finite, or incurable, which is why no insurance company will cover it if we put it down as our official diagnosis. Personality disorders are a unique category, apart from treatable things such as mood disorders and bipolar disorder.

Is a personality disorder ever manageable? If—and this is a big if—a person hates their diagnosis and really wants to tackle it, it may be manageable. They have to be really motivated and determined. In the end, it depends, but I am sure the success rate is low.

Places where people with personality disorders abound are in politics, entrepreneurship, upper management, entertainment, and any profession deemed high profile. Since being the center of attention is the drug of several of the most common personality disorders, you can see why those professions would have a higher rate per one hundred people than, say, teaching school or nursing.

People with personality disorders are difficult and unreasonable. Their perception is often inaccurate, and the problem is they don't get better. It is a finite problem like being on the autism spectrum or having Down syndrome, something where functioning can improve with the right therapies, but in the end, you have to deal with a bottom-line diagnosis that remains the same. People married to a person with a personality disorder who choose to remain in their marriage can read books and get therapy that will help them learn how to handle it on their end with solid boundaries and self-care.

Other Things to Know About Personality Disorders

If we meet ten people with the same personality disorder, such as narcissism, all of them may have similar characteristics, but how they present their symptoms and how severe their symptoms are will be different. Some are truly evil people, malignant and dangerous, and others seemingly harmless or at least under the radar. Ever heard of *covert narcissism*? It's narcissism, to be sure, but the covert ones are passive in their actions as opposed to the direct destruction a true narcissist engages in, and supersensitivity is a forte. The one truth is what I said before: The condition is incurable and will be a lifelong disorder. Another complication is that these personality disorders almost always present with other mental issues, such as anxiety disorders, depression, chronic illnesses, and more, making treatment and living with an individual who suffers from such a disorder extremely difficult.

If you choose to continue a relationship with a person who has a personality disorder, my best advice is to read up on it and learn the strategies that work the best. Don't compromise yourself; stay firm in who you are and what you're about. Think solid and firm boundaries all the way. You can find numerous resources that speak about this in books, videos, podcasts, and websites, many of which are free.

Bipolar Disorder

The person diagnosed with bipolar has serious mood swings from very high "manic" episodes to very low depressive episodes. In its more severe form, bipolar I, the highs and lows are super extreme, and in its milder form, bipolar II, less so. The person with this diagnosis may have extended periods of time when their moods are normal, and then they'll experience a crashing depression or manic episode. During a manic episode, a person with bipolar may do things like clean out closets for days or go on a shopping spree or dream up some grandiose ideas for fame or fortune. They appear endlessly energetic.

The way bipolar disorder shows up is also different for every person who has it. Some people who have bipolar disorder seem to be terribly mentally ill while others live very normal lives, and you would never know. An expert in bipolar disorder told me once that the tell-tale sign that can put a therapist on the scent to diagnosing bipolar disorder is that almost every person with it has sleeplessness issues. Another expert once told me that if you can't figure out what is wrong with a person, it's almost always bipolar. I don't know about that, but unlike personality disorders, bipolar is very treatable, and it should be treated. Untreated, the mental illness can get much worse, and a person can become psychotic. There is no shame in getting a mental illness treated and moving forward in your life, and if you are practicing the all-important self-care I have written about, you will.

A good example of how a marriage plays out when a person with a mental disorder chooses not to be treated is Kanye West, the world-famous rap singer who publicly talked in 2016 about being diagnosed with bipolar on David Letterman's Netflix show, *My Next Guest Needs No Introduction* (Murphy, 2019). He said that when he has a manic episode he may experience racing thoughts, sleep loss, and paranoia. He takes pride in eschewing medications.

"'When you're in this state, you're hyper-paranoid about everything,' West, now known as Ye, said during the interview. . . . 'Everything's a conspiracy. You feel the government is putting chips in your head. You feel you're being recorded. You feel all these things'" (Murphy, 2019).

Later, he infamously made headlines by announcing he would run for president in 2020 and began revealing private information about his marriage to his wife, Kim Kardashian. No one knows what really happened behind closed doors, but Kardashian reminded people at the time that West has bipolar and needs compassion and empathy. She divorced him shortly after, and to this day, West speaks unkindly about his wife and her family and friends on social media. This is certainly a reflection of his continuing instability, which is what happens when mental disorders go untreated.

Treatable Mental Disorders

I have seen many individuals with treatable mental disorders who refuse to be in therapy for the long haul in which they could really get healthy and make things right and many more who won't consider taking a medication that might make the difference in helping them save their relationship. Not wanting to get therapy speaks to the fact that so many people would rather sweep painful events and things under the rug rather than deal with them head-on. Too many choose to avoid any situation that might make them uncomfortable. If you or your partner are reluctant to seek answers for mental and emotional health issues when there are signs and symptoms waving in your face, then I must assume you want me and other therapists to do all the heavy lifting. In other words, you want us to fix you, when all we can do is show you the way. If it's not that, then perhaps you don't think you need it.

Therapy has evolved tremendously over the years, and there are ways of healing trauma that don't involve rehashing old wounds; you just have to find a therapist who is the right fit. Somatic experiencing is one therapy that works that way. It is the life work of Peter A. Levine, PhD, and is defined as a "body-oriented therapeutic model for healing trauma and other stress disorders from a nervous system lens" (Somatic Experiencing International, 2024). I trained in this about six years ago over a three-year period and got certified as a somatic experiencing practitioner (SEP). That's what I suggest you look for.

SEPs have clients focus on feelings in their body, which are symptoms of stress, shock, and trauma that accumulate and are seeking to be released. The techniques used, including touch, help release those traumas. It's very powerful.

Medications are another story. While I believe most people can function well if they manage their lives and situations in a way that keeps them thriving and that pills alone won't get you where you need to go, sometimes, and for some people, they are a godsend. As Dr. Bick Wanck says in *Mind Easing* (HCI Books, 2019, p. 193), "Medicine won't eliminate trauma caused by childhood adversity, but medicine may reduce the symptoms enough for you to resolve the trauma with talk therapy and other types of guidance. . . . It may also reduce your symptoms enough for you to more effectively address your current sources of distress and resolve old wounds that may have previously felt insurmountable." That is the gold standard for the best use of medications, in my opinion.

I haven't ever met anyone who wouldn't benefit from therapy, and if you need meds, take them. Therapists are well aware that therapy used with medications, as opposed to using just one of the two, is the most effective way to eliminate major symptoms of common mental disorders like depression and anxiety. These are the actions that people managing their health take, and they just might make the difference in what results at the end of your marriage crisis.

In any event, it takes men and women, not boys and girls, to heal broken marriages. What do I mean? Men and women, grown-ups, are willing to work and do the hard work now for the benefit of what they get later. Children want what they want now and may wail, carry on emotionally, or manipulate to get whatever it is they're after. One way works and can create the positive life change your partner may need to see, and the other does not.

Here are some common excuses for not taking meds:

- "I don't like medications."
- "I don't want to be on a bunch of pills like my mom."
- "I can tough it out."
- "My religion forbids it."

- "What I have is not that bad."
- "I don't want to become an addict." (Some of the most effective medications we have are nonaddictive.)
- "I read it increases your chances of suicide." (Extremely low chance.)
- "I don't want the sexual side effects." (There are meds available without sexual side effects.)
- "I don't want to be a zombie." (Modern meds are not like that.)
- "I tried it once and hated it." (Not all meds are the same!)
- "My spouse doesn't want me to."

A person living in fear of dealing with their issues or one who thinks doing so is selfish must consider the bigger picture: If you chose to have a family—a spouse and perhaps children—and you struggle with severe depression, paranoia, fearfulness, anxiety, moods, or other issues, these things don't just affect you. Yes, you may have a debilitating existence, but your illness and lack of self-care will seep into the entire family as if it were a virus. If a person who needs help doesn't get it, the dysfunctional family system will persist in its negative cycle until someone steps up and says, "No more!" I have little patience with family members who are not supportive of proactive mental health care and who do not want their partner to get the readily available and extremely helpful mental health care they need. Having seen the night-and-day difference a properly treated mental health client can experience, and relatively quickly, I find it irresponsible not to encourage a person you care about to do all they can to feel better. Inform yourself. Talk to your doctor and search well-respected sources on the web, such as the National Institute of Health, Web MD, and www.mentalhealth.gov.

Addiction Issues

"How do you know when an addict is lying?"
"It's easy. It's whenever he's moving his mouth."
—A joke therapists often tell

Few things can destroy the health of a family like addiction. Addiction shows up in all sorts of categories—alcohol, tobacco, shopping, food, drugs (illegal and prescription), gambling, religion, Internet, video games, and sex, love, and relationships.

In my intake forms, I ask a lot of questions so I can get to know my new clients, and quite a few of them are meant to poke around at the possibility of addictions as a problem in the relationship. It is absolutely necessary to know whether or not addiction is a concern, and it's so common that it would be extremely neglectful to not let your therapist know if you suspect there may be an addiction issue.

What Is Addiction?

Whether addiction runs in a person's family and likely has a genetic component to it or was picked up as a way to manage stress and the toxic shame of not feeling good enough, it involves an obsessive compulsion to do the addictive behavior, basically a craving that cannot and will not be denied. The activity is something that is pleasurable to a person, and the person keeps going back for more and more pleasure fixes until these fixes start affecting their ability to work and be a present and functioning family member. Addictive behaviors pass through stages, and the last stage leads to a disastrous end, which could be serious illness, incarceration, loss of your family, or death. The stages are:

1. Experimentation
2. Regular use

3. Risky use

4. Dependence

5. Addiction

A description of what cravings are like for addicts who eventually give in to abusing again is characterized by the world-recognized Cycle of Addiction (Recovery Connection, n.d.):

- Frustration and internal pain lead to anxiety and a demand for relief of these symptoms
- Fantasizing about using substances or behaviors to relieve the uncomfortable symptoms
- Obsessing about using substances or behaviors and how life will be after the use of these substances or things
- Engaging in the addictive activity, such as using substances to gain relief (acting out)
- Losing control over the behavior
- Developing feelings of remorse, guilt, and shame, which leads to feelings of dissatisfaction
- Making a promise or resolve to oneself to stop the behavior or substance use

When I deal with clients who, at least for a time, have used self-control to stop using whatever substance it is, I often hear them say, "I literally have no desire for it." I smile nervously for I know about the cycle of substance abuse, and without treatment, the cravings will return, and the addict won't have the knowledge or skills to stay sober. A website called the Recovery Connection describes the addictive cycle of substance abuse well: After a period of time, the pain returns, and the addict begins to experience the fantasies of using substances again. This cycle can rotate on a variable basis. For example, binge users rotate through this cycle more slowly.

Daily users may rotate through the cycle of addiction daily or several times throughout the day. This cycle can be arrested at any point after the addict or alcoholic makes a decision or is forced to get help. Sometimes, the consequences that arise (legal, financial, medical, or social) force the addict or alcoholic to stop using. However, in the absence of outside help, such as alcohol or drug detox followed by addiction treatment help, the substance abuse or addictive behavior is likely to return.

Marriage therapists think of addiction as a serious marital crime, and it is listed among the three marital felonies of abuse, addiction, and adultery. Marriages can recover from felonies depending on many things, but in the case of addiction, recovery would be an absolute must.

A Special Word About Addiction to Porn

Quite a few women come in and tell me they believe their male spouse is addicted to porn. If he is, I ask them if the porn is of something strange in a perverted way or illegal. If so, that's a huge problem. If his behavior fits the criteria of a compulsion that he cannot stop, affects his life in some negative way such as causing him to not be productive at work, or he stops being interested in connection, quality time, or a sex life with her, then it's very concerning and could be an addiction. Almost always, I have found this is not the case.

What is frequently the case is that the husband will be looking at mainstream porn movies on his phone or computer, perhaps pleasuring himself. This could be rarely or several times a week, but the compulsion and lack of productivity and connection are not happening. I have to explain to appalled wives that men are visual

creatures and have been looking at hard-copy porn—dirty magazines and Victoria's Secret catalogs—for years prior to the advent of
the Internet. Nothing has changed except that porn is on the Internet
these days, it is more readily accessible than it has ever been, and it
can be free of charge.

I consider looking at pornographic pictures normal male behavior, and no, the husbands aren't paying me to say that. I really
mean it. Women may not understand it, they may feel it's gross and
degrading, but if it's not affecting their lives personally, it's best to
look the other way, perhaps developing a policy of "don't ask, don't
tell." I think women in heterosexual relationships best choose battles
they can and should win, and this one would be far down my list of
priorities.

Don't misunderstand; I do have sympathy and empathy for the
wife's point of view. A therapist is supposed to honor your own belief and value systems and work around that; however, we are also
supposed to lean on and influence you if your values and beliefs are
so unbending or unreasonable that they needlessly cause family suffering. We can, at times, say something like "I respect how you feel,
but I have to tell you that you are asking a man not to do something,
in this case, to not look at naked photos or videos of women on the
Internet, that is completely natural and normal for almost every
man."

If you don't believe me, read up on it, but I side with the dudes
on this one. I don't believe a wife needs to spend too much energy
worrying about something like that. Only when it crosses that line of
distracting the man to the point that he doesn't want to do much else
should we get worried.

Dealing with Addiction in Your Decision-Making

The biggest problem I have experienced with addiction that is wreaking havoc in a marriage is getting people to admit they have an addiction problem, and when they *do* admit it, getting them to go for treatment is extremely difficult, whether in a long-term (thirty days or more) rehab center or a free, community-based twelve-step program. I have seen many, many individuals with the addictions previously listed, and the addiction is always the elephant in the room as the marriage hangs in the balance. In my opinion, you must deal with it, one way or the other—remembering the three choices.

You've probably heard the old saying that addicts have to hit rock bottom to finally get the help they need, and though there are those who disagree, it is usually true. Why? Because you have to understand what motivates people to change. People don't change just because someone wants them to. They change under two circumstances:

1. Either they have a health scare or something that causes them to take stock of their life, or they are about to lose something they value very much or pay a very heavy price.
2. They get so disgusted with themselves that they conclude they must change.

Addicts have a very strong voice in their heads that wants to keep the addiction alive and well. It tells them every reason why they shouldn't stop whatever it is they're doing. It knows every justification and excuse to throw at its host to keep the destructive behavior going. It takes a lot to quiet that voice long enough to reach a person's rational self where healthy decisions are made. Addicts are miserable, to be certain, but a person has to get *miserable enough* to change.

And yes, stepping away from an addict so they might reach that point of misery where they will give in to receive help could mean a person loses friends, a job, or life's basic needs, such as food and shelter, but what that typically means is the loss of family support. It's that spouse pulling the plug on being there for them until they get help that can create the motivation to actually do it. So often, it seems as long as one person, especially the spouse, is still sticking around, near, or with the addict, then the addict hasn't been pushed enough or made miserable enough to make the hard choice.

I have begged partners to not enable the behavior and to be tough on the addiction with firm boundaries, but that can be just as hard to achieve as getting the addict to quit. Enabling might involve monitoring how much your partner drinks, asking or nagging about it, talking about it with friends and family behind their back, minimizing the issue, buying the substance or using it with them, rationalizing it, covering it up so others don't notice, partnering in their lies about the behavior, trying to control them, treating them like a child, and more. I am reminded of one woman who came to see me alone with questions about what to do about her alcoholic husband. I'll call her Marie.

Marie and her husband, Tom, had two small children and were separated due to his alcoholism. When Tom told her the only way he would get help is if she let him come home, one of her first questions was "Should I let him come back?"

Tom was exhibiting typical addict behavior. He always tried to manipulate by bargaining and working out a deal, but the bottom line is that an addict always has a reason why they won't get help *today*. The healthy way to deal with an addict is to have them get the help first, let them spend some time being sober as a recovering addict, and *then* talk about putting the relationship back together.

When I talked to Marie about setting such healthy boundaries, she would cry and cry. She was one of the many hundreds of enabling spouses I have seen in my office over the years who somehow believe it is mean and cruel to set firm boundaries with a sick person who lies, abuses, threatens, and pushes whenever confronted about "the problem." I suggested some books to her, such as *Facing Codependence* and *Facing Love Addiction* by Pia Mellody, and one other crucial piece of moving toward health, and that was to attend Al-Anon meetings. Al-Anon is a twelve-step program for friends and family members of alcoholics. It was a perfect place for Marie to learn about her part in the family dysfunction and how to never repeat the pattern. Marie's husband was an alcoholic, but I also suggest family members go to Al-Anon no matter what kind of addict their spouse is. The meetings address common denominators that hold true across all addictions, and attending those meetings will teach you about the codependent dynamic. You will see people just like yourself all over the room and find relief from the fact that you're not alone.

Everything would be so easy if people didn't have to go through all that, but that way has the highest success rate over any others, including quitting on your own, which has an extremely low success rate. If I were miserably married to an addict and strongly considering separation or divorce and knowing what I know, I would insist on completion of a twelve-step program, ongoing involvement in the program, and continuing long-term individual and family therapy to follow as a precondition to discussing marriage therapy or reconciliation.

In the end, anyone who works with addicts knows that when dealing with one, toughness is the only way to go. I have no problem with a client saying, "It's me or your addiction." It's a painful ulti-matum to make, but ultimately, it is the most loving.

A Word About Marijuana

I have a love/hate relationship concerning the use of marijuana. On one hand, it is now widely available legally, and when prescribed by a physician, it has helped thousands, if not millions, with legiti-mate health issues such as pain and nausea. I'm all for that.

But what I see as a marriage therapist is the person who prob-ably has a major anxiety disorder using it to calm themselves down. A therapist would much rather a person deal with their anxiety in proven ways that have nothing to do with self-medicating. When it comes to adolescents, the National Institute on Drug Abuse warns that marijuana is thought to change a teen's brain in a way that in-creases negative emotions, psychopathology, and feelings of alien-ation (NIDA, 2019). Don't forget that adolescents grow up to be husbands and wives.

Human Brain Waves

All of us have five channels in our brains, and if we are hooked up to a neurofeedback monitor, they can be seen. At any given moment, your brain is on one of the five channels. The channels/waves and how each works (Pearce, 2022):

1. Gamma is intense concentration and focus, a place most of us reach only occasionally. Also known as the "genius brain."
2. Beta is everyday functioning and our thinking mind. This is the channel we use for thinking, processing, working, and playing.
3. Alpha is relaxed and chilled out.
4. Theta is awake yet extremely relaxed. This is the wave that hypnosis reaches so your subconscious mind can be attained.

5. Delta is sleep.

Each channel can be overaroused or underaroused. A person with anxiety may find their beta waves are not in balance and are overaroused. People don't like this feeling, of course, so they may medicate themselves with various medications, including marijuana, to take them to a more relaxed brain wave. When a person uses marijuana, for example, it will move them out of beta, which in their case is overfiring, and move them down to an alpha/theta level, where they are extremely relaxed. There are other ways besides medications to achieve this, like using neurofeedback, breathing exercises, meditation, yoga, hypnosis, and many more.

Marijuana has been widely researched and has also been traced to altering the brain, especially when a mother uses it during pregnancy, or the user begins use when young. According to the Centers for Disease Control and Prevention (CDC), "Using marijuana before age 18 may affect how the brain builds connections for functions like attention, memory, and learning. Marijuana's effects on attention, memory, and learning may last a long time or even be permanent, but more research is needed to fully understand these effects. Youth who use marijuana may not do as well in school and may have trouble remembering things" (CDC, 2020).

My issue with it, however, is anecdotal, meaning what I have seen with clients. When a husband or wife comes in and claims that their spouse is a "pothead," I'm less concerned about that than with what the spouse's marijuana use is doing to the marriage and family. My experience has shown that when a person is under the influence of marijuana, they are having a solitary experience and cannot be relational and intimately connected. In addition, it kills motivation in otherwise productive human beings because the user is in such a relaxed state that they don't want to do anything else. Both are relationship killers, and my experience is backed up by research: "Recent marijuana use (defined as within 24 hours) in youth and adults has an immediate impact on thinking, attention, memory, coordination, movement, and time perception" (National Academies of Science 2017). The CDC has lots of information on marijuana use and how it affects the human brain, and I urge you to take a look.

With medical marijuana, doses are calibrated in a way that a person knows exactly how much they've had, and a person can choose between strains that either energize and increase focus or relax them. In marijuana bought illegally, people cannot guarantee what they are getting, and some will smoke it all day long and up until bedtime. This is a long time to be disconnected and unmotivated. When your brain is forced to stay mostly in a super-relaxed zone, your brain will change over time.

With all that said, I have friends and acquaintances who use it frequently, and it seems to have a positive effect on their ability to engage with others. I suppose the important thing is how you or your spouse use it, what its effects are in your particular case, and whether use improves or detracts from your ability to engage as a couple.

Abuse and Family Violence

When I was a counseling intern, I worked at the Family Violence Center in San Antonio. I am thankful for this invaluable experience as I use what I learned there nearly every week with my clients.

Abuse affects every race and socioeconomic background. My clients are professional people for the most part, but they, too, can be verbally, emotionally, physically, and economically abusive. It breaks my heart to see otherwise reasonable and functioning people live in these situations of being victimized when they do not have to. The reason people stay or go back after leaving is complicated, but most of it involves the abused partner holding out hope for change. The average woman leaves an abusive man seven times before she finally leaves for good because it takes that long for her to realize what he promises is not what he is going to do in the end.

There is so much wonderful research about the abusers themselves, including that no matter what an abuser may tell you, they *can* control the behavior; they simply choose not to. Even if an abuser does want to change, the amount of time and work that it takes to change abusive behavior, and the many facets of thinking and behavior an abuser must tackle, are the change equivalent of climbing Mt. Everest, and very few people will see it through (NDVH, n.d.). If you are in one of those types of relationships, let it be said loud and clear here: It is exceedingly difficult, and probably impossible, for an abuser to change. I think that is very important for you to know as you try to make decisions concerning your marital crisis.

Abusers love to tell their victim that they are not abusive and that the victim "makes" them act that way. Nothing could be further from the truth. So that you have no doubt, let me describe what an abuser is: a person, usually but not always a male, who does what they can to attain power and control over another person. The most common behaviors are any sort of name-calling, put-downs, threats, blackmail, controlling who the partner sees and where they go, withholding money, intimidation, spying or stalking, not allowing a partner to work or do the things they love, pushing, shoving, hitting, sexual assault, telling them they're crazy, isolating them from family and friends, and more.

Check the Power and Control Wheel (Duluth, n.d.) on the following page. The circle represents a violent and/or abusive relationship. Inside the wheel are the behaviors that are abusive. The center core of the circle represents what the abuser is trying to achieve.

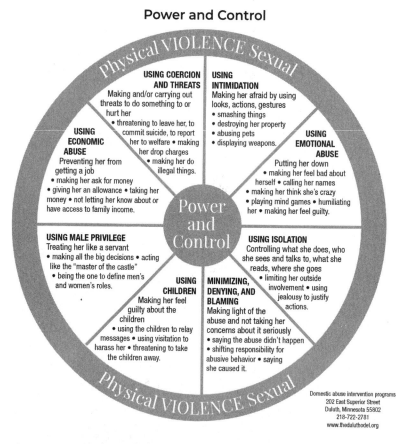

Power and Control

The Power and Control Wheel is used in every domestic violence center in the United States as a tool to show women clearly what constitutes abuse. It is a diagram of tactics abusers use in the middle "pie" pieces, and the outer ring represents the acts of violence.

Abuse is a very common thing, and it is excruciating for a therapist to identify it to a client beyond a shadow of a doubt and then watch how long it takes them to leave the relationship. A client of mine, Sheree, who looks like a New York runway model, has a history of being drawn to successful and ego-driven men who end up being abusive. She told me she thought that it would be "mean" to leave the man who continually screams at her and kicks her out of the house and tells her he is done with her. On many of her visits, Sheree had bruises on her body and stories to tell that were as shocking as they were devastating.

Following his abusive tirades, her lover wooed her back and became lovey-dovey, followed by a week or two of great times. Feeling the *all clear,* the tension built, and finally, he exploded again.

Every abusive relationship has a cyclical nature to it, and each part of it is considered dangerous. For example, there may be a period when tension builds and an explosion occurs, followed by a period of making up and wooing, or there may be no making-up period at all. The idea is that the behavior patterns in an abusive cycle repeat themselves until the end of time. Unfortunately, many victims tell themselves the lie that when the relationship has a period of calm, if it does, the abuser will remain calm, and things will improve. But an abusive person, who likely has a personality disorder, never will because they can't do it. If you are in an abusive relationship, know that the factors to consider are multifaceted. I urge you to learn all you can about it; begin with Promising Futures, hosted by the U.S. Department of Health and Human Services, to create a future without family violence. You'll find more information in the Resources section.

After five years of on-again, off-again, my client married her abuser—just after a major breakup that lasted six months. Just as I was hoping she had broken the spell for good, he began an intense process of wooing her back. When she called to tell me they were marrying, my heart dropped.

"Everything I taught you about abuse and how this will play out still remains true," I said, "though I know that's not what you want to hear."

"Really?" She laughed. "Okay."

Women under the spell of a charismatic and abusive man are often not reachable. Most have to learn it all the hard way. It is my wish for you that you will heed the wise information and advice available that has helped millions of women throughout the world.

Can He Change?

Every victim wants to know, "Can he change?" and I just told you, no, he cannot. That is my opinion after working at a domestic violence center in San Antonio and counseling dozens of women in abusive relationships. All counselors are trained in understanding family violence dynamics prior to getting their first clients, and we must understand and underscore to our clients the dismal chances of an abuser changing, as that is the big question every woman wants to know.

Family violence centers strongly recommend against marriage therapy until an abuser has accepted responsibility for their actions and completed extensive individual and group work designed specifically for abusers. Knowing how few will agree to do that, you should be getting a pretty clear picture of how your relationship is likely to play out should you stay together. In his book *Why Does He Do That? Inside the Minds of Angry and Controlling Men* (2023), Lundy Bancroft, a renowned consultant on domestic abuse, says that abusive men don't make lasting changes if they skip any of the steps listed on the facing page. He also says that the process is difficult, and many end up "throwing in the towel."

1. Admit fully to their history of psychological, sexual, and/or physical abuse toward any current or past partners.
2. Acknowledge unconditionally that the abuse was wrong.
3. Acknowledge that their behavior was a choice, not a loss of control.
4. Recognize the effects the abuse had on their partner and children and show empathy for those in detail.
5. Identify in detail their pattern of controlling behaviors and entitled attitudes.
6. Develop respectful behaviors and attitudes to replace the ones they are stopping.
7. Reevaluate their distorted image of their partner and replace it with a more positive and empathetic view.
8. Make amends for the damage done.
9. Accept the consequences of their actions.
10. Commit to not repeating their abusive behaviors and honor that commitment, no excuses or conditions.
11. Accept the need to give up privileges and do so, such as no more double standards.
12. Accept that overcoming abusiveness is a lifelong process.
13. Be willing to be accountable for their actions, past and future.

One more thing is important to note: If you plan to leave your abuser, there is a way to do it and a way not to do it. Abusers can be at their most dangerous when their partner leaves, and this fact should not be taken lightly. I strongly urge you to devise an exit plan with a therapist who is experienced in dealing with the abuse dynamic, or you can call the National Domestic Violence Hotline at 800-799-7233. Do not do this alone.

For more information on domestic abuse, see Appendix II: Recommendations.

Attachment Styles

Much has been written about attachment styles and how important they are to understand when it comes to relationships, but in my practice, few have ever heard anything about it. As you ponder what to do about your marriage, it is vital to take into consideration the attachment styles of you and your partner.

When I first learned about attachment styles in school, it blew my mind. Of course, I thought, this explanation makes relationship dynamics that seem foggy turn into something clearer. I wouldn't even mention it here if it didn't play a gigantic role in why couples go around and around with their issues. The round-and-round pattern I refer to is the one where one person is constantly trying to attain more time, love, attention, and affection from the other person while that person tends to touch the base and then avoid and run away. It's a pattern of push and pull, and it drives the person chasing the other bonkers. Of course, in the ideal world, both partners would be physically and emotionally available to the other on an as-needed basis and would absolutely respond and make it a priority when the other person really needs them, but except in rare instances, that's not the way it is. In the most common pattern, one is running toward, and the other is running away.

For years, I seemed to attract men who were what I called "emotionally unavailable." We'd start to date, and if I really liked what I was seeing and started to feel like this could be something, he'd pull back, leaving me to wonder what was going on. I'd obsess about if I'd hear from him again, feeling quite a bit of anxiety and sometimes sleeplessness, and about the time I was going to give up, here he'd come as if nothing had happened. For me, knowing the object of my interest might bolt at any time increased my anxiety and obsessing. This was my first taste of two people dating with completely different attachment styles, and my guess is that every person reading this has experienced some form of this, too.

What Is Attachment?

Attachment is a "lasting psychological connectedness between human beings" (Bowlby, 1969). It's the emotional bond between two people, a sense of connectedness. Attachment theory, which plays a large role in the world of psychology and revolutionized the way we understand close human relationships, was conceived by Thomas Bowlby in the 1950s and was enhanced by the work of Mary Ainsworth in the 1970s.

Bowlby's studies showed the importance of a close and continuing caregiver relationship between an infant and their primary caregiver, usually a mother (Bretherton, n.d.). When the child gets too little (neglect) or too much (smothering) attention from a caregiver, it can cause all sorts of attachment issues in adulthood. For example, a child who was smothered might be avoidant because they equate intimacy with the anxiety of being engulfed. A neglected child might be desperately trying to attain a connection with another to be completely and wholly tended to and loved.

When couples come in, I can usually tell by their stories what attachment patterns they have, and there are three. These descriptions are from the book *Attached: The New Science of Adult Attachment and How It Can Help You Find—and Keep—Love* by Amir Levine and Rachel S. F. Heller (2012).

1. **Avoidant.** It is very important for an avoidant attached person to maintain their independence and self-sufficiency, and they prefer autonomy to intimate relationships. Avoidants do want to be close to others but feel uncomfortable with too much closeness and tend to keep their partner at arm's length. Avoidants don't spend too much time worrying about romantic relationships or about being rejected. Partners tend to complain that they are emotionally distant. Avoidants are often on high alert for any signs of control or impingement of their territory by a partner.

2. **Secure or ambivalent.** Being warm and loving in a relationship comes naturally to the secure attached person. These well-balanced individuals can happily connect with their partner or give them space. They enjoy being intimate and take things in and do not get easily upset over relationship matters. This type effectively communicates their needs and feelings to their partner and is strong at reading their partner's emotional cues and responding to them. Secure attached individuals share their successes and problems with their mate and are able to be there for them in their times of need.

3. **Anxious.** The anxious attached person loves to be very close to their romantic partners and has the capacity for great intimacy. They often fear that their partner does not wish to be as close as they would like. Relationships tend to consume a large part of the anxious-attached person's emotional energy. They tend to be very sensitive to small fluctuations in their partner's moods and actions and can take their partner's behaviors too personally. Anxious attached individuals experience a lot of negative emotions within the relationship

and get easily upset. As a result, they tend to act out and say things they later regret. They can learn to feel content and safe if their partner is good at helping them feel secure and reassured.

Take the test at https://www.attachedthebook.com/wordpress/compatibility-quiz/ to learn which attachment styles you and your partner have. What I usually see, of course, is a couple where one person is anxious and needing constant reassurance married to an avoidant, who is always looking for more space. The question becomes, can this marriage be saved? Yes, but it's hard. The goal, of course, is to see if we can get both to be consistently stable instead of having the "stably unstable" relationship that Levine and Heller describe. In the meantime, it is almost always the anxious partner who has to make concessions just so the relationship can keep puffing along.

If you do find that you both have the motivation to turn this pattern in a new, more secure direction, then educating yourself about the dynamic and what must be done to bring both people into the zone of secure attachment is a great first step. For our purposes here, you now know that this theme is often a real obstacle to couples being able to visualize continuing the relationship; it can be helped if you both care to do the work.

Today, I am married to a secure attached man. He will give me all the love and attention and time I desire, and he is fine with giving me space; these are the healthiest partners to be in a relationship with, needless to say. The beautiful thing about him being securely attached is that his calm nervous system calms my nervous system, and all the symptoms of anxiousness I once experienced with avoidant men are long gone.

Attachment styles are difficult to change, but they can be changed, or at least improved. For instance, when I have clients who are anxiously waiting for their partner to connect, I advise them not to rely on that elusive moment to feel okay; I encourage them instead to entertain and/or nurture themselves. We simply must not rely on others to fix what is wrong with us or fill our emotional voids. When we aren't feeling right, it is our own task to fix it, not our partner's. Sure, sometimes it is nice to have a partner be there for you, but we must not rely on that as the only solution. That wounded child we all have inside will calm down when they feel tended to in a nurturing way, whether it is by our loved ones or ourselves.

Avoidant people want connection, but they feel a need to regulate it to maximize their comfort level. Too much closeness is overwhelming, and when that feeling kicks in, they feel the need to run. I coach avoidants to tell their partners, "I love you, you are my person, but I need some breathing room. I won't be gone long." Reassuring their anxious partner before withdrawing can work wonders rather than just withdrawing and leaving them wondering when that next moment of connection will arrive.

People with both avoidant and anxious attachments can do trauma work to help their nervous systems tolerate much more connection and distance, which by definition is to become more secure attached. Interestingly, those who have worked extensively with trauma, such as Pia Mellody, teach that while an anxiously attached person appears outwardly to fear abandonment, underneath it is a fear of intimacy. This may mean that if someone with an anxious attachment finally caught the avoidant and got them to stick around, they might not know what to do next. Conversely, the avoidant person appears to fear intimacy while underneath it is a fear of abandonment. This tells me that if they stayed around and allowed their partner to come close, they might start needing it too much.

Wrapping It Up

As you ponder what to do about your marriage, ask yourself how much you see yourself or your partner changing. Knowing things can never be perfect and that you will never get 100 percent of what you want, ask yourself if the percentage you are getting is enough. Look at the list of things we went over in this chapter, and knowing what can be worked on and what has a low success rate of improvement, can and will you get the help you need to become more functional in relationships, and will your partner do the same? Are the issues you deal with the type that rarely improve? Are you in denial about your partner's ability to change? Are you willing to give them a chance? Will your partner give you the chance to show that you will become healthy and functional and take care of yourself moving forward? All these things should be considered as you ponder the question "Should I stay or should I leave?"

The question the Leaning-In partner should ask is "Knowing what I do now and that what I may learn in the future may affect the outcome of this marriage crisis, am I willing to be proactive in my self-care and address the issues I have not yet addressed in my life?" This question and the answer will weigh heavily in the days and months to come. My advice to you is to get to work, and don't ever stop.

Deciders can examine their decision-making process and make sure their thinking is rational. You should be seeing what is changeable and what isn't while looking at what you are willing to live with and what you aren't. If I were in your shoes, I would want to work on what can be changed. If my partner had too many issues that rarely change and wasn't willing to do the work to become better, it might make my decision to leave a tad easier.

CHAPTER FIVE

Dealing with Infidelity

Almost every married person tells their friends, "If my spouse ever cheats, I'll [insert some terrible act of cruelty here] and divorce them," but when it actually happens, it's a different story. Why? Because cheating on your spouse, though in the top tier of bad things to do in a romantic relationship, is a very complicated dynamic, too complicated to result in following through on your promise to torture your partner or divorce them immediately, no questions asked. Though we believe it when we declare our intention to be harsh, in truth, I believe humans threaten these things as a warning to their partner that there will be, at the very least, emotional blood to spill if they ever cross that line, and there will be.

Any time there is an affair, a marriage crisis ensues, though there could be numerous different scenarios. A Leaning-In partner discovers the affair, or in rare instances it is confessed to by the person having the affair, who at this point cannot be defined as a Decider as we still don't know any details about the betrayal. Both spouses' sympathetic nervous systems get activated, and they feel the fight, flight, or freeze response. At some point soon after, a conversation takes place. Typically, a Leaning-In partner rises up into a rage-filled response and peppers their cheating partner with machine-gun rapid questioning, sometimes without waiting for an answer: "Who is it? Are you in love? Is it serious? How long? Do I know them? Where did you meet? How many times? I hate you! How could you do this to me? You've been lying to me!"

If leaving someone who cheated was black-and-white, then how do we account for the fact that approximately 60 to 75 percent of marriages survive infidelity (Soloman & Teagno, 2018)? It's because there are so many reasons to work it out. The attachment we feel toward our partner cannot be turned off like a bath faucet. Your head can tell you to throw the bum out, but your heart won't allow it. Then there are kids, extended family and friends, a history together, money, property, age, religious and other beliefs, an aversion to dating again or being alone, the idea of being a failure, worrying about what people will think—these concerns and others intertwine to make a victim of cheating torn about what to do.

I always tell couples there is no justification for cheating whatsoever. It is selfish, cowardly, and stupid, and when it happens, it causes untold pain to every person involved plus children, extended family, and friends. Still, it happens quite frequently. Getting accurate numbers on how many married people have cheated is exceedingly difficult because most married people who've cheated don't want to talk about it. From my experience, cheating is rampant, but the stats available usually report what I consider to be shockingly low numbers. For example, according to the American Association of Marriage and Family Therapists (AAMFT), "Some national surveys indicate that 15% of women and 25% of men have experienced intercourse outside of their long-term relationship" (AAMFT, n.d.). In my opinion, you can raise both those numbers by 20 percent when it comes to nonphysical, emotional cheating, such as talking online with someone who lives far away.

If people could see what I have as a couple's therapist who sometimes manages an affair crisis, they would vow to never be a part of something similar. It is one of life's most painful experiences, igniting anguish and despair rivaled only by losing someone dear through death or some other means. A high percentage of my clients who cheated report regretting it deeply and wish they could take away all the pain and nasty consequences that came with it. The others were so far gone and out the door that humility, remorse, and the ability to accept responsibility were not to be found.

What Is an Affair?

An affair is any secretive relationship outside marriage that involves chemistry, attraction, and romantic or sexual intention. Part of the power and allure of affairs is the secret itself, which may give a betraying partner, who perceives themself as a long-suffering spouse, a sense of autonomy and power (Perel, 2017). For example, a woman who has not felt power or equality in her marriage may feel she is taking her power back by the act of having an affair, as will those who feel they have sacrificed in marriage and received little in return. For those who have played it safe most of their lives, it can be an act of risk, danger, and rebellion, says Esther Perel in her book *The State of Affairs*. Perel, a psychotherapist, says that "affairs sometimes involve sex, and sometimes not, but they are always erotic." Couples may quibble over whether sexual or erotic texting, social network messaging, phone calls, and video calls rate as an affair, and the answer is yes, they do; an affair does not have to be physical to be what it is: an affair.

Why Do People Cheat?

It is vital to understand the "why" part so if we get the opportunity to work on the marriage, we can correct and heal the issues that led to one partner looking for solace outside the marriage. The problem is so many people either cannot or will not be forthcoming about why because they do not want to injure their partner, or the why is so revealing of their own shortcomings that they don't have the ego strength to own up to it. It's a rare person who will truthfully and candidly reveal how very low they have fallen, although I highly recommend it. Most people like to think of themselves as a *good* person, and for many, the ability to esteem themselves depends on it, so they deny any negative traits they may have or keep them buried deeply because acknowledging faults is excruciatingly painful. But the truth is we are all flawed and imperfect, and we all have negative traits that, if brought to light and faced, will cease to have as much power over us. I have engaged in this process myself and found it profound and life-changing.

It's ironic, of course, that a cheater doesn't want to injure their partner emotionally by pointing out the reasons they cheated when their partner is already as injured as a person can be by the betrayal. But there are a lot of strange dichotomies when it comes to this subject. In her practice dealing with infidelity, Perel notes that clients are often more hurt by the lies and deception than the affair itself, and indeed, getting a cheating spouse to reveal the brutal, ugly truth is hard if not impossible.

In my experience, 95 percent of people who cheat became disgruntled in the marriage and entered the deterioration process described earlier in the stages of a dying marriage. In Stage Three, as you may recall, a person detaches and finds distractions and activities away from the marriage to maintain some sense of personal satisfaction. This is the stage when affairs are most likely to happen.

Most people who are losing faith in the relationship along the way tell their partner about it, but there are a handful that don't speak up and instead just silently seethe. The future cheater sees that their partner doesn't make the relationship a priority, they feel alone or lonely and left to fend for themselves emotionally and physically, and the clock ticks to a day and time when they will become vulnerable to someone's kind and loving words and arms.

All the Married Men

Before I married my husband, I was single for about ten years. I can't count the married men who shared with me during that time that they were unhappy in their marriage. As a marriage therapist, I suspected this was a form of trolling to see if I was available as a shoulder to cry on—and perhaps something more. If a person who is turning away from their spouse as described in Stage Three finds a willing and/or sympathetic shoulder, the listener will likely begin to feel sorry for the person and will hear about how bad their spouse is, creating a villain not to be concerned about, and it'll be off to the races in a full-blown affair. I was never about to go for anything like that, but I appreciated seeing how it's done in action.

It is in that interpersonal sharing where bonds are built and caring begins. It's why I tell any person who will listen, single or married, that should they share or be willing to receive personal details, griefs, and sorrows with or from a married person, it is the marital betrayal equivalent of playing with fire. Don't go to lunch, drinks, or anywhere alone with the person, and if you are married and need to do it for work reasons or similar, make sure your partner is fully aware of who you are with and is comfortable with it, and/or make sure a third party is there. If someone tries to unload life's burdens and starts to dive in to their personal life, which can lead to caring and bonding, simply say, "I think you ought to work that out with your partner, not me," or "If you want to have coffee and have a shoulder to lean on, I'll see when my husband [or friend] and I are available."

I feel compelled to add that this advice is not meant to enable unreasonable and jealous spouses who want to know every detail of their spouse's life to control their partner. This means that a partner who must meet with others as part of their job (or another reason) is being respectful to their partner by telling them about meetings with a boss, coworker, or other known people, so it is understood that the meeting is completely on the up and up and all mates know about it.

As a partner nears the decision to betray, their ability to see much good in their spouse becomes more and more difficult, and the amplification of their spouse's negative traits increases. A phenomenon in human beings described in the 1960s by psychologist Peter Watson (1960) is known as *confirmation bias,* which describes our tendency to hunt for and favor facts that back up any hypothesis or fact we may hold to be true. If a partner decides their mate is a cheapskate, they will find all the instances that can back it up, even if some of the facts are a stretch, while ignoring the times it isn't true. As a spouse's stock drops and an affair becomes imminent, the Decider will find every particle and morsel available to back up their theory that the relationship isn't serving them and is hopeless and irreconcilable. The negative things they tell themselves about their spouse provide the justification they need to have an affair without remorse as a sort of narcissistic "I deserve this" attitude forms.

So much of what entices a person who is disillusioned with their marriage is the longing to feel desired, special, seen, and connected (Perel, 2017). After being with the same partner month after month, year after year, have they noticed that you lost that sparkle in your eye when you look at them? When they want to make love, do you groan as if it is a huge inconvenience? Do you avoid physical or emotional connection?

Sexual Addiction

While most spouses who betray are disgruntled in their marriages and seeking validation of some sort outside their marriage, the other 5 percent of those are dealing with sex addiction. That is an estimate based on the thousands of couples and individuals I have seen.

In the same way an alcoholic uses booze to numb the emotional pain they feel due to toxic shame and not feeling good enough, a sex addict uses the high of pursuing a sexual conquest to do the same thing. Sex addicts are usually shame filled and remorseful following an episode, just as an alcoholic might be after going on a bender, but to overcome the remorse, they often just hop back into the cycle to distract themselves. Of course, when either is asked to get the help they need, there will be resistance; addictions don't surrender easily.

In the other cases I've had where either the husband or wife turned out to have a sexual addiction, getting information out of them was next to impossible prior to them taking ownership of the problem. Indeed, the truth about what they have done doesn't come out unless and until they are working a twelve-step program, and that usually won't happen until a person's life has become completely unmanageable.

Jorge was one of the first clients I ever worked with in marriage therapy who had this issue. His marriage was on the rocks, and when he and his wife came in, she was dressed for her powerful career, but as a career woman, mother of three, and wife to ever-demanding Jorge, she was obviously tired and haggard.

"My husband is wearing me out," she said. "Is it normal for a man to want sex three times a day? Do I have to do this? Don't I get a say?"

"Of course you do," I replied.

"Then there's this thing about him texting women," she said. "He says it's harmless fun, but I don't like it. He says I'm a prude, but am I?"

Jorge clammed up and didn't say a word. It was time to meet with him alone.

Handsome and wearing a power suit of his own, Jorge proudly described his life as a businessman and politician. He said he loved the people and the power his office gave him. People now cared about what he had to say; it had helped his self-esteem, he said.

"Holding office provides a lot of opportunity," he said. "I get a lot of benefit from it."

"Well, aren't you worried about texting with other women and what might happen if it became public?" I asked.

"Sure," he said. "That's not the half of it, but I'm good at not getting caught. The fact is that I have a high sex drive, and my wife can't meet my needs. She complains about me pursuing her. I love her, we're soulmates, but she's not enough. She can't be who I need her to be, and I have to get my needs met."

Afraid to hear what was coming next, I braced as he began to describe dozens and dozens of meaningless affairs he'd had.

"I'm having three affairs right now," he said calmly, watching for my reaction. "I have to do it. There is no way one woman can meet my needs."

"How do you find the time for all that?" I asked.

"It does take a lot of time, but I manage," he says. "I have to. I have to have it all, that's just how I am."

Jorge taught me a lot about how a sex addict thinks as he shamelessly described his many conquests. If he met a desirable woman in a restaurant, his goal became to get her phone number before leaving.

"If I get the number, let's say, on Wednesday night, my next goal will be to see if I can be in bed with her by Sunday. It's a game I play, and I play it very well."

When I told Jorge he needed help and we needed to tell his wife about what was going on, he said he wasn't ready and refused to return. I never saw either of them again.

Jorge is not a representative for every sex addict; he is one version, and every person is different. What was remarkable about him was that he was willing to share every detail with me, almost as if he wanted someone to know. He seemed proud of it. Not every person with this issue does what he did the way he did it. I do believe Jorge's life was headed toward becoming unmanageable, and perhaps it was already there.

If you believe your partner has a sexual addiction, you should be in a program yourself, like Al-Anon or Codependents Anonymous, to learn how to be healthy within that. Al-Anon (n.d.) has a phrase called the *Three Cs* that will give you an idea of what will be asked of you: I didn't cause it, I can't control it, and I can't cure it. I interpret that as don't blame yourself, stop talking about and evaluating their problem, stop trying to fix it, and my added advice: start living your life for yourself and your other immediate family members.

While you're (hopefully) doing that, you can be sure your spouse won't change unless they are honest and get the help they need. Most people won't get help unless faced with a huge obstacle like loss of relationship, career, reputation, or whatever it is they value. Working a twelve-step program for the rest of their lives will be a crucial piece to staying sober. It is a very difficult issue to overcome, but it can be done with hard work and a determination to be healthy. Until they do this, don't believe a word they tell you, and make decisions based on your needs and the needs of your children if you have them.

Sex addiction is the most difficult type of cheating to overcome, in my opinion. It is not something someone can just stop doing, and most people I have worked with resist the extensive treatment that would be necessary for them to go into recovery, which, at a minimum, would be participation in an ongoing twelve-step program for sex addicts and working with a sponsor.

My Spouse Is Acting Strange and Insists They Aren't Cheating

Perhaps you suspect but don't know for certain if your spouse, the Decider, is cheating on you. Their behavior is different, even weird; they turned their back on the marriage, so you wonder what on earth is going on. Is it a midlife crisis? I imagine you have asked them if there is someone else, and they have said absolutely not, but what I can tell you is that 999 out of 1,000 cheaters will lie about cheating, so a denial of cheating in a marriage crisis is not a very valued piece of evidence. This is a situation where you need to look at what the Decider is doing and not what they're saying.

Even if your spouse is normally a person of great integrity and you've never known them to lie or deceive, they will lie and deceive about this. Why? Because cheaters are judged very harshly in our culture, and who wants to subject themselves to that? Also, in a marriage crisis, the Decider can be seen by some as a sympathetic character as they tell the tale of being neglected and aggrieved at the hands of their spouse. And, by golly, they've got the Leaning-In partner on their knees begging to work things out, willing to do anything they ask! If it is discovered that they have cheated, the tables will turn, and the leverage will turn back to the Leaning-In partner in two seconds flat. Cheating spouses instinctively know this and want to stay in the marital driver's seat with their hand on the button of whether to stay or go.

Leverage in marriage is attained by having a legitimate grievance against your spouse along with a demand for change. It is a "You have treated me wrong, do this thing I ask or else!" sort of stance. This puts a Leaning-In partner back on their heels in a defensive posture. In a marriage crisis, the Decider has all the leverage, or power, and since they can pull the trigger on the marriage at any time, the onus is on the Leaning-In partner to get busy working on their mind, body, and spirit self-care so they can be a healthy partner moving forward. Once an affair is revealed, the Decider loses their power and ability to control the situation and the power shifts back to the Leaning-In partner, at least for a while, as the betrayed spouse points the finger at their own legitimate beef against the Decider. Upon a realization that the Decider has been using the Leaning-In partner's faults as a cover for fooling around, a Leaning-In partner is likely to think, *How disgustingly convenient and shameless.* It may be easier now to see why a Decider who is cheating has no good reason to tell the Leaning-In partner that they have met someone else. Understand that this choice has nothing to do with what is right or wrong. The Decider with a conscience knows it is wrong but has created justifications for it in their own mind that make it understandable and acceptable. It is a stretch of information processing to say the least, like a person who has good reasons for why it's okay to cheat on a diet. If a person has lost enough integrity to cheat on their partner, then what is the harm of a lie that a Decider may well justify to themselves by saying it is merciful to all not to tell?

Is There a Way to Find Out If My Spouse Is Cheating?

In a marriage crisis, there are signs and symptoms that scream, "Affair!" if you will just open your eyes and ears. The tell-tale sign is when the Decider's back is turned away from the marriage and they have no interest in working anything out. They are against marriage therapy, may be seriously tilting toward the divorce decision, and want to be left alone by the Leaning-In partner. They also often seem to be faring well despite the fact that their life of marital and family domesticity is crumbling all around them.

What, worry? they may think. *Not at all, as I have love drugs coursing through my brain that have me feeling high as a kite. I am intoxicated and feeling courageous, buoyed by plenty of verbal and emotional validation and very possibly inspired physical intimacy, and the last thing I want is to return to my dull life of sacrifice, lack of appreciation, and sexual drought.*

What does a Leaning-In partner do when they are confused about suddenly being thrust into a marriage crisis and much of it doesn't make sense? In my experience, when something doesn't make sense, it's because we don't have all the information. Typically, the Leaning-In partner will take stock of the situation: "Out of the blue, there was a shift in my partner's behavior. What is going on?" they ask. "Are these the tell-tale signs of betrayal? My spouse thinks they want out of the marriage, they've been working on their appearance, their schedule has changed, they've become more private, and their inter-personal exchanges with me have become more disrespectful. What the heck is happening here? What do I do?"

The answer? Snoop, of course.

Perhaps you are shocked at my answer. And being a person de-voted to teaching and practicing appropriate boundaries, this idea is somewhat shocking to me—but only for a second or two. Under normal to fair marital weather, I would be totally against snooping into a spouse's business. Their e-mails, texts, phone calls, mail, where they go, and what they do in the normal course of a day should all be respected as private unless otherwise mutually agreed upon, though in healthy marriages, both partners should have no issue giving their partner access to this information. For example, if I asked my hus-band, he would have no issue letting me look through his digital communications, but why would I want to? There's nothing there. In marriages where both partners are monogamous, trolling through their private communications is controlling and unnecessary.

But if a spouse has noticed changes and has evidence and a sense that something isn't right, I believe it opens the door to what I call *allowable snooping*. If you consider what is in the higher good of this marriage and family, I believe dismantling the secret of an affair is a positive thing to do, as one of the most appealing things about an affair to a betrayer is the danger and secrecy. Taking away the secret and exposing the marital crime will instigate change one way or the other that was in need of happening anyway, and if the Decider is gaslighting or playing the Leaning-In partner for being a fool, then of course I am going to recommend taking action to uncover that.

When it comes to allowable snooping, my Leaning-In clients who choose to go that route absolutely amaze me with their amateur private detective skills, and it proves that if there is a will, there is a way. I often say how I have seen everything in marriages and nothing surprises me anymore. This still holds true. What stuns me even more than their skills is that if my clients do pull up the goods on their cheating spouse—and sometimes it's outrageous and really, really bad—it is rare for the cheating spouse to drop the sword of defense and say, "Okay, I did it." They'll almost always minimize the cheating with a caveat like "It was only one time," or "The pic was photoshopped," or "We never had sex," or "It was just texting," or "It isn't what it looks like," or whatever minimizing defense tactic they can think of.

I don't buy it, and I tell Deciders that I don't. Their integrity on the line, they usually shrug their shoulders and say, "Whatever, what I'm telling you is true," though I know it isn't. How do I know? Experience. As a younger therapist just getting started, I used to buy into the stories, but after I was played the fool over and over, I realized the only sane thing to do for myself and the Leaning-In partner was not to quibble over the details and just treat every indiscretion as a worst-case scenario. Now, no matter what the busted cheater says about what they've been doing, how much they minimize or gaslight, I treat it as if it is really bad, like a long-term physical and regularly intimate love/emotionally intense affair and leave it at that. That way, all the bases are covered, and the Leaning-In partner and I won't have to sit and listen to the baloney the Decider will surely send our way.

They Are Cheating! Now What?

And so a cheater is uncovered in a marriage crisis. Caught red-handed. What do we do next? Sad to say, if a Decider is involved in a serious emotional and/or physical connection with another person, they may promise to end it, but my experience says they won't. Oh, yes, many have sincerely believed they can stop their love drug cold turkey, but rarely does the abstinence last. I know this, so I tell Deciders they may mean well, but I don't want them to make promises they can't keep. The intelligent thing to do is speak to them about all the reasons they should stop it and devote their energy to saving their marriage and family. Then we bide our time and allow the new relationship to play out. Fizzle. Dwindle. Die. And it almost always will, bringing the Decider to a place where they may return to their rational thinking brain, end their relationship, and become willing to possibly work things out with the Leaning-In partner. This is a bitter pill to ask any Leaning-In partner to swallow, and most won't do it.

If there was an emotional connection and the Decider really does promise to end it, then they must be held accountable to staying away from their drug, aka the Other Person (OP). If they work with the person, then they need to either (a) make plans to leave the job or see if the OP will, or (b) move to another area of the job where there will be no contact, or have the OP move. My attitude about this is if you do the crime, you must do the time, and the time may be leaving a job you enjoy or depend on and allowing yourself to be monitored by the Leaning-In partner for the indefinite future. The last thing we want is for the Leaning-In partner to live in insecure terror every day knowing the Decider is in contact with the person who has hurt them so.

More times than I can count, the cheating spouse refuses to leave a job or release or move an underling employee with whom they had an indiscretion. If it was me, this would be a no-go, but I have seen many Leaning-In partners who deal with or tolerate it even though it prevents them from healing and moving on. That's how much they do not want a divorce.

When There's an Ongoing Emotional Connection

If the OP is married or in a serious relationship, and the relationship involves an enduring emotional connection that is still ignited, I believe the Leaning-In partner should let the OP's partner know, though many resist my advice. In this case, there is therapeutic value because we want the emotional or physical affair to be stopped (see below), and if the other partner knows about it, they will be your ally in achieving this. I want to be clear that if it was not an emotionally connected affair and it was a one-off situation, I do not think you should tell the OP's partner, as there would be no therapeutic value in doing so because the person is no threat to your marriage.

Let me explain my thinking for why a person should tell if there is an enduring emotional connection.

1. Nothing kills the allure of an affair like having it exposed to all parties involved. Often, the secret itself is a large part of what makes it so potent.
2. The OP's partner will likely be a great ally for the Leaning-In partner moving forward as they begin to manage their own relationship crisis and watch every move their betraying partner makes. I have seen OP

> partners share information with Leaning-In partners
> as they cross-check excuses, lies, and other outrages. If
> either betraying partner is caught contacting the other,
> it is likely one of you will find out about it.
> 3. The Golden Rule. Wouldn't you want to be told if
>   someone knew your partner was cheating on you? In
>   most cases, I am sure you would.

Kimberly was a beautiful blonde wife of a successful physician. They had been in love since high school, and she had seen him through college, med school, residency, and more. She described their relationship as special and her life with their two young children as ideal—until he started getting too close to his nurse.

"It's like he's turned into a completely different person," she said through her tears. "He used to adore me, and now he won't talk and snaps when I try to talk to him. Help us!"

I met with them together. Her husband, Stephen, was young and handsome, and while she had told me that he was normally hospitable and engaging, he didn't appear that way now and had absolutely no interest in talking to me about a marriage crisis or affairs. The only thing he would tell me was that Kimberly was too needy, and anytime he tried to do his own thing, like travel to visit a friend, she'd freak out and he'd have to cancel his trip; she vehemently denied his version of the story. He was shut down, shut off, and not in the game. We quickly concluded that I would work with his wife alone.

When I see men like Stephen, I think they have become possessed temporarily by some dark entity in a true Dr.-Jekyll-and-Mr.-Hyde scenario. They are caught in a sudden storm of self-centeredness, digressing to between ages four and fourteen. "I want to do what I

want; leave me alone!" When he shut down in our session and refused to engage, I visualized a child throwing a tantrum. My goal was
to figure out a way to break the spell he was under.

Other employees at the clinic where Stephen worked began to
call Kimberly and tell her about how he was spending inappropriate
moments with his nurse, who was married and had children herself.
To bring the crisis to an end, I implored Kimberly to call the nurse's
husband and to call the head doctor of the clinic where they worked.
She would not do it. She felt certain it would make matters worse,
but I disagreed. It wasn't long, though, before a disgusted employee
went to the head doctor, and the head doctor took charge of the situation: He moved the nurse to a different clinic, called the nurse's
husband, and then called Kimberly saying that he was going to bring
an end to the situation that was disrupting their office's functioning
and turning it into a nest of gossip. *This had to have been divine intervention on Kimberly's behalf,* I thought.

Kimberly's husband remained defiant a little longer and moved
to a hotel suite for a month but by the end was ready to come home.
A world-class pleaser, Stephen had most likely caved under such
negative scrutiny and prematurely returned home. I wanted him to
consider reconciliation for the right reason: He regretted his actions
and wanted to patch things up with Kimberly because of love, who
she is, and what they've had. This quick reconciliation smelled fishy
to me. Kimberly answered my call when I checked in for an update
and said the crisis was over.

"He's back to the wonderful man I married," she said.

I recommended they get couples counseling moving forward to
shore up their relationship cracks and rebuild trust, but he still was
resistant to facing any of it, and she wasn't going to push. I nervously

accepted that they weren't ready to work on their relationship and told myself that I hoped they would at some point because in my view, the coast was still not clear.

You'd think a marriage crisis specialist would applaud any reconciliation, but we do not, especially if they are cut and pasted together too quickly. Reconciliations must be managed correctly—both parties working on the issues that created the crisis in the first place and having a history of being better and being motivated to continue working on it—before moving back in together. All the evidence shows that when a couple reconciles too soon, without working on the issues that got them into the situation in the first place, the reunion will be built on quicksand. The research-based book *Splitting Up* by Alvin Pam and Judith Pearson (1998) discusses this in detail, saying that when a Decider suddenly wants to patch things up and return, they are likely returning "not in a spirit of hope and love, but rather with a sense of frustration and failure" (p. 350).

- The Decider often returns after concluding there is no one better and settles for the partner they have after bitter defeat as a single person. "It is precisely this type of reunion that is most common," Pam and Pearson write, "and also offers the most flimsy chance for success" (p. 349).
- Quick reconciliations are usually the result of problems with a new partner or due to the downfall of financial or other plans.
- Most Deciders aren't eager to return if their life away from the Leaning-In partner is going well.
- Men who return quickly often have realized they have an inability to manage well without a partner.
- Leaning-In partners are often eager to reconcile if substantial letting go hasn't occurred.

Lessons Learned

It isn't wise to assume that either partner has *learned a lesson* from the separation experience unless that lesson learned has been demonstrated over time. This is not a time for telling your partner what you plan to do to be better; it is a time to show it through your actions over weeks and months, and that includes therapy. It is estimated that of the partners that do reconcile, 50 percent of those part again within a year (Weiss, 1975, p. 123). This is because the couple has not changed the marital system enough to lead to mutual satisfaction moving forward. If it were my life, knowing what I know as a therapist and a person who has been through it, I would insist on individual counseling for each person; working together on the relationship by engaging in trauma-based couple's counseling, workshops, and seminars; and spending time implementing the change before I would agree to a full reconciliation. Date each other, yes, but based on my experience, when a Decider or Leaning-In partner comes home too soon, with promises made but no work demonstrated, each partner will lose motivation to do the work necessary for the reconciliation to stick.

Do you believe Kimberly and Stephen's reconciliation will last? Do you believe she fully trusts him and can completely relax in knowing that their marriage is back on solid ground? I personally don't think so, either.

Why is it that people like Stephen run from counseling like the plague? Why is Kimberly unwilling to demand it? Fear, no doubt, but fear is never our friend. If you understand the dynamics of codependence as described by Pia Mellody in *Facing Codependence*, it's because people who are suffering from childhood developmental trauma—and 99.9 percent of us are—do not want to face uncomfortable truths or feel discomfort in any form. They will sit in a swamp of unhappiness and suffer for a long and miserable time before they will put a stop to it, and some never do. Being in recovery from codependence means facing things head-on proactively, as they come up. It is the ultimate self-care necessary to be a healthy adult. I heard a saying once that "people often resist what they need the most," and I believe this was true in Kimberly and Stephen's case.

Post-Revelation Crisis Management

Most betraying partners understand there will be a period when the injured spouse will be obsessed with what just happened, will be peppering them with questions and details, and, if they stay together, will want to monitor their every move and communication. The questions should be answered for the most part, and honestly. Do tell them how you met, where you met, how many times you met, how emotionally involved you are or were. The questions that should never be answered are sexual details, physical and sexual acumen comparisons, and anything that will create haunting visuals for the Leaning-In partner or will make them feel worse about themselves than they already do.

The questions will come by the truckload, and the Decider should humbly answer. However, I often see the ability to tolerate the interrogations does not outlast their spouse's need to know. Deciders often become belligerent, resentful, and basically *resist the bridle* of being held accountable to anyone.

Again, there is only room for humility here from the betraying spouse. No pride, ego, or attitude about having to be watched like a child. My message to the Leaning-In partners is yes, for a while you are the *hammer* and the cheater is the *nail*, but don't hammer too long or too hard or the tables may flip. You must use a soft hammer and wield it with compassion. There is a very fine line about how much any human will tolerate, so don't take advantage of this brief period when you have the upper hand—the Golden Rule is a good thing to keep in mind as you obsess about what just happened.

Other Things to Consider

If the Decider cheated with a family member or close friend, those people should be extinguished from your circle, whether you leave the group, or they do. Do I need to remind you that a family member or friend who would do something like that with your spouse is not really a friend at all? Once again, we are talking about retraumatizing the Leaning-In partner over and over by having to come into contact with someone who has a history of showing no regard for their marriage. I think it is cruel to ask your life partner to deal with that.

Another issue is whether to tell anyone about your spouse's cheating. Many people who have been caught cheating have pleaded with their partner not to tell anyone, and I completely understand why someone who betrayed their spouse would want no one to know. Maintaining a certain image as a good person is very important to a lot of people for a variety of reasons, which can include the ability to support or contribute to the family.

Even so, most injured spouses feel a longing to share what they are going through with a trusted friend or family member. They need the support. I am not talking about telling people who then proceed to create an alliance against the betrayer and try to pressure the betrayed spouse to end the marriage or punish them in a scorched-earth way. This type of person is not a friend of the marriage and should be kept out and avoided during affair management.

Friends of the marriage are another story. Friends of the marriage are supportive of your healing, understand your desire to reconcile and work on and repair the marriage, and won't be talking about your situation with others.

As you consider which path is best for you, think about the dynamic of the prerecovery alcoholic who wants to keep that problem a secret because of the shame involved in not being perfect. Some betrayers would also like only their partner to know and carry the burden of the truth alone, when the truth is we are all flawed and imperfect and do things we wouldn't want others to know. Once an alcoholic is in recovery, they learn the adage "You are only as sick as your secrets." Twelve-step programs encourage people to face their issues head-on, taking full ownership of them within their trusted group or those they feel comfortable with. They believe keeping the addiction a secret will hamper recovery. Likewise, even if you are not a sex addict and you are just a disgruntled spouse who had an affair, I believe that shameful secrets in general leave the door cracked to the potential for future indiscretions. This is why I coach Leaning-In partners that they should not feel obligated to keep their partner's betrayal secret, and ideally the two spouses together will inform age-appropriate children, which is over the age of eighteen, keeping in mind that not all eighteen-year-olds are mature enough to receive such information.

Sometimes, the betrayed spouse threatens to immediately tell children younger than that, sometimes saying things like "I want the children to know what a whore their mother is!" I shut down that idea right away and want to say now that for a betrayed spouse to do that is such a selfish (appropriate use of the word here) act of cruelty that I can't find the words to properly describe it. You must protect your younger children from your marital garbage at all costs; there is no benefit to exposing it at all, and if you overrule good sense and do it anyway, it will damage your children and backfire on you sometime in the future as they mature and realize that you chose not to protect their innocent hearts and minds.

Telling trustworthy people, if you feel you need to, and having their kind support may help clear a major obstacle on the road to potential healing and recovery and lead you in the direction of the peace and relief you both no doubt long for. There is nothing like compassionate and empathetic support. If the betraying spouse refuses to understand why it may be best to tell a few people, then I leave the decision to the Leaning-In partner alone. If they want to tell certain people they consider safe, meaning people who have their best interests at heart and would not use it to harm them, they should.

Also know that if the betraying spouse decides to end a love affair, they will likely grieve the loss. Since the Leaning-In partner is not likely to want to hear about the betraying partner's sadness and longing, I recommend not going through it alone and processing it with a therapist. It does hurt, and there will be a lot to unpack. The same goes for the Leaning-In partner. Don't do it alone.

Which Marriages Can Be Saved After a Betrayal?

If the relationship the betrayer was in was not significant and no emotional connections formed, they may be more than willing to stop their temporary bout with insanity, end the affair, and never look back.

Whether your marriage will make it or not after that has to do with:

1. **How remorseful your partner is.** The more mortified a betrayer is with themselves and the humbler they are throughout the process, the better the chances for a full recovery. If a betrayer huffs and puffs in frustration at any or all that is asked of them as if their partner is a pain in the backside, the chances of recovery lessen significantly.

2. **Is the betrayer able to understand and validate that this episode was a *big damn deal*?**

3. **If your partner downplays the seriousness of the cheating, minimizes it, and tries to quickly move on and not talk about it, the less likely the chances of a successful outcome.** We really need the betrayer to get how huge and hurtful the episode was, express that clearly, and be willing to talk about it spontaneously when appropriate.

4. **Does the betrayer accept that they will have to be totally transparent?** During the recovery and healing process, the betrayer must answer most of your questions (not questions about sexual details or comparisons of the OP to yourself) and sometimes the same questions over and over.

5. **No contact with OP.** Is the betrayer willing to have zero contact with the OP, and if unintentional contact is made, will they inform their spouse?

6. **Patience is necessary—this will take time.** Does the betrayer understand it can take more than two years for things to normalize (Fife et al., 2023)? Does the betrayer understand that normalization means obsession with the affair has dissipated, but the marriage itself won't/can't be the same as before.

We know most marriages that experience an affair recover and move on, the marriage intact (Lindner, 2023). This does not mean everything gets healed and all is forgotten. It is a long, painful, multi-pronged process that, if done right and with a little luck, will lead the couple down a path to mutual understanding and empathy, healing conversations, learning healthier ways of communicating, growth, recovery, and a stronger, richer marriage.

It must be said, however, that a post-affair marriage will be fragile for a very long time. A study of post-affair marriages five years later showed that 47 percent of couples were still together using a type of therapy called behavioral couple therapy, which is a form of couples therapy that incorporates abstinence from alcohol or drugs (Marín et al., 2014). Though this study wouldn't apply to everyone, it shows that even in heavily challenged marriages, the statistics remain close to 50 percent of marriages remaining intact.

The anguish felt by a Leaning-In partner is deep and wounding when an affair is revealed. It is tremendous, and a moment never to be forgotten. Their world stands still as they wait to find out how serious a betrayal this really is, and though the pain felt is serious beyond question, most betrayed partners instinctively understand that there are different degrees of affairs, some more marriage-threatening than others. What does this mean? The more emo-tionally attached the betrayer is, the longer the affair has gone on, the more serious it is. Add factors like the affair was with a family member, business partner or assistant, or best friend, and the diffi-culty to recover rises exponentially. Here is a spectrum of betrayal crimes to consider:

1. **Best-case scenario:** A one-time, spontaneous, meaningless union between a spouse and someone else.

2. **Really bad and difficult to recover from:** A long-term love
   affair. A workplace affair between a spouse who refuses to
   quit or leave their job and a former love who also refuses to
   quit or leave.

3. **Even worse to recover from:** Long-term betrayal with a
   friend, family member, nanny, babysitter, or any person who
   betrayed the Leaning-In partner's trust.

4. **Worst-case scenario:** A sexually addicted spouse who has
   had numerous liaisons, usually found online or in bars, and
   is regularly in pursuit of his next conquest.

Anytime you have a cheating episode in your marriage, you really
must process it with a mental health professional. The professional
will be knowledgeable and have expertise in helping you navigate the
slope in a way that won't damage the relationship more than it already
is, will increase your chances for a successful reconciliation, and will
lead you on the journey to healing. Part of that is not allowing the
betrayer to minimize or downplay what they did, preventing them
from either telling too much or too little about the details of the affair, coaching the betrayer on being transparent moving forward,
and helping you assess what's possible and what isn't.

There is no way one chapter in a marriage crisis book can cover
every base about affairs, and there is a lot of great information available dedicated entirely to that subject. I urge you not to allow your
family and friends to have a say about what you should do; instead,
inform yourself and work with a professional who has experience in
helping couples in an infidelity crisis. The books I use and recommend are *After the Affair* by Janis Abrahms Spring, a marriage and
family therapist who has been a clinical supervisor at Yale University
and whose own husband cheated on her, and *Not Just Friends* by

Shirley Glass, also a marriage and family therapist who was referred to as the "godmother of infidelity research" by the *New York Times* (Hooper, 1999). Esther Perel wrote *The State of Infidelity* in 2017 and offers some unique ideas and insight into the subject. If you read these three books, you will know most of what there is to know about infidelity. I want you to do your research, consider all options, and take your time in taking any action because whatever you decide to do, you need to be as sure as you can be about it so there will be no regrets down the line.

Healing and Forgiveness After an Affair

It is possible to mostly recover from an affair, as it is possible to recover from a broken leg or other serious injury. You can heal, but there will likely be scars. As one spouse said after deciding to remain with their partner who had cheated, "I'm moving forward and I'm going to stick with my marriage, but I don't think things will ever be totally the same." That's a pretty typical response.

Exercise: Discerning If Recovery After an Affair Is Possible

As you make your decision to try to work this out or not and whether healing and forgiveness are possible, I want you to be considering the following questions:

1. Is your spouse humble and remorseful as opposed to defiant and defensive?

2. Is your spouse willing to tell you the truth, the whole truth, and nothing but the truth? (No sexual details allowed, by the way.) Example: "How many times did you have sex?" is acceptable. Comparison questions such as "Was she better in bed than I am?" or physiological ones such as "How big, small, etc.," are a no-no.

3. Is your spouse requesting forgiveness?

4. Is your spouse accepting responsibility for their actions?

5. Does your spouse have insight into why they took this action?

6. Is your spouse willing to be completely and totally open and transparent for a long time to get your trust back?

7. Is your spouse willing to go to marriage therapy regularly to discover the root causes of the issue and correct them? If it is sexual addiction, are they willing to get extended treatment in a twelve-step program such as Sex and Love Addicts Anonymous (SLAA)?

It really is all about attitude, humility, and the willingness and motivation to do some serious self-inventory and an inventory of the relationship that will make redemption and recovery possible. And as much as people whose spouse has cheated on them hate to hear it, many times the marriage will become better than it ever was in the aftermath.

How Do I Know If the Betrayer Is Going Through a Midlife Crisis?

When I am managing a couple in crisis caused by infidelity, the subject of whether the erring spouse is having a midlife crisis often comes up. I'll explain what a midlife crisis is, and the person who cheated will most likely be able to tell you if it sounds like what they are feeling.

A midlife crisis is a rebellion by a person who perceives themselves as giving and sacrificing much to benefit their family while not receiving enough appreciation, love, and support in return. When I see a young couple come in and one or both individuals brag about how hardworking they are and how little time they make for relaxation,

I always warn them that they are a midlife crisis in the making. It is about the perception of the sacrifice made and what is received in return that creates the perfect environment for a future crisis.

Suzanne had been a pleaser for as long as she could remember. Raised in a traditional family in the American South, she was taught to step back and let the man take the lead. When she married Ronald at age twenty-four, she agreed to go along with his choices in life and to be as supportive as she could, molding herself into who she thought he wanted her to be.

"He just really wanted to become something in his life and was as hardworking a man as I've ever seen," she said. "Although I'd ask for more quality time with him, he could only do it here and there, then he'd drift back into his busy schedule where I hardly ever saw him. He bragged about what a good provider he was, and he was, and how I should be happy with that, and for a long time, I felt guilty about griping and complaining."

They had two children in three years, and Suzanne began to feel like a single mom who couldn't date, she said. Ronald left the kids to her most of the time.

"I'd go to a bunch of events with friends or family, and he could never join me," she said. "I was always apologizing for his absence at whatever event it was, and people teased me about being a widow and having a mystery husband. Then I'd see all these other dads involved with their kids, and there was my husband who left before the kids got up in the morning and came home around bedtime. When he was off, he was too tired to engage in romance, would eat, and go to bed. On the weekends, he usually had some project that took him away. He posed for photos with the kids that gave the impression he was there, but he wasn't. I guess at some point, I began asking myself, 'What is this we're doing?'"

Suzanne's resentment built up. Complaints and requests for improvement were ignored or dismissed as a lack of appreciation of what he was building for the family.

"I'm doing all of this for you guys," he'd say, "to provide you the best life."

"If this is your idea of a best life, I don't think I want it," she'd say.

Suzanne was married but getting few of the benefits of marriage. She felt like a house manager and nanny, and she longed for more. She wanted to be held, loved, and have someone look in her eyes like they were happy to see her. She started to think about how she had gone along with the life Ronald wanted from the beginning, putting her hopes and dreams aside. When she asked for him to treat her as his equal and as a partner so she could feel included, he resisted. Not long after, Suzanne began little spurts of flexing her independence muscle. She took money from her budget and bought a sports car, though Ronald had implored her not to do it. She got a dog for her and the children against his demand of no pets and began refusing to attend his all-important work social events with him. "I don't want to give the appearance we're something we're not," she'd say to him.

Doing what she wanted for herself for once felt good, and just getting a taste of it seemed to make her crave more.

A midlife crisis involves a person who previously conformed entering into a process in which they now refuse to conform. The conforming, pleasing, and accommodating got the person nowhere with very few needs met, they conclude, and so as an antidote, "I will now do for myself."

In my graphic (to follow), you can see how it starts. I created the typical steps and evolution of the midlife crisis based on my professional experience:

1. From birth to around age twenty-eight, the person conforms to family, religion, or other influences.

2. By age twenty-eight, the brain is fully developed, the person has often completed or nearly completed their education, had their own life experiences, and begun to form their own opinions.

3. Between ages twenty-eight and thirty-two, they question whether it is okay to think and be who they want to be or whether they are supposed to keep conforming.

4. In a marriage, they may feel unappreciated, diminished, or invisible. They may conclude the sacrifices they've made for the benefit of their partner aren't worth the payoff. If they married young, they are growing up, maturing, and seeing the world through an adult's eyes. Their training wheels are off—has their partner made way for their new, evolving self? They begin to deeply resent how things have played out.

5. Sometime after age thirty-two (though it can be decades later), in what appears to be a spontaneous moment, though the situation has been brewing for years, the person throws up their hands and says, "No more!" They suddenly want to change their life and focus on their own enjoyment. This could mean an affair, a fancy new sports car, getting in shape, or many other things.

6. The spouse panics and says the person has lost their mind; they want them to come to their senses, but the person has not lost their mind. They are finding themselves, albeit in an unpleasant, extreme, and sometimes self-sabotaging way.

7. In my professional experience, the person in a midlife crisis will usually not be reachable for any rational conversations for around two years. At some point, they will return to balance, and like a tornado that has just left a town, it will

be time to survey the damage. Whether or not a marriage survives a midlife crisis can fall either way, but one thing is certain: the sacrificing partner will not be sacrificing with little or nothing in return anymore.

The Midlife Crisis Model

Beginning of Life:
A period of conforming to what others expect and want us to be.

Midlife examination begins between ages 28–32, when we begin to question the idea of being who we want to be or who others expect or want us to be.

A person might say, "Do I have to believe and act like my family and culture advise, or can I believe and act on what I feel is right for me?"

Midlife crisis: A person feels and acts upon a sudden and intense pull toward extreme self-centeredness that will balance out in time, but the person will never return to the conforming and out-of-balance self of their younger years.

Authenticity and individuality will be a new and necessary theme for living that will take them to the end of their life. To friends and family, it looks like they have lost their mind, but the truth is, they are finding themselves.

Beginning of Life	Ages 28–32	End of Life

What happens: If a person is out of balance in their younger years, with too much work and sacrifice and not enough play and/or freedom, the subconscious mind will propel them into a period of self-examination about how they really want to spend their life. The question is: "Do I continue conforming and sacrificing, or do I find something in this life for myself? What do I want?" The person will feel an enormous pull to find balance and be true to themselves. If this is not acted upon organically, an ungraceful midlife crisis that masquerades as temporary insanity will ensue that confuses and confounds family and friends.

- This model applies to both genders.
- The more rigid and sacrificing the person is early in life, the more they are setting themselves up for the midlife crisis.

In a midlife crisis, the gray line represents a person's life. The first part of life was spent conforming to what others wanted. Between ages twenty-eight and thirty-two, many conformers question whether to stay conforming or jump into living for themselves.

Suzanne's husband could not handle her newfound autonomy and enlisted friends and family members to join him in pressuring her to come back into the fold. Suzanne resented being ganged up on and became even more determined to find her way on her own—with her children. Her marriage would not survive.

I spoke with Suzanne a few years after her midlife crisis had settled. She was divorced and said she had not been happier in her life. She found a career, formed her own identity, had new friends, her children were happier, and she had no regrets. She said those who pressured her to go back to her old life had been cut out of her life. Then she added, "My ex remarried pretty quickly," she said, "and my kids tell me that about half the time, his wife sleeps on the couch!"

Now you should be able to answer the question of whether you or your spouse is having a midlife crisis or not. If they are, learn from Suzanne's example. Let your spouse find who they are and do for themselves. Those who stand in their way will likely be discarded. Your spouse will come back to balance, and though it is hard to stand by someone when the self-focused part of their inner child is at the helm of their personality, it is the only thing you can do if your goal is to save your marriage.

CHAPTER SIX

I'm Trapped in Ambivalence: Should I Separate, Divorce, or Stay?

We have spent a lot of time talking about what leads to the destruction of marital contentment and how that destruction plays out. Now that you're fully informed about what is going on, how it happened, and what you need to do about it, we'll look at things you can do as you decide whether you want to remain married or leave or if you are trying to figure out if your spouse might be persuaded to stay.

I get a lot of calls from frantic Leaning-In partners who, when hearing the idea of separation, act as if they have just received the news of a terminal illness. Some have even begged me not to say the word *separation*. Their partner wants out of the marriage, and the Leaning-In partner is looking for a miracle cure or at least to buy more time before going down the final road to divorce.

Why do so many resist separation? Many Leaning-In partners see separation as the first step to an inevitable divorce—but it is not. In this chapter, we'll talk about your options.

Many issues couples face are correctable if they are willing to put in the time and effort. If there are no serious mental disorders or chronic illnesses that might be caused by the Leaning-In partner's lack of self-care or unwillingness to learn how to be an emotionally healthy adult (or both), then there's a chance the Decider *can* see a way back to the marriage. This is not to say the Decider has nothing to work on—I'm sure they do—it's just that in the phenomenon known as a marriage crisis, the onus is on the Leaning-In partner to begin to correct the things that caused the Decider to become disgruntled in the first place. There is no fairness and equality when a marriage is swinging toward a divorce decision. If all goes as we hope, and we can come out of crisis management and work on the marriage, the time will come to address the Decider's issues.

One obstacle in a marital crisis can be getting two people motivated to work on their marriage at the same time. In addition to digging into resources such as this book, a marriage therapist, therapist websites, and other publications, the decision about what to do is so important that I highly recommend you also lean on professional help. This help should come from an experienced marriage and family therapist, who can offer insight and suggestions and help you mull over your decision. Whether you choose to stay or not, no one knows what hangs in the balance more than a therapist who spends their days in the trenches of marital and postdivorce situations.

Beware of Random Books and Websites

Books and websites dedicated to getting your partner back can be found all over the Internet. Some are written by therapists who know a lot about the subject, and others have been put together by people who got dumped and then devised a successful way to get their spouse back. Perhaps impressed with their success, they now market themselves as an expert on the subject and, for a price, reveal their secrets. I've also seen a lot of social media sites where people ask for advice from the general public. More often than not, the advice is cringeworthy and, at times, dangerous—please steer clear.

I promise you there are no secret potions, spells, or strategies that haven't already been thought of, tried, or written about by people who understand true research—not the kind found on Google and Wikipedia, which are sources I wouldn't use exclusively for any sort of important decision-making. I'd veer away from the amateur relationship experts who believe their unique situation applies to everyone, and instead look toward the therapists and academics who have studied legitimate sources and research studies and who have personal experience working with couples. The stakes are high, and the quality of the help you receive should be high.

If I were in your shoes of seriously considering whether to stay with my spouse, separate, or divorce, first and foremost, I would want to do whatever I could to save the relationship or at least thoroughly explore if this is possible. I have been through divorce with and without children involved, and I know the pain, shame, and anguish that are sure to come with it; I assure you that the pain will last through your lifetime. The wildcard factor in trying to work out what choice to make is always the other person, of course. You may have all the will and motivation needed to bring your marriage back to life, but if your spouse only wants out, nothing can be done. If you're that person who wants out, I hope my words have persuaded you to take your time and mull through every possibility before giving up on your marriage. No matter what path is chosen by a couple in crisis, it's a good day when a final decision to end a marriage can be slowed down.

There are strategies available to help couples with differing stances concerning their marriage get clarity about whether it can and should be saved. One method that is very popular right now is *discernment counseling*. The other is a method I created called *managed separation*, which is a strategy to separate intelligently, deliberately, and with a plan. Then, of course, there is divorce, which I will discuss at the end of the chapter.

Discernment Counseling

When therapists think of discernment counseling, they think of its primary creator, Bill Doherty, a well-respected colleague in the field of marriage and family therapy and a professor in the Department of Family Social Science at the University of Minnesota. Doherty has long worked with troubled couples, and he lamented that in our field, there was no in-between place for couples who were in a marriage crisis (Doherty & Harris, 2017). The choices of the past were either do marriage therapy or get a divorce. *Mixed-agenda couples,* as he calls them, are when one spouse is leaning out of the marriage and strongly considering divorce and the other is leaning in and strongly wants to save the marriage—this is the same situation I describe as a *marriage crisis.*

With children's lives hanging in the balance and the reality of numerous lives changing irreparably in a divorce, Doherty longed to find a third choice that could turn a disgruntled spouse, someone with little or no motivation to work on the marriage, toward taking a deeper, more considered, and weighted look at both staying and leaving the marriage.

Doherty got the idea for doing things differently when he watched a presentation by family therapist Betty Carter (Doherty & Harris, 2017). Doherty listened as Carter described how she managed mixed-agenda couples in the 1980s, and he began to incorporate her strategies into his practice. He continued to hone his process and began to create and test a short-term therapy for mixed-agenda couples that takes place in five sessions or less, using both individual and couple sessions. The process is designed to give couples clarity and confidence about the next steps for their relationship. He calls the process discernment counseling (p. 14), and one of the important strategies he espouses is helping each person in the marriage have a deeper understanding of how each partner has contributed to the negative state of the marriage.

In discernment counseling, three choices are presented: (1) Stay in the marriage and keep it as it is, (2) get a divorce immediately, or (3) spend six months of concerted effort in marriage therapy, and then decide to stay together or divorce. Though couples come in together in this process, the intensive work is in individual, separate conversations specifically orchestrated by the discernment counseling process.

While marriage therapy aims to improve a relationship, discernment counseling aims for "clarity and confidence about a next step"

(Doherty & Harris, 2017, p. 14). Doherty says his method is not to solve marital problems but to see if marital problems can be solved (p. 15). When Doherty examined one hundred couples who went through the process with him, he found that 12 percent chose to keep the marriage as it is and stay together without therapy, 41 percent chose to divorce immediately, and 47 percent chose to take the six months and work on their marriage in therapy (p. 36). The information on one couple was lost, so the data came from a total of ninety-nine couples.

Questions asked in a recommended two-hour first session with the couple together are "What's happened to your marriage that's gotten you to the point where divorce is a possibility?" and "Can you tell me what you've done to try and fix the problem in your marriage, whether on your own or with help" (p. 56)?

The emphasis is on each person's part in the marital breakdown; these questions also delve into the issue of how the couple typically deals with conflict. Are they fighters, fliers, freezers, or fixers? The process also has partners focus on what part their children play in their decision-making and what their relationship was like in the best of times (pp. 58–59).

If the couple continues with the process, the first joint session will be followed by several individual sessions, and finally, by a last meeting as a couple, when a path is chosen. At any point in the process, a divorce decision can be made, and in that case, the Decider will choose path two, and the discernment counseling will end (p. 118).

I believe discernment counseling is a helpful tool for some couples and is certainly worth exploring, especially when the Decider refuses to go to any type of marriage therapy or marriage crisis manager (like me). Even though things are bleak, many Deciders intending to divorce will agree to a short-term process like discernment counseling. It is another tool that helps couples get the thing they most report they'll need to tell themselves if the marriage does end: "I did all I could to save my marriage, and we just couldn't get it there."

Another thing I'd like to add is if a couple chooses discernment counseling, there is still work that will need to be done on the other side, no matter what course of action is taken. I feel my managed separation process, either to work toward healing and reconciliation or an amicable parting, is the perfect place for couples in this situation. A therapist trained in helping people reconcile or uncouple will ensure that the process is done in the healthiest possible way for the family.

If You Plan to Separate, Do It the Right Way

If you are considering a separation, promise yourself you will do it the right way or not at all. Separating on your own, with no timeline and no purpose, is almost always a fool's game. Because of this, I created a plan for separation around 2010 when practicing in San Antonio, Texas. Texas has a lot of interesting laws when it comes to divorce and separation, and one of those is that legal separation is not available, as it often is in other states. Suppose a person wants to separate in Texas and they have a partner who is not willing to move out or support them or continue to contribute financially or agree to divide time with the children. In that case, they must file for divorce and get temporary orders that will make their partner accept separate residences, stay in their supporting financial role, and provide enforceable custody rules to follow. For many of my clients leaning toward separation, the idea of filing for divorce was overkill, demoralizing, and very frightening. They wanted a smart way to separate that didn't involve lawyers, judges, and something as intimidating and unnecessary as filing for divorce.

Using Managed Separation to Separate the Right Way

I created the managed separation agreement to offer a plan for separation that has a reason, purpose, and timeline. It addresses all the negatives that doing a separation on your own does and prevents couples from ending up in separation limbo, where they don't want to reconcile but they're not ready to end the marriage altogether. Here are the things I don't like about disorganized, unplanned separations:

1. **No purpose.** Why are you parting? To take a break? To wake your partner up from their marital coma? To experiment with being single and free? How do you plan to achieve your purpose, and how will you know when you're there?

2. **No timeline.** Separation limbo comes from what I described above: Not ready to reconcile or get back together, and so the separation continues indefinitely. The reason is that neither person has been working on the things that got them in this marital mess in the first place. There has to be growth and forward movement to pull you out of inertia.

3. **No plan.** What will you be doing during the separation? Have each of you agreed to get individual counseling, begin a self-care regimen, and talk to a couple's therapist together

regularly to discuss your marital patterns, discontentment, and what you are hoping for?

4. **No guidelines.**

Controlled Separation

I'm not the first person to realize that helping people during separation was a well-needed tool. Controlled separation is a process created by therapist Lee Raffel as an answer to what a Decider should do when caught in the middle between "I can't stand my marriage" and "I hate the thought of divorce." I found Raffel's work when I was researching ideas for my own separation plan to use with my clients. She and I found the same frustration in watching couples unnecessarily make a mess of their marriages, separate without a plan, end up in limbo, and create a situation in which they destroyed the "last salvageable shreds of their relationships" (Raffel, 1999, p. 9).

She created a twelve-step process for couples to separate that involves time limits; fair management of money, children, and household items; whom to tell; and a negotiated answer to the question of whether it's okay to date others. Like me, Raffel understands the wisdom of slowing down the decision-making process, clearing the air of intense emotions, and getting a couple to a point where they can better assess what they really want to do moving forward.

Her plan is a bit different from mine, as I have created two different plans for couples: one that recognizes the Decider's ambivalence about wanting to go and wanting to stay and creating a separation that leans toward the hope to reconcile, and a second plan for those in which the Decider is certain they want to end the marriage, which is in the next chapter.

Does Separation Feel Like the Beginning of the End?

A word to terrified Leaning-In partners who think separation is the beginning of the end: Please understand how terrible things really are when it comes to the state of your marriage. Your marriage is on life support, and anything could happen. The Decider will divorce you if you are not willing to give them the space they need to come out of activation. In my view, it is your only option to save your marriage. Please trust me that I know what I am doing here and know this: fear is not your friend right now.

One more bit of advice for you as you consider your options: If you are not in a situation that involves abuse or addiction, do not listen to the advice of anyone who is not a supporter of doing all you can to possibly save your marriage. Anyone who would encourage you to throw in the towel on your marriage, especially if there are children involved, is not a friend to you or your family. In-laws or friends who aren't big fans of your spouse may take the opportunity of your marital crisis to tell you things they haven't felt were appropriate to say before. You may be barraged as your spouse's detractors verbally pile on and put them down. I hope you will put a stop to this as soon as it occurs. If you do reconcile, this will backfire on the critics, and your spouse likely and justifiably will never want to see them again. I would hope that, knowing it takes two partners to bring down a marriage, you would not allow others to blame one person or trash the mother or father of your children. Sitting around diminishing other human beings is not an adult activity anyway; it's for arrogant folks who have a robust and uncontrolled AC—remember our inner fourteen-year-old? Even if you divorce, you will still be a family, and staying political—meaning taking into consideration the long-term ramifications of things said and done today—will be a decision you won't regret.

Deciding to Separate

In my practice, there have been numerous times when a Decider has brought in the Leaning-In partner to try to get me to talk to them about managed separation. The terrified Leaning-In partner often thinks I am the devil, and the idea of separation is something they don't want to entertain. Some have said, "I don't like you because you encourage separations. I don't want to separate."

I do not encourage separation for all couples—only the ones for which I believe the marriage will fail without it. It is a last-ditch Hail Mary pass to "win" the game of marriage. Without the pass, there will be no chance of winning. The marriage is already gasping for air. Staying in the status quo is not an option. Instead of remaining stuck and ultimately divorced, I created a hopeful path to try first.

Sometimes You Think You Need a Separation, but You Don't

A few years ago, a couple came to see me so I could manage a separation for them, but after speaking with them, I knew it wouldn't be a fit. Why? They were high school sweethearts, now in their late thirties, who loved each other dearly and wanted to be together, but the wife's controlling ways and temper were something the husband was not willing to tolerate anymore. Separation was not going to change that, but trauma therapy could.

I told Sam and Sophia that I would not manage a separation for them because they didn't need it, but we could do marriage counseling and probably take care of the issues altogether. When I looked at them, I didn't see a Decider there, nor a clear Leaning-In partner. The husband was happy-go-lucky and madly in love with his wife. They had three teen children they adored. He just wanted to motivate her to stop being so moody and stop trying to control the entire family. She loved him, too, but I saw a woman who had not found her identity away from being a wife and stay-at-home mom. She also thought that riding herd over children was what being a good mom was. It isn't.

Part of Sophia's journey was to find a life that interested her away from her family. Her kids were older and didn't need her as much, so she became a health coach and now helps people with various ailments find the right nutrition for their situation. She learned that having healthy boundaries means never trying to control another, and with children, it means nurturing them along as they unfold into who they are instead of molding them into who you want them to be. She reported that as she changed her own life and perspective, her family changed, too. Her children wanted to spend more time with her now that she wasn't "up in their business" all the time.

We worked together for about eighteen months, and their marriage improved so much that they felt good enough to move back to their busy lives. I wanted to tell you this story so you could understand that separation is not something for everyone. Your marriage may need a few tweaks, or you may need a little knowledge and work on childhood-development trauma issues. If you're locked into the pattern of your WC getting activated and your AC being your responder (as described in Chapter 2), then go see a Pia

Mellody–trained therapist or a therapist trained in the Meadows Behavioral Health model, and then get to work. You will see what I see in my practice every week: couples going from dysfunctional to functional, and quickly.

For others, maybe you, a separation is exactly what you need. Read the criteria for those who should consider a managed separation and decide if it's right for you. Remember, I have two plans, one for when the Decider is trapped between not being able to tolerate the marriage as it is and not wanting a divorce, and the second for when the Decider knows they want to end the marriage but want to separate and slow down the process and proceed in the most amicable way possible.

When the Decider Is Tilted Toward Saving the Marriage

I understand that separation is a major life event, and I never suggest it unless I really feel it will be beneficial to a couple in crisis and their decision-making process. To that end, I have criteria I look for, based on experience, and here is my list—consider a managed separation *tilted toward saving the marriage* if:

- The marriage would definitely end if the couple did not try something drastic.
- The Decider feels they won't be able to cope if they don't get away from the Leaning-In partner.
- The Decider is caught between the ambivalence of "I can't stand this marriage anymore" and "I hate the idea of getting a divorce."
- The Decider is not motivated to do marriage therapy at this time but recognizes they might at a later point.

- The Decider feels confused about what they want and need.
- Prior to the crisis, the Leaning-In partner was resistant to change and is now willing to do almost anything to save the marriage.
- There is no affair going on, or it is at least a meaningless affair that will be ended prior to the separation, and dating third parties is off the table for now.
- Both parties are prepared to do regular therapy individually and together at intervals for the purpose of managing the separation.

On the facing page is the Managed Separation Agreement Version One. Version Two is for Deciders and Leaning-In partners who intend to divorce and is found in Chapter 7. Read through it, see what it requires, and get a sense of whether it's right for you. Everything in the document is negotiable, but a word of caution: I have tweaked the agreement many times over the years to make a loophole-free document that answers every issue a couple is likely to face during a separation. Changing anything too much will decrease your chances of success, so change it at your own risk.

What to Do If the Decider Refuses to Do Managed Separation

I occasionally work with Leaning-In partners whose Decider spouse refuses to meet with me for marriage crisis management, or with any marriage therapist. The Decider, they tell me, is stuck in limbo, with no movement in any direction, and is not interested in working on the marriage, but also not ready to say they want a divorce. Often, this situation has been going on for an uncomfortably long period of time, and the Leaning-In partner wants to know what to do that might get movement forward.

If your marriage is stuck, and the Decider refuses marriage crisis management and managed separation, or to work on the marriage, I suggest you use marriage crisis management or managed separation guidelines, unilaterally. With separation, you could leave for a while, temporarily, or ask them to. During this time, you would follow the rules of the agreement of no contact and no marital benefits and spend the time working on yourself, going to individual therapy, and staying quiet. If you have children and do this, you can follow the guidelines I provide for temporary child custody.

For there to be change, we have to move the relationship out of the status quo, and doing the unilateral separation achieves this. This shift could motivate the Decider one way or the other, and it could also change your perspective in unforeseen ways. I always hope during a separation the Decider will realize how hard life is without you, how much they love, need, and miss you.

Now, onward to the agreement, which is designed to nudge couples toward intelligent action and decision-making.

Managed Separation Agreement Version One: For Those Stuck in Ambivalence
Doctor Becky Whetstone's Managed Separation™ Agreement
Date: _____

This is a Managed Separation Agreement between parties **Spouse 1 (insert name here)** and **Spouse 2 (insert name here)**, a married couple, who will be referred to in this agreement as *the individuals.* It is understood and agreed that the purpose of Managed Separation is to create the possibility that a broken marriage may be restored to a state of health and wholeness.[1]

---

1 Note: This agreement was created by Becky Whetstone, PhD, a licensed marriage and family therapist in Texas and Arkansas. Becky Whetstone has provided this nonbinding agreement for the purpose of helping a couple desiring to separate in a structured manner that may increase the likelihood that they will reconcile and/or to assist them in making the best decision for them regarding whether to stay in or end their marriage. It is understood that Becky Whetstone is *not the couple's therapist.*

Purpose and Spirit of a Managed Separation. A Managed Separation is for couples whose marriage or relationship is in crisis and would most certainly have ended with a permanent split or divorce if not for the Managed Separation intervention. Managed Separation is indicated when one partner, the Decider, has turned their back on the marriage and is leaning strongly in the direction of permanently ending the relationship. Typically, the Decider will describe an urgent feeling of needing to get away from the other partner in the relationship, referred to as the Leaning-In partner. Although the Decider feels extreme stress, they describe feeling uncertain, confused, and ambivalent (as if they both want and do not want the relationship) about their feelings for their spouse.

Research shows that many individuals make the decision to divorce during this period of time, only to find later, when the stress lessens, that they wish they had done more to save the marriage. In a postdivorce study of Deciders, more than 50 percent, knowing what they know now, wished they had done more to save their marriage (Hawkins et al., 2013).

In several states,[2] there is no legal separation. Where there is legal separation, a couple may not want to enter into a legal process too soon or at all, and the Managed Separation Agreement is meant to bridge the gap between a couple separating without purpose and a plan or going the legal route. It is also mutually understood that whichever party is the one to leave the family home where their spouse and children (if there are children) may currently reside will not be described as having abandoned the home and/ or family but is merely taking part in a therapist-recommended separation and intervention for the purpose of trying to bring the marriage back from the brink of divorce into a functional and workable space where they may thrive moving forward.

---

2 States with no legal separation are Delaware, Florida, Georgia, Mississippi, Pennsylvania, and Texas.

This is a Managed Separation Agreement between parties who are a married couple, who will be referred to in this agreement as *the individuals*. The facilitator or manager of the Managed Separation is **(enter name of licensed therapist here)** _____.

This Managed Separation Agreement is unapologetic about its bias and preference that the marriage will be saved if possible. The purpose of Managed Separation is to imitate the atmosphere of what divorce would be like, a "trial divorce," so to speak, so the Decider may experience the positives *and* negatives that come with divorce as opposed to divorcing first and seeing how it feels afterward.

The agreement also slows down the divorce decision-making process and creates space and buys time for the Decider to hopefully turn back toward the marriage if that is possible. For example, sometimes, during Managed Separation, the Decider may not like being away from the family, may miss their partner, or see that life on their own is not for them, creating the possibility that the marriage may be brought to health. In addition, Managed Separation eliminates hasty decisions during a time of stress and also allows individuals to be able to say they did all they could to make the best and wisest decision regarding their relationship.

Ending the agreement early to divorce. Time apart is meant to bring clarity to both partners. Once Managed Separation begins, occasionally it becomes clear to the Decider, the Leaning-In partner, or both that a decision to permanently separate and divorce is in the best interest of both parties and that to continue Managed Separation would be needless. In these cases, the therapist recommends that the couple transition to Divorce Therapy to facilitate the healthiest possible divorce process in the best interest of both parties.

Ending the agreement early to reconcile. This contract is not meant to be used by couples without the guidance and supervision of a licensed marriage and family therapist (LMFT) or licensed professional counselor (LPC) trained in marital therapy. Research shows that couples who separate without getting professional guidance and therapy for the situations that caused the estrangement in the first place ultimately will almost always face divorce and/or permanent estrangement and/or separation, and reconciliations that occur without working on the issues that created the marriage crisis in the first place are likely to fail.

Terms of the Managed Separation Agreement

The terms in the Managed Separation Agreement are not meant to punish, and this agreement is not about who is right or wrong but is about creating the space needed for a person who is tilting toward the divorce decision to possibly realize the permanent and irreversible effects of such a decision and create the motivation to become involved in marital therapy. (A person who is feeling the enormous stress that leads to such a separation, it is agreed, is not motivated to work on the relationship.)

The following are the terms of the Managed Separation Agreement. Couples may negotiate different or compromised terms with their therapist.

1. The individuals agree that **they will live apart**, but financial arrangements between the two will remain the same as when they lived together. There will be no capital purchases, hiding, hoarding, or moving finances around during the separation period. Bank accounts will remain the same; property ownership will remain the same; there will be no running up credit

cards, canceling credit cards, sudden remodeling projects, or changing of any bank accounts; and if a major expenditure comes up unexpectedly, both parties will be fully informed.

Note: It is not recommended that a couple separate under the same roof. Keep in mind we are trying to create motivation to work on the marriage, and it is our hope that the Decider does not enjoy living on their own, especially over the long term. Though they may initially feel euphoria at getting away from the tension and stress they have been feeling, trust me when I say what goes up will come back down. When things settle in, we hope they don't like it and will reach out to the Leaning-In partner to work on the marriage.

This may sound like it is the Decider who should leave the family home, and that is always my first choice. Why? First, they are the one wanting space. I want them to miss the home, their stuff, their family, the pets if they have them. If we make them too comfortable, separation may not have the result we are hoping for.

If the primary caretaker of the children is the Leaning-In partner, you will definitely want the Decider to be the one to move. This way, things stay as normal as possible for the children.

Some couples choose to take turns living in the family home while the other goes to an apartment or some other location when it's not their time with the children. This has worked very well for my clients.

2. Feeling safe and secure during this period of Managed Separation is of utmost importance and is crucial to the process. Therefore, **individuals agree that they will not file for divorce without notice or warning or engage in any covert actions**

that would likely negatively affect their spouse mentally, emotionally, spiritually, or financially. This includes but is not limited to actions such as (again) filing for divorce, filing any sort of litigation procedure, hiring private investigators, or filing restraining orders. Do not post cryptic, direct, or passive-aggressive messages on social media during this process; it will not be helpful and may well hurt what we are trying to do.

3. **The process will continue for a minimum of 2 weeks, 30 days, 60 days, 90 days (choose one) and may be extended from month-to-month but in no event will exceed 6 months.** Work with your therapist to decide an appropriate length of time for your unique situation. Hopefully, the Decider will have a strong sense of what they need, but in any event, remain flexible about the time frame. On occasion, one jolt of the battery charger with a two-week parting will be all that it takes to create motivation, but we never know.

Extension date _____

Extension date _____

At the end of each one-month period, a decision will be discussed regarding whether to continue the Managed Separation, end the relationship, or move toward possible reconciliation via a concerted commitment to marital therapy. Couples may decide to reunite prior to the 90-day period and to begin marital therapy, but this decision should be made with the therapist to ensure the couple is not returning to old, dysfunctional behaviors.

Note: Just because the selected time is up or the 6-month mark is reached does not mean that the spouse who has moved out of the family home may return. This decision will be negotiated in couples therapy as the time nears.

At the end of 6 months, if the Decider is still feeling ambivalent about whether to stay or go, all parties agree that the final decision defaults to no and they will not reconcile. Understand that if the Decider wants to return home, there will be marital work to be done in a therapist's office, and many times, it is best to continue a separation while the couple dates again and goes to therapy. If the Decider doesn't want to return and doesn't want to do marriage therapy, then you can say you have done all you could do, but the decision is to split for good.

4. Throughout the process, so long as each point is followed in this agreement, **each individual agrees not to mention the word *divorce* or say "I'm done" or say anything regarding the marriage being at an end unless** they are absolutely certain that the marriage being over is what they want.

5. The individuals agree that **they will not contact each other** via phone, face-to-face meetings, text, e-mail, social media messages, or in any other way except to facilitate logistics regarding children (specific terms regarding children are listed below) or unless a medical or family emergency is faced. The only contact they will have other than facilitating child logistics is in the Managed Separation meetings with their Managed Separation manager.

Explanation: In a divorce, individuals alone must take care of situations such as flat tires, water leaks, and an inability to find one's keys or lost earring. Such is the case in a Managed Separation. A person tilting toward divorce needs to see and experience what it is like not to have that partner available in times of need. Hint: most don't like it.

6. **The individuals agree to meet together with their managing therapist weekly or every other week** (circle one) to check the

progress of the Managed Separation and to address any questions or concerns regarding the process. The individuals agree that the state of their relationship, or anything regarding their relationship, will be discussed together only in these sessions.

7. **The individuals agree to be involved in regular, ongoing individual therapy** with the therapist of their choice. Be honest about your part in the marital breakdown, as well as your partner's. Do not just go to therapy and go through the motions; instead, work to understand yourself. The most powerful changes come when we get deeply honest with ourselves about who we are and what we're doing that even we don't like. Look in the mirror.

   Make certain you do quality work in the areas of self-esteem, boundaries, perception, dependency, and self-control, the five core issues Pia Mellody writes about in *Facing Codependence*.

8. The individuals agree that **neither party will have contact with or date a third party for romance-related purposes.** It is agreed and understood that a Managed Separation will not be successful, and the relationship will most likely stand no chance of being saved, if a third party is involved. Honesty and transparency in this regard are absolutely necessary. **Read this:** Do not agree to a Managed Separation and do not put your partner through the stress of following such an agreement if you cannot abide by this rule!

9. **This agreement assumes trust; therefore, individuals agree that they will respect the other person's privacy** and will not spy on or interfere in any way with the other individual's bills, mobile phone, texts, e-mails, phone calls, or mail. Mind your own business; focus on your own healing; do not tattle on your spouse to your therapist without your spouse present; and if

you have any concerns, bring them up in the Managed Separation sessions with your partner and therapist.

10. **There will be no romantic pressure, contact, or pursuit by one spouse of the other spouse.** This includes no verbal, written, physical, or romantic pursuit of any kind toward each other or in any other way. No cryptic social media posts, no asking friends or children about how your spouse is doing. Leave each other alone.

11. The individuals are aware of and understand that the best policy is honesty. . . . **This means that telling friends, family, and coworkers about the Managed Separation is acceptable** and, in most cases, advisable, although whether to tell others is a personal decision made by each individual.

12. The individuals understand and are aware that **speaking about their spouse negatively to friends, family, and coworkers will not be helpful and may be damaging to the Managed Separation process.** This is a concept you need to learn anyway. **Such conversations are best worked through inside a confidential atmosphere, such as with a therapist.**

13. **Planned holidays and vacations together should be canceled or postponed.** If you were planning Christmas together, it should now be spent apart. If it's your birthday, do not include/invite/contact your spouse. Trips are now taken without your partner; rituals are celebrated alone. (See clause regarding children and holidays below.)

Note: Why? Because we want the *Decider to strongly dislike being separated and being away and not included in family activities. Trust me on this.*

14. **When the going gets tough, contact your therapist.** The Managed Separation process is difficult, and it requires enormous amounts of self-control and discipline. Each person will experience highs and lows. When the lows hit, or if you are angry about something, or you find it hard to make it through, **call your therapist.** She or he will coach you through it. If you need the lifeline, use it.

Amendments (write any additions or changes here):

_____

_____

_____

_____

This Managed Separation Agreement is not legally binding, cannot be used in a court of law as proof of anything, and is meant to provide a framework for a separation that may create the space necessary for a couple to work on saving their marriage through marriage therapy. This agreement is the copyright of Becky Whetstone, PhD, is for your use only, and is not to be shared with others without Whetstone's written consent. By signing this agreement, you are making a good-faith agreement to abide by its terms.

Signed and agreed to by:

_____

Partner 1: _____

Date: _____

Partner 2: _____

Date: _____

Witness: _____

Date: _____

In Appendix I, I've included suggestions for each of you to track your thoughts and feelings during the separation. See the one titled "Understanding Your Problems." Start there, and work through all the exercises in Appendix I. It is such a stressful time that memories aren't going to be very accurate. Tracking your thoughts, fears, struggles, and feelings from day to day is never a bad idea, and it will force you to face what's going on each day. Since humans love to avoid discomfort, I'd like to encourage you to face your discomfort and see what it's trying to tell you. This will help you get to know yourself, which is something we want you to do anyway.

Couples with Children

Books have been written about healthy parenting in general and also about how to handle a separation or divorce with kids of all ages so they may experience the best outcome. Most of us who didn't know any better made a lot of mistakes in raising our children during and postdivorce, and this is your chance to be better and get it right.

Both parents should read the following books to get a sense of what is in the best interest of the children while going through this process: *Helping Your Kids Cope with Divorce the Sandcastles Way* by M. Gary Neuman and Patricia Romanowski (1991) and the classic *Helping Children Cope with Divorce* by Edward Teyber (1992).

Telling the Children

When your decision to separate or divorce is made, do not tell your children who live at home until about ten days before Mom or Dad moves out. This will give them time to normalize what's happening and prepare mentally and emotionally. When you talk to your children about the separation, it is important to *do it together.* Stress that the situation is not their fault, and the decision has nothing to do with them but has to do with your marriage and the relationship between the two of you. Reassure them that you are doing what you can to make the best decision for your family; for younger children, for example, you might say you're taking your marriage to the doctor. Reassure them that no matter what happens, they will have access to you always, and that although they will not see both of you every day, you will still be hands-on, involved completely in their lives, and will always love and be there for them.

While it is important to *be honest with your children* about what is going on, it is also important to *leave out dirty details, negative comments, or blame.* Separations and unhappy marriages are a part of life, and it is important not to shield children completely from life's realities. However, as a family therapist who mops up divorce messes all the time, I can assure you that each time you talk negatively about your children's parent, you are damaging your children and the respect and admiration they have for you, *so do not do it.* Your children need the space to feel loyal to both of you. When you provide them with negative evidence against the parent they love, you confuse this process, and it is a crime against your child's self-esteem and sense of safety in the world. So do not speak about your spouse positively, negatively, or in any other way except having to do with logistics— for example, "Mom is caught in traffic and will be ten minutes late to pick you up today." Period. *Do not say things like* "You know how Mom is always late, so of course she's late again today. What do you expect? She cares about no one but herself."

Got it?

Can I Talk to My Kids when I'm Not with Them?

Yes, you can. As far as the separation goes, do allow the children to receive phone calls and make contact with Mom or Dad by phone if it brings them comfort. You may just let them know that while you will make every attempt for them to talk every day, they may sometimes miss a day, and that's okay, and it doesn't mean anything is wrong or they are not thought about or missed. To avoid contact with your spouse, and to meet the requirements of the "No Contact" clause (see #2) in the Managed Separation Agreement, many couples add an additional kid's cell phone so the child may have direct contact with the parent they are away from. For little ones, try to set up a daily call time, perhaps after dinner or bathtime. Mom or Dad will have to set it up, so stick with the purpose of the call, and that's it. When it comes to phone contact, when you first sit them down and talk about the separation, also let your children know that phone calls once or twice a day are reasonable, but calling all day and night is not. Tell your child to leave one message for Mom or Dad, and they will call back when able. The same goes for Mom and Dad: Leave one message. Refrain from calling over and over. When in the trenches of the separation, help children find a balance when it comes to this.

Do Not Put Your Kids in the Middle

Many of my clients have heard the phrase "Don't let your kids become pawns in the divorce or separation process." What does that mean? I've created a list of examples so you can get a clear idea about it.

- **Do not allow your child to be an informant.** Do not ask your child about Mom or Dad. Nothing. Nada. Not how Mom or Dad is doing, who they are hanging out with, not if they're happy or sad, not how much beer they're drinking, not how much they're sleeping, or anything else.

- **Do not use your child as a go-between for information.**
  Examples: Don't tell your child to tell your partner you love or
  miss them; don't tell your child to tell your partner you need
  more money; don't use your child as a messenger at all!
- **Do not manipulate your child to be on your side.** Let children figure out who is to blame on their own—and believe
  me, they will. If you try to influence or sway the vote, it'll always backfire, and it often ends in resentment and many years
  of estrangement from you. Don't do it.

Other Do Nots

- Do not allow your kids to parent or take care of you.
- Do not allow your kids to feel responsible for your happiness.
  Encourage them to continue with their lives, activities, and
  friendships, even when it's your time to have them.
- Do not buy their love or buy them things because you feel
  guilty. "Disneyland parenting" filled with numerous activities
  is not advised—occasional cool vacations are fine, but otherwise, just live a normal, balanced family life, sometimes with
  activities, sometimes not. It is not good for kids to be enter-
  tained 24/7, and you should not allow yourself to take on the
  role of the tour or entertainment director. It's okay for kids to
  get bored occasionally and learn how to entertain themselves.
- As little change for kids as possible is advised at this time. If
  at all possible, do not move the child or children more than
  thirty minutes away from the other parent during the Managed Separation process, and keep them in the same schools
  and activities as much as possible.
- Do not threaten your spouse in any way if they do things you

don't like or approve of with the kids when you're not there. Each parent deserves an equal say in how the children are raised, and in healthy marriages, these decisions are negotiated. If you get a divorce, you will have no control over your former spouse and their parenting decisions, and judges don't take kindly to motions that involve petty disagreements.

- Do not threaten to take away custody. Angry, wounded, and hurt partners often threaten to take children away from a parent or report them to the child welfare authorities. Before you tell your spouse something like this, read up on it. It takes a very bad, negligent, abusive parent to lose custody or equal access to children, and infidelity, social drinking, pot smoking, and taking them around your in-laws whose politics you don't like won't cut it. Also, look into and clearly understand what kinds of things get the attention of child abuse authorities—it's a relatively high bar. I don't take kindly to individuals who cruelly threaten to take children away over relatively minor infractions, and it should not take place, especially if your hope is to save your marriage or to raise healthy children. It is not in your children's best interest to take them from their parent unless what the parent is doing is horrific. In case you didn't know, if you report the other parent to the authorities, the children will be pulled aside and interrogated separately, and it will scare them. Don't do it unless it is absolutely justified, and it usually is not.

Do

- Always be pleasant, friendly, and respectful with your partner when making the kid exchange. Believe me, your kids will be watching this like a hawk—make them proud.

- Attend school and sporting events that your child is involved in, even when it is not your day or week to have the kids, but don't sit with your partner when you do unless invited. Be pleasant, wave hello, and smile if you see each other there.
- In couple's sessions, *do* bring up what your child is *voluntarily* telling you about Mom and Dad's parenting skills while you're away. What kids say should be taken with a grain of salt, as many times, the child is actually trying to manipulate you in some way when doing this. If the problem becomes a continuing one, we may end up having to do a family session over it, but the idea is not to allow your child to create "splitting" or alliances with Mom or Dad that leave the other parent in the cold. Parents should be united against splitting.
- Stay on your side of the street when it comes to boundaries. If the parent who moved out provides a place, bed, or situation that the other parent feels isn't adequate, mind your own business. It's okay for kids to sleep on pallets on the floor (they usually enjoy it!) or in a one-room studio with a parent and not enough space. To them, it will be an adventure. What is not okay is moving in with a strange adult or leaving them alone with that person—ever. Get a place on your own, and if you have to live with someone they don't know, then when it's your time to have the kids, take them to a hotel or family member's place to spend the time together.

Custody and the Managed Separation Agreement

The model for the Managed Separation Agreement with Children is the traditional divorce decree arrangement, which has long since proven to be a fair-minded proposal (though not perfect) that keeps the children's best interests in mind. Couples may negotiate different or alternative terms together with their therapist, but the traditional model is a good place to start.

You will find the traditional setup outlined below, but some couples I work with find it more convenient to use the seven-day-on, seven-day-off model, which means each person has sole custody and responsibility for the child or children every seven days. The advantage of this is less disruption for the children. This will be discussed in the first Managed Separation Agreement meeting with your therapist.

Managed Separation Agreement with Children

Definitions:

Partner A = Partner remaining in the family home

Partner B = Partner moving from the family home

In most cases, it will be Partner B's responsibility to pick up and drop off the children from their "home base" when it is their turn to have the children.

During the times Partner A or Partner B has the children, it is their responsibility to get them to school, get them picked up, and provide for their care if they must go out of town or need a babysitter.

In the best separations, Partner A and Partner B are flexible and helpful to each other in these cases. For example, if Partner A needs to go out of town on business or something unexpected comes up, they should ask Partner B first if that parent would be available to take care of the children. If Partner B is unable to do it, however, the responsibility falls to Partner A to find and pay for (if applicable) care for the children.

Traditional Custody

The partner (Partner B) that moves away from the family home shall:

1. Have custody of the children each first, third, and fifth weekend from Friday following the end of school (if there is school) until 6:00 PM on Sunday when they shall return the kids to the other parent. If the children are not in school, the parent shall pick the children up on Fridays at 6:00 PM.

2. Have custody of the children each Wednesday (choose one):

    ☐ Following school, the children shall be picked up by Partner B from school or at the bus stop, spend the night with Partner B, and be returned by this parent to school Thursday morning.

    ☐ From 6:00 PM to 8:00 PM for dinner. Partner B picks up and drops off.

Holidays and Birthdays

Although traditional divorce decrees are not written like this, Managed Separation Agreements can command a more casual and friendly arrangement.

Children will spend one half day on Thanksgiving and one half day on Christmas Day with each parent, with details to be decided in the meetings with the therapist.

Regarding the Thanksgiving and Christmas Holidays as a Whole

One parent shall have the children the entire Thanksgiving holiday, from the time school gets out or from Wednesday afternoon through Sunday at 6:00 PM, while the other parent shall have them the entire Christmas holiday from the time school gets out for the holiday break until December 26 at noon, when the children will then be returned to the other parent for the rest of the holiday until school resumes in January. During these times, the first, third, and fifth weekends and Wednesday night custody agreements will not be followed unless agreed to and amended by Partners A and B in Managed Separation therapy sessions.

"Santa" should still come to the home where the child is on Christmas Eve and morning, and each parent can also give individual gifts.

Partner A and B Birthdays, Mother's Day and Father's Day, and Other Celebrated Holidays

Each partner shall have full custody of the children on their own birthday, no matter what day of the week it occurs. If the birthday falls on a school day, the parent having the birthday may pick up the child from school at the end of the school day and return the child to school the next day. If the birthday falls on a weekend, the parent may pick the child up that day at 9:00 AM and return the child at 9:00 AM the following day or take the child to school, whichever is applicable.

The same arrangement is in effect for Mother's Day and Father's Day. If the child is scheduled to be with Dad on Mother's Day, the child will instead be with Mom from 9:00 AM on Mother's Day and return at 9:00 AM or to school, whichever is applicable the following day.

Child's Birthday

If the parents agree, either parent may attend the child's usual birthday celebration held at the other's house, depending on who has custody on that day. If the parents cannot agree, the child may spend (on weekends) one half day with Partner A (from 9:00 AM to 2:30 PM) and one half day (from 2:30 PM to 8 PM) with Partner B. During the school week, the child may spend from the time school gets out until 6:00 PM with Partner A and from 6:00 PM to 9:00 PM with Partner B. If the child is in after-school care or activities, Partner A has the option to pick the child up after school, forgo after-school care, and spend time with them until Partner B's time begins, if applicable.

Amendments (write any additions or changes here):

_____

_____

_____

_____

We understand that this is not a legal or binding agreement, does not make claims about who is the best parent, and does not assign fault, guilt, or blame, but is an agreement to follow during our Managed Separation that is in the best interest of our children at this time. We also understand that the agreement content and format are copyrighted by Becky Whetstone, PhD, and will not be shared with others. By signing, we agree to follow the terms of the child custody part of this agreement.

Signed and agreed to by:

Partner A: _____

Date: _____

Partner B: _____

Date: _____

Witness: _____

Date: _____

Managed Separation Agreement, Copyright 2008 Becky Whetstone, PhD. www.doctorbecky.com.

In Appendix I, I have included custody calendars showing the custody arrangements I just described. You will find the traditional model, with every other weekend and a dinner visit on Wednesdays for the noncustodial parent, and you will find two models that represent sharing the children 50/50. One is keeping the kids for seven days and switching, and the other is an expanded version of the every-other-weekend model. Depending on your schedules, you should be able to find something that works for you, and remember, you can create a custody arrangement that works for both of you.

I also reiterate my suggestion that if either one of you cannot keep the child on your assigned day, turn to your spouse first as a potential babysitter before asking anyone else. To see you helping each other out and being flexible with each other is always in the best interest of your children, and kids would almost always rather spend the extra time with their parent or another close family member than someone else.

Waiting Until the Children Are Grown and Gone

It always fascinates me that people will say they want to wait and divorce when their children have grown and left the nest as if somehow that will be easier for them. I can assure you it will not. If you are staying for yourself so you can be with them on a daily basis while knowing you are counting the minutes to leave their other parent, then shame on you. I'd much rather you spend the negative energy you are feeling toward your partner in a more positive direction, seeing if there is anything you can do to save your marriage. Dealing with issues directly instead of passively is always the better path.

Toxicity Overload

Years ago, my parents separated a few times. I was in my teens when it all started, and it went off and on through my college years. They had one of the worst marriages I could ever imagine, and their separations were just as toxic.

My dad told us we were such bad people that he was compelled to go away and would never come back unless we fixed ourselves. He insisted on secrecy, and we couldn't tell anyone he was gone. We weren't allowed to know where he was staying (it was with a secret mistress, I learned years later); we didn't have his phone number and could only reach him at work. He'd come home from time to time, unannounced, and have deeply romantic evenings with my mom that embarrassed and repulsed me to see. Then he'd vanish, and we wouldn't know when we'd see him again.

They ended up staying unhappily married for sixty-two years. My mom was completely love addicted and dependent on him, and she never would have left. I would caretake her when she was alone, as her depression was dark and deep, and she had no one else to talk to. I got deeply depressed as well.

Their dysfunctional situation was so toxic that when I was fifteen, I begged my dad to divorce my mom so we might have relief from the craziness. He'd always say, "I will if your mom wants to." The reason I am telling you this story is to acknowledge that some children desire their toxic parents to part, and understandably so. Some marriages, whether on-again, off-again, or not, are just so filled with negative energy that the family can feel it. In my opinion, it's okay if you want to destroy your own life, but don't drag your children down with you. It is sometimes best to cut off the gangrenous leg your marriage has become and move on. For those of you in similar situations, consider that sometimes, divorce is in the best interest of all involved.

An Overview of Blended or Binuclear Families on Children of Divorce

If you are considering living with a new partner postdivorce, whether married or not, the issue of raising young children in newly formed families must be addressed. I wanted to put this section here, where couples are considering whether to divorce, because this information may influence your decision-making process, and I hope that it does.

First and foremost, if you choose the path to divorce, know that it is a path that primarily suits the parents. Unless their daily family life is unbearable, with fighting and negative parents, children will not wish their parents to live apart. It is stressful for them, and their stuff ends up all over the place. It is important that you understand the burden you are placing on them if this is the path you choose. Most children would prefer to grow up in a healthy, intact family with two parents they are comfortable with and attached to, and hopefully, everyone understands this is not always possible.

Children's tendency in a divorce is to put their needs last and the parents' needs first. Most parents I've worked with do the opposite: They put their needs before their children's. Families who continue this cycle will pay a painful price. Using common sense, consider what it may mean to a child's life if you bring a stepparent and potential stepsiblings into their life. A child enters a home that is new with people they don't know well or feel attached to. This situation will likely result in a child feeling like an outsider, a person who does not belong but goes along.

We have all heard of people who, as children, witnessed their parent have numerous live-in boyfriends and girlfriends passing through or a parade of stepparents. This type of situation is completely unacceptable and, thankfully, not the norm.

Mostly, though, it isn't a parade of new people entering the household; it's usually one new partner or two at most that the children must contend with, but either way, in the best cases, a child usually goes from a family where they felt grounded, secure, and safe to one that doesn't feel that way. No matter how old a child is, there will likely be challenges. I have clients from ages twenty to sixty who still feel the sting of their parents' divorce and ask me how to deal with the challenges stepparents bring.

If you look for studies to back me up on my belief that children would prefer to not deal with stepparents and stepsiblings, you might not find many. Most of my evidence in this case is, admittedly, talking to hundreds of people, now grown, who had this experience as children, and to those who have struggled in their roles as stepparents and single parents. My therapy room is where people can tell me the truth about their experiences and feelings—feelings they might never want their other family members to know. A child may not be able to express their true feelings about a situation until much later when their brain and critical thinking skills are more developed.

In younger children, the difficulty adjusting will likely show up behaviorally, through moods, acting out, grades dropping, and even physical ailments. My own children experienced things like this. If only I could go back in time and handle things differently knowing what I know now.

The way I think about it is this: How many of us would enjoy having a permanent houseguest? Someone we likely do not know, or know well, moves into your family home, or you all move into a new home, and the houseguests never leave. They may even bring children. How long do you think it would take for you to relax and feel comfortable in your home with the new guests? Keeping in mind that you recently had a major change where instead of living with your entire family, you now go between two households, dragging stuff back and forth? A psychologist friend told me once he'd read research that said it takes at least five years for a child to become comfortable in a blended family if they ever do. I have a lot of compassion for that on behalf of the child.

The work of Patricia Papernow, PhD, director of the Institute for Stepfamily Education and a psychologist in private practice in Hudson, Massachusetts, is profound, and I strongly suggest you read her research-packed books: *Surviving and Thriving in Stepfamily Relationships* (2013) and *The Stepfamily Handbook* (2020) I have seen hundreds if not thousands of couples in stepfamilies who are having marriage issues, and almost every time, the role of each parent combined with the other person's children plays a huge negative part. My clients make the very mistakes that Papernow points out and corrects throughout her work. If you decide to marry someone with children, or you have children and remarry, it is imperative to read her work so you can be aware of what works and what does not work in the stepfamily dynamic.

Also, it is vital that parents considering divorce understand that statistics show sexual abuse in the household is most often perpetrated by a new mate or stepparent. Interviews with 930 adult women who came from divorce in San Francisco revealed that one in six had been sexually abused by their stepfather (Phelan, 1986). Knowing what I know today, if I had the opportunity to create a stepfamily, I wouldn't risk it.

If divorce and separate households it is, children will want to spend significant time with each parent alone or with their siblings and not always with your boyfriends, girlfriends, new stepparents, or stepsiblings. However, they will often go along with whatever situation you put them in because they want you to be happy, especially younger children.

Although some children fare well in a stepfamily, they are at higher risk for the adjustment issues I mentioned earlier. The more children involved from either side, the more difficult it is likely to be. Research shows that stepmother and stepdaughter relationships are the most difficult, and adolescents have a harder time adjusting than children under nine. Girls have more issues than boys (Papernow, 2013, p. 62).

Stepfamilies bring five key challenges to a family, according to Papernow, and a huge part of it is that someone seems to end up feeling like an outsider compared to the other group, depending on what's going on. As you consider all possibilities for your family in the coming months, I think it's helpful to have a basic understanding of what Papernow says are the basic challenges for remarriage and stepfamilies.

Challenge One: Insider vs. Outsider. Stepparents feel like outsiders when their spouse's children are present. The most stressful times are when the entire stepfamily is together at one time. Pushing to have too much togetherness at one time with the new family exacerbates insider/outsider pulls (Papernow, 2013, p. 67). Think of the better option for combining families as tiptoeing into a pond rather than diving in headfirst.

Challenge Two: Children struggle with losses, loyalty binds, and too much change (Papernow, 2013, p. 90). Gains for the new couple become a loss for the children. Children struggle with feeling disloyal to their other parent.

Challenge Three: Parenting tasks polarize adults. Different parenting styles collide. Stepparents who move too quickly to a disciplinarian or authoritative role face resistance (Papernow, 2018, p. 12).

Challenge Four: Creating a new family culture. Children are used to one way and now must adjust to new ways (Papernow, 2018, p. 14).

Challenge Five: Ex-spouses are still part of the family. Children feel torn between the people they love. Conflict makes it worse. The more banished the other parent and their family is, the worse it is for the children (Papernow, 2018, p. 15).

Numerous books have been written about how to best handle the many land mines in combining families after a divorce, but they boil down to this: If a blended family works successfully, it will be because insider parents and outsider stepparents find empathy for one another and work together to support one another (Papernow, 2018, p. 68). I have found empathy and an ability to have the children's best interests come first after divorce hard for many to attain.

In the case of infants, the issues are not as difficult. Obviously, an infant has no history of the intact original family, so if you want to remarry, it's not as egregious and can be a positive thing. I still would not recommend bringing a parade of suitors around a young child because they become attached to people. If people they get attached to leave over and over, it can harm them greatly and cause them to avoid attachments moving forward.

Since the only adult in the room is you—and I am calling for us all to be better at how we decide to divorce, divorce, and handle our children after a divorce—I believe the price you should pay for not working things out with their mom or dad is getting them raised with your full attention until they reach the age when they start to focus on freedom and friends and don't care whether you are dating or not. That is when they are well into their teens.

The other thing, especially if you are a Leaning-In partner and have to face an unwanted divorce, is do not let your children see you wallow in despair. Do everything you can to bring a healthy self to their daily life. It's okay to show a range of emotions at times; we are human, after all. But if you fall apart or become unable to function for long periods, it will have untold negative effects on your children.

When I started studying complex trauma with Pia Mellody, I learned that children have no boundaries or the ability to protect themselves from an adult's intense emotions, so they absorb it. For example, Timothy's mother's fearfulness, anxiety, and anger during his parents' divorce were expressed openly and without restraint. Unknowingly, he absorbed all of it, and as he grows, his own fearfulness, anxiety, and anger will begin to show up in various situations. This is what Mellody calls *carried emotions*; a child absorbs their parents' negative energy and carries it into adulthood. Ask the adult why they are so anxious or angry, and they may not be able to tell you, but a trauma therapist will know and also understand how to help the adult release the burden of that carried energy. In addition to the tragedy of carried emotions, many children take it upon themselves to try to soothe or fix their parents' woes. Whatever you do, do not allow them to become your caretaker.

My unusual stance on raising children postdivorce comes from visiting with thousands of children (now grown) and young adults who considered themselves very damaged from their parents' divorce. Of course, there are amazing stepparents out there who have made a positive difference in the lives of their stepchildren, and I hear about those, too. But how it will play out is such a crapshoot that I believe in erring in favor of the children.

In the next chapter, I will talk about what to do if your decision is to divorce, and I will provide you with the Managed Separation Worksheet Version Two. Though it is sad, there is a way to do it that is healthy, and there are things you can do to avoid animosity and vitriol. I implore you to take the high road if you decide to end your marriage. Let's see how that's possible.

CHAPTER SEVEN

If You Decide to Divorce

Anyone who has divorced has war stories to tell. When it comes to stress-inducing things that can happen to people, divorce is right up there with losing a loved one or your home or possessions, or a life-threatening illness. One of the reasons it is so terrible is that our brains process it as a threat to our lives. Being in a marriage crisis does the same thing, of course, as described in Chapter 2— your sympathetic nervous system fires up, your WC and AC ready themselves for action, and add to that the adversarial legal process and nothing good is likely to happen.

Most individuals who tell me they plan to divorce also say they want it to be as peaceful and amicable as possible. Although couples may enter the process with good intentions for peaceful and nego-tiated outcomes, my experience is that sooner or later, the divorce process brings out the worst in people. It is one of my life goals to put an end to that, and it is my hope that you will dedicate yourselves to not going low if divorce is the path you choose.

I jokingly have told single girlfriends for years, "Choose your future ex-husband well, and make sure he's the kind of guy who will do right by you and your children should you divorce." I think I had this thought in the first place because, looking back, I think by the time we married, most of us who have divorced could tell if the person was a reasonable, rational person of integrity who wouldn't go nuclear if we were to part. Obviously, the more prone a person is to drama, vengefulness, and harsh reactions while married, the more likely they will want to take a pound of flesh in a divorce. When a Leaning-In partner facing divorce says, "I don't get mad; I get even," I feel chills down my spine, and I talk to them about how I've never met a sane person who regretted taking the high road in divorce.

Priorities in Divorce for Families with Kids

If you're divorcing and don't have children, I guess it's your decision about how to handle yourself. But if you have children, there is no excuse whatsoever to do anything but be reasonable and rational and conduct yourselves in a way that is in their best interest. Know this truth right now: Children come first during separation, divorce, and postdivorce; what you want and need comes second, and that will remain so until they are raised. If you want to keep yourself in the number-one spot, stay married to the mother or father of your children and maintain the hierarchy most healthy families follow: parents at the top of the totem pole, then kids, then biological family, the last one being optional. For divorced folks with kids, it's kids first, you second. More on this and what it means coming up later in the chapter.

For Leaning-In partners, when it sinks in that your spouse is going to divorce you whether you want it or not, it's scary and painful, and you are probably going to want to protest. Like a family dog that is normally friendly to almost everyone, if it gets hit by a car, it will be afraid and in pain, and when you go to assist that dog, it might growl, lash out, or bite. People are the same way. You can growl, lash out, or bite, but I'd much rather see you practice self-care, be tender with yourself, and surround yourself with compassionate and nurturing friends and family. You're about to go through a tough time, and you're going to need a caring support system.

For the Decider, understand that your soon-to-be ex is going through one of life's most painful experiences. You most likely will, too. If you're feeling up now because you are finally coming out of limbo, I would predict a major fall in the future, so don't be surprised. As far as your soon-to-be ex, be as kind and understanding and fair as you can be while remaining firm that your kindness does not mean you want to reconcile. If you have children, you are setting the tone for an amiable postdivorce relationship, which is vital to how your children will fare.

Going Rogue: Misbehavior During Divorce

If either partner decides to misbehave in the divorce process, it's usually because one threatens to take the children and destroy their partner's life, refuses to share fairly, or decides to make them miserable in some egregious way—I've heard nasty threats hundreds of times. Let me be clear: There's absolutely no excuse for that. Judges are not going to take children away from parents who aren't perfect, that is, those who drink, smoke pot, cheat, lie, don't have much money, or have a crazy family. If they did, almost all children would be taken away. You will not be able to control how your ex manages the children when they are with them, so you need to learn to soothe yourself when things go on that you don't like. Unless it's abuse and bona fide child endangerment, stay out of how the other parent parents. Neither the Decider nor the Leaning-In partner has any business deciding what's best for a child over the other parent. You may think you're the better parent and should have the most say, and perhaps you are far more responsible than your soon-to-be ex, but the law doesn't look at it that way. Remember this: If divorce it must be, you will no longer be able to have any say over what the other parent does when your children are with them. Children need equal access to both parents until they are old enough to decide for themselves, and mediocre parenting is better than having no parent at all.

All of that aside, once lawyers get involved, things will likely happen throughout the divorce process that will send you through the roof with rage. That is because lawyers are trained to be adversarial, meaning warlike, drawing blood to win. They wear you down with nasty letters labeling you in a derogatory way, an initial offer so low and unfair that your ability to survive postdivorce is threatened, and attempt to limit your time with children or remove access to beloved possessions or shared properties. The stories are endless. How is one to get through it in one emotional piece?

In 1994, the late psychologist Constance Ahrons wrote a groundbreaking book titled *The Good Divorce*. Divorced twice herself, she insisted to critics that she was not encouraging divorce but instead accepted it as an inevitable truth in our culture, and with that in mind, she wanted to provide a pathway into it that limited upheaval, even strongly suggesting that couples who have children who divorce should be "encouraged—even expected to maintain civility when they split up" (Ahrons, pp. xv, 10). Not a bad idea, for it is the acrimony between parents that creates the divorce nightmare for children that books, poems, and plays have been written about. If we could all get along during a divorce, it would go a long way to help with whatever stigma remains around it today, but it's not lost on me that if you can't get along in marriage, why should postmarriage be different? Why? Because if you have children, it has to be.

No Such Thing as a Broken Home

If you are a couple divorcing and you have kids, you will remain a family until the day you die. The only true divorce occurs when it involves a couple with no children; they can part ways and never see or deal with each other again. But when there are children, the family remains; only the living circumstances and time spent together change. For the family to function in a healthy way, there will need to be structure, rules, compromise, and mutual understanding. Many rules and structures are usually delineated in a divorce decree, and that is there for you to use if your ex decides they don't want to follow the rules.

The compromise and mutual understanding will come from your humanity, from a humble place, without pride, ego, and stubbornness. I will present you with a nonlegal divorce decree in this chapter for couples with and without children to use as a guideline. It is similar to the separation agreement in the previous chapter but has none of the strategies I use to encourage the softening of hearts and reconciliation. You can save yourself a lot of money and heartache if you negotiate a fair agreement before presenting it to your lawyer for final approval. My goal is to leave lawyers out of this process as much as possible. Remember, they are trained to be adversarial and will use any means to win without regard for how their nasty daggers affect the family moving forward. For example, in my own divorce from my children's dad, I was portrayed as a woman who wanted to be supported and didn't want to work. Never mind that we had mutually agreed that I would stay home with the children while he focused on his all-consuming career. Now that was being used against me, and I was being characterized as a woman who lazed around the house reading romance novels and popping chocolates in her mouth at the man's expense. That would be angering to anyone who knows themselves well enough to know they do not mind working. Rather than wear each other down in the adversarial process, I prefer a kinder, gentler approach in the higher interest of all involved rather than having a winner or loser.

Mediation and Collaborative Law

Thankfully, I'm not the first person who wanted to stop the acrimony that often comes with divorce. Years ago, judges tired of hearing couples nitpick over ridiculous things and encouraged them to go to mediation before bringing their issues into a courtroom. The mediation process involves two rooms, your lawyer, your estranged spouse's lawyer, and a mediation attorney. Usually, each side sits in a separate room, and the mediation attorney goes back and forth between the rooms with offers to settle the case. Hopefully, an agreement will be reached at some point, everyone signs off on it, and afterward, the official papers are drawn up and signed, and the divorce will soon be granted.

All it takes is one stubborn, uncompromising spouse or one who doesn't want to be fair to make this process a waste of time. In some states, mediation is required, but my warning to you is that if you want to get the divorce process over with, come in prepared to be fair and reasonable to save your time and money. I am also telling you that you must be fair and reasonable if you have children because we want to put their needs and wants above your own, remember? Kids' needs first, your needs and wants second.

In 1990, a Minneapolis family law attorney named Stu Webb began a policy of refusing to represent a client if the opposing party resorted to disputing the case in a courtroom, and this ultimately influenced the development of a new type of divorce process known as *collaborative law*. As described by the American Bar Association, collaborative law is a process in which both parties agree to negotiate everything outside of the courtroom. As collaborative attorneys are hired, a written agreement is signed by all lawyers and clients, agreeing that no one makes use of or threatens to use the court process. If any person breaks the agreement, both lawyers are fired, and the clients enter the adversarial process with new lawyers, and things will no doubt get ugly and damage will be done.

In my mind, collaborative law is the only sane way to go in divorce. Other advantages to it are that mental health therapists, neutral financial consultants, and other specialists often join with the couple to help them come to the healthiest outcome that is in the highest interest of all. By all reports, judges like working with couples who choose this route, as it helps keep their courtrooms "from being cluttered with litigation cases" (American Bar Association, 2018).

Discuss the idea of collaborative law with your estranged spouse as a healthy option for families who are going through divorce. If you can both agree, search for collaborative lawyers in your area and get the process started. You won't regret it.

Dealing with Anger

Even if you choose the collaborative law option and want to remain amicable during the divorce process, it does not mean that you won't feel the extreme emotions that the divorce process usually ushers in. Anger, for example, is a normal emotional response to perceived injustice, and there is no way a Leaning-In partner is going to process being led into divorce any other way. Deciders will experience anger, too; it's unavoidable. Understanding that anger is normal and nothing to be ashamed of is helpful, but what is even more useful is the idea that adults can control what their response is to the anger they feel. One choice might be to shoot up the town, which is a terrible idea; another might be to delay a response while in the heat of rage, then learn how to extinguish the anger through focused energy release techniques I'll describe.

Once the anger has lessened, you can respond to whatever a situation is in a calmer and more thoughtful state, which is the state we should always communicate in unless there is a house fire, car wreck, or some other life threat. Don't get me wrong, your brain will most likely perceive the divorce process as an existential threat, and that's why couples get activated frequently in the process. Whether you tell yourself all the normal divorce catastrophe thoughts like *There won't be enough money to survive, I won't be able to live without my person, I'll never meet another person and will die lonely and alone, I'll never be able to retire,* your sympathetic nervous system will be firing. What I am asking for is that when you do get activated, take care of it on your own or with the help of a therapist or supportive and trustworthy friend, and don't vomit negative garbage on your soon-to-be ex or anyone else. Taking out your rage on someone else is not the right answer in divorce.

When I am in a rough spot of frustration or anger, I often ask, "What is healthy for me right now?" Ask yourself the same question, then choose an anger-release technique for yourself. Ask, "When I am feeling super angry, what might help me extinguish the negative energy that is not harmful to anyone, including myself?" Do the same for the self-soothing ritual: "What will make me feel calm and nurtured in this moment?" Having ideas in your back pocket for when you need them will save so much impulsivity and needless ugliness. You cannot have the amicable divorce that most families say they want without learning to deal with the anger you will most certainly be feeling.

How couples prefer to deal with each other during the divorce process is not one-size-fits-all, either. Some people will need to take time and space and not interact very much, and others are able to talk amicably with their estranged spouse throughout. When I was divorcing my children's dad, for example, I would have liked for us to be friendly; it would have helped my nervous system stay calm, but he wanted to stay as far away from me as possible. There is no right or wrong here, just what you need to move through the process. If one of you wants to stay away, that boundary needs to be accepted; trying to push through another's walls will usually result in a nasty confrontation, so be respectful and don't do it.

Also keep in mind that you are divorcing because you are incompatible, can't get along, or some other reason that makes continuing a lifetime together untenable. Don't expect your partner to suddenly be easy and wonderful to deal with in the divorce and postdivorce process if they weren't when you were married.

One Option: The Slower Divorce

It is time to refashion the way divorce is done. Does anyone doubt that the way we've been doing it for years isn't working? People come out of it emotional and financial wrecks, which isn't good for anyone, and yet it's completely understandable. Divorce is not a single event; it is a series of events (Kitson, 1992, p. 14). It means lots of change, decisions, and choices, and doing it all in a short period of time might not be the wisest of decisions. Why? Because when everyone is upset and constantly activated, and then feeling intense emotions, we cannot process important decisions rationally. I'd like couples to wait and settle the details of a divorce until they both feel more solid, when our best decisions can be made.

In graduate school, almost every therapist learns about the Holmes-Rahe Life Stress Inventory test, created in 1967 by psychiatrists Thomas Holmes and Richard Rahe, who were looking for ways to relate stress to illness, whether physical or mental. They examined the medical records of more than 5,000 medical patients and then asked them to select from forty-three potential life situations and to check the ones they had experienced in the previous twelve months.

Holmes and Rahe assigned a point value to each of the forty-three situations. For example, the death of a spouse is 100 points, the most stressful thing that can happen to someone according to this test. Divorce is 73 points. The lowest stressors on the test are parking tickets, 11; major holidays, 12; and vacations, 13. Midrange stressors are being fired, 45; major business readjustment, 39; and in-law troubles, 29. The idea is to check the things you've experienced in the last twelve months, add up your score, and if you score 150 to 300 points or more, there is a significant chance (between 50 and 80 percent, depending on your score) of experiencing a major health breakdown. This teaches us that too many life stressors in a short period of time are very unhealthy for us. Divorce often packs quite a few of life's major stressors into a short period of time. Here's a typical list of what divorcing individuals go through in one year:

Divorce...73 points

Separation...65 points

Marital reconciliation with mate...........................45 points

Major change in health or
behavior of a family member ....44 points

Major change in finances.......................................38 points

In-law troubles..29 points

Major change in living conditions..........................25 points

Change in residence ....20 points

Change in family get-togethers...............................15 points

354 points

Three hundred points or above increases the odds of a serious physical or mental health illness by 80 percent within two years; 150 to 300 points increases it by 50 percent; and 150 points or less means an emotional or physical illness due to stress is low.

The test is widely available, and anyone can find and take it online with a simple Internet search. I like it because it wakes people up to see that there is a limit to how much one human being can take before they experience some sort of mental or physical illness. This is because there is a powerful mind and body connection that I urge you to respect. For example, many chronic pain patients were injured, and their bodies didn't heal as they should have because of whatever stressors they were under or things they didn't deal with emotionally, which compromised their immune systems (Wyns et al., 2023). It becomes an endless cycle of never getting better.

With all that in mind, what if, for our own mental, emotional, and overall health, we tiptoed into the divorce process in a way that people had the time to adjust to change and had time to sort through what works best and what's really important to them? I envision it as bringing a family through a major change process by letting them down easy rather than the approach of kicking the person out of the car and burning rubber down the highway.

As we know (and based on my personal and anecdotal experience), couples are usually activated for up to two years because of all that happens in the divorce process (Rice & Rice, 1986). When we are activated, our brain (again) is in survival mode, and rational decision-making isn't possible. What if a couple planning to divorce went to their separate spaces and began their lives apart but put off going through the legal process until more calm and reasoned thinking was possible?

There is a lot of wisdom behind this idea. First, if you never separated but moved straight into divorce, it will be quite a shock to your system. "With no gradual period of separation for the actual physical parting, the shock and distress of dissolution may be great," say Joy and David Rice, authors of *Living Through Divorce: A Developmental Approach to Divorce Therapy*. Though a couple may know in their mind that the separation or divorce is imminent, "relief and respite are likely to be mingled with feelings of depression as one comes to the final realization that the relationship loss is likely to be permanent" (Rice & Rice, 1986).

The Rices recommend a period of separation during which each person receives individual therapy, and the couple enters a divorce therapy process that will facilitate rational and equitable problem-solving and compromise on all the issues the couple are facing, such as custody, support, and property division. In the divorce therapy process, feelings and resentments will be worked through, and each person will focus on their own growth and understanding rather than that of their estranged partner. Divorce therapy is most successful when a therapist can get each individual to steer away from blaming each other and move toward what's best for the family. This is the strategy I recommend, as it is all about emotional healing and having support, getting two people to a place where they are calm and rational enough to make wise decisions. I wish it were required for all divorcing families.

I recognize that Leaning-In partners are likely to grasp this idea of slowing the divorce process down, and Deciders may just want out as soon as possible. What I am asking the Decider to do is, so long as their estranged partner isn't abusive and suffers from no major addictions, to consider a more humane approach in the interest of what is best for the family.

Adjusting to Divorce

Years ago, a psychologist friend told me that on average, it takes one year for every five that a couple was married to fully adjust to the effects of divorce, but I can't find any research to back that up. And anyway, how do we define postdivorce adjustment? Does it mean we get over it? We never think about it? For me, it means feeling like yourself again and not thinking about the loss so regularly that it interrupts your quality of life. When I was single, I could tell when my dates weren't over their divorce as it was all they'd talk about.

What I don't think it means is that a day will come when you feel apathetic about it and your heart won't hurt or you won't feel anger. For most of us, feelings of all kinds will linger for decades to come.

There have been studies on the subject, of course, and just defining the term *adjustment* is an issue in itself. We know it is not a black-and-white thing, meaning a person is either adjusted or not adjusted or over it or not over it. It is far more complicated than that. The divorce process is traumatizing for both parties, and the pain, anger, fear, and sadness that come with it cannot be turned off like a bath faucet, although all of us wish it could. It's a process.

Whatever adjustment is—let's say it is doing or feeling better— some people are more resilient than others, which we'd expect. For example, Deciders tend to do better than Leaning-In partners, and women tend to do better than men thanks to their social support systems, emotional intelligence, ability and experience with daily household management, and ability to talk about their feelings. Not that some men don't have those characteristics, but because most women in our culture are used to "doing it all," they tend to do better (Rice & Rice, 1986, p. 22).

The factors that affect adjustment to divorce are personality, self-esteem, mental health history, who was the Decider, gender, race, support system, and socioeconomic situation. Obviously, someone who was mentally or emotionally unstable during the marriage is not likely to experience the same sort of adjustment as would an emotionally stable person.

Judith Wallerstein, a psychologist and researcher who served as the executive director of the Center for the Family in Transition in Corte Madera, California, which she founded in 1980, was one of the best-known researchers on the effects of divorce. Though critics complained that she mainly focused her work on heterosexual middle-class families (Woo, 2013), her work was a game changer in the understanding of the effects of divorce on the individual members of the family. She published sixty to seventy articles in psychology and law journals and five popular books, including *The Unexpected Legacy of Divorce* (Woo, 2013).

A 1985 *Los Angeles Times* article, "Effects of Divorce Last Indefinitely: Study Shows How Family Members Fare 10 Years Later," reported that "Wallerstein presented new findings from an intensive follow-up study of 60 middle- and upper-middle-income California couples who divorced a decade ago" and found:

- Overall quality of life had improved for both partners in only 10 percent of the couples.
- Fifty-five percent of women had improved the quality of their lives, compared to 32 percent of men.
- More than half the women felt they bore no responsibility at all for the marriage breakup compared to 30 percent of men.
- Ninety percent of women and 70 percent of men still felt it was the right decision.
- Few wanted to reconcile.

Wallerstein cited intense anger as the reason couples may have not been interested in reconciliation; 44 percent of women and 20 percent of men remained intensely angry ten years later. None of the divorces studied involved custody or visitation issues, and some had even moved on to successful new marriages. The bottom line of adjustment is that those whose lives don't change that much socially or financially do better than those who experience drastic differences.

In 1992's *Portrait of Divorce,* author Gay Kitson describes the first year of separation and divorce as a heightened state of stress, followed by gradual adjustment over a four-year period. I sometimes tell clients going through a divorce that in five years, you'll likely tell yourself, "Man, divorce is horrible, but in my case, I have to say it was for the best" (p. 319).

Almost all married couples have developed a strong attachment or bond to their partner that is like an emotional umbilical cord between two people. In divorce, the umbilical cord is severed, and that is a painful process that takes time to recover from. There just isn't any way around it. In my experience, we all go through the stages of grief—shock and denial, bargaining, sadness, anger, and acceptance —in no particular order and repeat a few of the stages along the way, but it isn't until we get super angry with our estranged partner that the emotional umbilical cord can at last be severed. I always feel relieved when one of my divorcing clients gets angry because I know the sun is about to come out on the other side.

Monica is forty-two and was married to Roy for twenty years. I sat with her for hours and hours while she cried buckets of tears over her crumbling marriage. Roy was an alcoholic, and he was abusive when he drank. She was extremely attached to him and tried to leave him numerous times over his drinking, but attachment kept pulling her back in. "We grew up together," she said. "When he's sober, he's the sweetest man in the world. Plus, I didn't know who I was without him."

During Roy's last drinking binge, he had slugged Monica in the face. That was her final straw, and she asked for a divorce. Roy moved out of town, and the process began. Six months into the separation, Monica described herself as "still a wreck."

"Then, on my birthday I woke up and said, 'It's a whole new year, a whole new life, a fresh start, it's going to be all about me now.'" That happened nine months into the process.

"He was an alcoholic, and I do mourn sober Roy," she says. "I feel like he died but he's still breathing. The person I loved doesn't exist anymore. I still love the man he was."

Two years later, Monica still weeps about the divorce occasionally, though she has a new boyfriend and a higher-paying job, and life is looking up. "I'll never completely disconnect my feelings to Roy," she says. "We went through too much together. But I do know that our divorce needed to happen. I talk to him occasionally, and he's still drinking, of course. Now he's become like a ghost to me. I no longer feel the urge to reconcile that I used to have when we were apart. I guess I'm as over it as I can be."

And so goes adjustment to a new life and a new reality.

Preparing to Divorce

I have not given up my quest to get you to stay away from the adversarial legal process in divorce. In a 2019 national survey conducted by Martindale-Nolo, a do-it-yourself legal site, the average cost of getting a divorce using attorneys in the United States was between $15,000 and $20,000. Costs vary from state to state, but a site like Martin-Nolo, with do-it-yourself forms for every legal situation imaginable, has every reason to talk people out of going the divorce attorney route. Still, we all know that the process is expensive, usually $200 per hour and up, and when we go ugly, it ends up making most of us angrier, poorer, and left to deal with the muddy mess left after the attorneys have cashed their checks and gone away.

To minimize the use of attorneys, there are forms online that can help you make a checklist of assets, liabilities, and every other thing you can think of. Use these to get started. Negotiate what you can without involving lawyers. Get in divorce therapy and start working on it there.

I mentioned earlier that hiring collaborative divorce attorneys is the only way to go when it comes to having as amicable a divorce as possible, and one service they offer in addition to each one of you having a collaborative lawyer is adding two neutrals—one who goes over each person's finances and the other a family therapist who is an advocate for the children. This team will work together to get you to where you need to be in the healthiest possible way. I highly recommend it.

For those of you who don't want to spend the money to do this, understand that having an attorney set everything up for you is far more expensive, and your inability to get along and communicate peacefully will cost you even more. Later, postdivorce, your children will be picking up the emotional tab for your ugly divorce, and you will pick up the tab for the family therapy they will need, and there is still no guarantee about how well they'll fare. So do it right, pay a divorce therapist, get most of your work done there, consider also adding the two neutrals to your collaborative process, and you'll thank me later.

Also, know that you will most likely be dividing things in half unless you have signed a prenuptial agreement with different terms. Don't ask your partner to take less than 50 percent of the assets or custody of the children; just know that although you don't want to hand over half your estate, you need to do it. When you have children and will continue dealing with each other for many years to come, it is the best thing for everyone. Messing with custody and paying less than your fair share in support and dividing assets will hurt your ability to get along moving forward, so just do your 50 percent, as the law says.

Over the years, many Leaning-In men in traditional relationships, who were the primary breadwinner and supported a stay-at-home mom, end up bucking and bristling at the idea of handing over half of what they've made to a partner that wants to leave them. I totally get why that is distasteful; I've heard all about it in my office, but don't even go there. As the years have ticked by, I have also seen more men be stay-at-home dads, and when divorce is imminent, the sole supporting female spouse squawks, too.

A man or woman who has chosen to put a career aside, raise a family, and has no personal wealth is going to be very concerned about how they are going to survive financially moving forward. They may have been out of the workplace for years or never did have a serious career, and entering the workplace will be daunting. Be compassionate and as helpful as you can if you are the primary provider. It will harm the children and your family if you allow your former partner to drown financially, and it will come back to hit you in the face as your children get older. Be kind and compassionate. Treat them as you would want to be treated if the shoe was on your foot. This may mean that they get a leg up while getting training or education to get where they can support themselves. Do the right thing; you are a family.

The bottom line of what I am saying is that every person in a divorce should be able to receive all that the law allows and should not short themselves, and there should be no shame in doing so. Find out what the law allows in your state, go to a divorce therapist, get a checklist of how to divide property, hire collaborative lawyers and the two neutrals, and create fertile ground for a family that will flourish as much as possible during a very difficult time. You will never regret it.

Suggested Divorce Agreement Template

As promised, here is my agreement for you to use as an idea of how to begin a separation process with the future intention to divorce. For the time period the couple will be separated but not yet divorced, I recommend it last six to twelve months. During this time, a couple should be receiving divorce therapy, hiring collaborative attorneys, and working on their checklist of assets and liabilities. Finances should stay the same during the initial process unless mutually agreed otherwise. In the meantime, figure out monthly budgets and see what you'll need.

The divorce process itself should end at the twelve- to eighteen-month point.

Managed Separation Agreement Version Two: For Those Planning to Divorce

Doctor Becky Whetstone's Managed Separation™ Agreement

Date: _____

This is a Separation Agreement between parties **Spouse 1 (insert name here)** and **Spouse 2 (insert name here)**, a married couple, who will be referred to in this agreement as the *individuals*. It is understood and agreed that the purpose of the Separation is to serve as a stepping stone that will ultimately lead to divorce. The purpose of the separation is to give breathing room and space to the individuals involved, so that they may have time to gradually enter into the new life experience and change that divorce brings. During the separation period they will have time to adjust and begin the process of divorce without the pressure the legal process often brings, demanding decisions and choices to be made when the individuals may be in a state where rational decisions aren't possible. The two individuals agree that this is the healthiest process for families with children, as too much change during a short period of time has been shown to be detrimental to the health and well-being of the family as a whole.

Purpose and Spirit of the Separation. A separation is a first step for couples whose marriage or relationship is at an impasse and incompatibilities cannot be reconciled. A separation is indicated when one partner, the Decider, has turned their back on the marriage and has decided to permanently end the relationship.

In Texas and other states, there is no legal separation, where details of a separation regarding finances, property, children, etc. would be written out and adhered to. This separation step may fill that void for couples in those states but is also helpful to couples planning to divorce who have legal separation available but do not want to delve into the expensive legal process it requires.

The purpose of separation in this instance is to imitate the atmosphere of what divorce would be like, a "trial divorce," so to speak, so the *Decider and Leaning-In partner may experience the positives and negatives that come with divorce.* It creates a lived experience and allows time for adjustment to such changes for the family. This should ensure the certainty of the divorce decision that the Decider *has made rather than the stressful experience of diving straight into divorce without experiencing what it all entails.*

It is strongly recommended that this contract be used in conjunction with the guidance and supervision of a licensed marriage and family therapist (LMFT) or licensed professional counselor (LPC) trained in marital and divorce therapy. Couples who separate without getting professional guidance and therapy will most likely ultimately face a worst-case scenario when it comes to being able to communicate about children in the future.

The Separation Agreement

The terms in the Separation Agreement are designed to lead a family to the most positive outcome possible by steering them away from the adversarial legal process that is known to create resentments and negative outcomes that affect families for years to come.

The following are the terms of the Separation Agreement. Couples may negotiate different or compromised terms with their therapist.

1. The individuals agree they will avoid the adversarial legal process by hiring collaborative lawyers and a divorce therapist as soon as possible to help guide them during the separation to a divorce with the most amicable outcome.

2. Each spouse should also strongly consider having an individual therapist to help them through this difficult time, and if children are involved, a family therapist where the whole family can work through issues throughout the process.

3. The individuals will agree to a time that **they will begin living apart.** Children will be informed approximately 10 days before the move takes place so they may get used to the idea.

4. Financial arrangements between the two will remain the same as when they lived together until other terms are reached with the divorce therapist and collaborative lawyers. It is understood that the process may involve neutral financial experts who may be helpful in sorting through complicated finances if that is appropriate.

5. Feeling safe and secure during this period of separation is of utmost importance and is crucial to the process. Therefore, **individuals agree that they will not file for divorce without notice or warning or engage in any covert actions that would likely negatively affect their spouse mentally, emotionally, spiritually, or financially.** This includes but is not limited to actions such as (again) filing for divorce, filing any sort of litigation procedure, changing any bank accounts, hiring private investigators, running up credit cards, canceling credit cards, selling things, making capital purchases, transferring ownership of property, or filing restraining orders. The individuals will not invest in anything during this time unless agreed to together.

6. The process will continue for a minimum of 6 months and not exceed 12 months.

7. By the twelfth month we hope that the couple has adjusted to their new reality, have worked through the terms of their divorce, and will be prepared to enter the legal divorce process. If there is a waiting period for divorce in your state, you may work out details and timing of when papers should be filed with your divorce therapist and collaborative lawyers.

8. Divorce is a way of saying, "I don't want to have you as a close person in my life anymore." To help each person adjust to that and begin the healing process, the individuals agree that **they will not contact each other** via phone, face-to-face meetings, text, e-mail, or in any other way except to facilitate logistics regarding children (specific terms regarding children are listed below) or unless a medical or family emergency is faced. They will communicate via divorce therapy. The purpose of this is to work toward breaking the attachment felt between two people

who have spent significant amounts of time together. It is especially important for the Leaning-In partner, who will have more difficulty "letting go" emotionally if there is more contact. At some point in the future, it may be possible for a divorced couple to be friends, but the time for that will be best after all the adjustments and legal issues have been sorted through. **There will be no romantic pressure, contact, or pursuit by one spouse of the other spouse unless it is mutually agreed in divorce therapy. This includes no verbal, written, physical, or romantic pursuit of any kind.**

9. **The individuals are aware of and understand that telling friends, family, or coworkers about the separation is acceptable** and, in most cases, advisable, although whether to tell others is a personal decision made by each individual. The individuals understand and are aware that **speaking about your spouse negatively to friends, family, and coworkers will not be helpful and may be damaging to the amicable separation process.** Such conversations are best worked through inside a confidential atmosphere such as with a therapist or divorce therapist.

10. **Planned holidays and vacations together should be canceled or divvied up between the two of you.** If you were planning Christmas together, it should now be spent apart. If it's your birthday, do not include/invite/contact your spouse. Trips are now taken without your partner; rituals are celebrated alone. (See clause regarding children and holidays below.)

11. **When the going gets tough, contact your therapist.** The separation process is difficult, and it requires enormous amounts of self-control and discipline. Each person will experience

highs and lows. When the lows hit, or if you are angry about something, or you find it hard to make it through, **call your therapist on weekends if they allow it, even if it is just to leave a message.** If you need a lifeline, use it.

12. **Children.** Each individual agrees to not talk neutrally, positively, or negatively about the other parent to the children. Ever. The only thing discussed with children about the other parent is pickup times or changes in schedule.

Amendments (write any additions or changes here):

_____

_____

_____

_____

This Managed Separation Agreement is not legally binding and is meant to provide a framework for a separation that may create the space necessary for a couple to work on saving their marriage through marriage therapy. This agreement is a Copyright of Becky Whetstone, PhD, and is for your use only and not to be shared with others without Whetstone's written consent. By signing this agreement, you are making a good faith agreement to abide by its terms.

Signed and agreed to by:

Partner 1: _____

Date: _____

Partner 2: _____

Date: _____

Witness: _____

Date: _____

Recommended Reading for Couples with Children

Both parents should read the following book to get a sense of what is in the best interest of the children while going through this process: *Helping Children Cope with Divorce* by Edward Teyber (1992). I discovered Teyber's work when I was learning about children and divorce beyond what I was taught in graduate school. I realized there were so many facets to it, and I couldn't afford anything but giving my clients the best information I could find. Not only did Teyber have the credentials—he was a professor of psychology at California State University in San Bernardino—but he had done a significant amount of research on the subject. I read what he had to say, and it concurred with everything I know about healthy families and handling separation and divorce. Teyber shows families how to create a best-case scenario and answers virtually every question a person might have along the way, from handling the first days of a separation all the way through coparenting and stepfamilies.

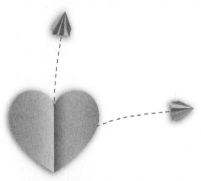

CHAPTER EIGHT
Healing from Divorce

During and after a divorce, almost everyone asks, "When will I feel better?" Humans don't like negative feelings and will go to a lot of trouble to avoid them. However, in divorce, feeling like you were hit by a bus in the aftermath is probably inevitable, as is obsessing about what happened. My period of obsessing led me to the education and career I have today and ultimately to writing this book. I had more *why* questions than could be answered in the regular therapy sessions I was in at the time, so I just kept searching and digging, and before too long, I knew more about it than most people. I'd like to encourage you to use what energy you are feeling in beneficial ways, too.

The process that a divorced couple will go through after the papers have been signed is predictable, but that is not a synonym for smooth. For Leaning-In partners, the ego has been blasted out of the water. The person who chose to spend their life with you changed their mind. You've been rejected, embarrassed, and thrown into a new life you didn't want, you may think. Then there's the all-important social connections: A good number of friends and former loved ones have likely run for the hills. They've either chosen to remain loyal to your ex because of blood or choice, or they just don't like to be around messy things. This is why, when someone I know gets separated or is the rejected partner in a separation or divorce, I always reach out and make sure I'm consistently there for them. We all need a strong support system of people who care when we're going through the worst of times. Most of us who've been through it never forget who was there—and who wasn't—when we were in our postdivorce basket-case phase.

The Decider may feel a period of elation following the initial separation, but in my experience, that almost always comes crashing down into distress and depression and a period of feeling bad about yourself. Looking around at all the damage that has been done, some may even question why they got a divorce at all. In an informal survey I ran a few years ago on the social media platform Twitter (now X), 25 percent of Deciders said they wished they had done more to save their marriage, and this is from the perspective of seeing how things played out for everyone involved. Indeed, approximately 6 percent of divorced individuals end up remarrying their former spouse (Bieber, 2024).

My experience backs up that regrets do happen. I've had quite a few Deciders over the years who absolutely, positively wanted a divorce and then called me a year or so later to ask if it was too late to reconcile. In all the years I've done therapy, only one Leaning-In partner agreed to reconcile (they remarried); dozens of others had moved on and were no longer interested. This fuels my need to persuade couples considering divorce to take the process slowly and try every option before pulling the final plug on their marriage because once that happens, it's not easy to get it back. For those interested in reconciliation, I'll provide more information later in this chapter.

Divorce Grief

There is no right or wrong way to do grief, no matter what kind of loss you are experiencing. Our bodies seem to know what we need at any given time, and they lead us that way. What is important in the first stages of divorce grief is to feel exactly what you feel the way you feel it. No one needs to fix or try to change it; the quickest way is straight through. Don't let anyone tell you what you should be doing or feeling; this is your pain and loss and yours alone. The problem is that finding the care that will support you in this and that you will benefit from may not be in plentiful supply. Lots of people are uncomfortable with those who are going through a bad time or feeling what they believe to be negative emotions, and they may have a misguided belief that it must be quelled or stopped. They may tell you to "Get over it" or "Don't be sad/mad," and that's unfortunate. A person coming through and out of divorce needs a caring presence, someone who witnesses what they are experiencing and says, "I'm sorry, and I care." These are some of the most powerful words anyone can say to an emotionally injured person; don't hesitate to tell your friends and family this if they try to put a stopper on your emotions. Tell people what you need and don't need.

As you come out of your acute stage, which usually begins to happen around the six-month mark, a good friend or divorce therapist might help with the practical, immediate consequences of the divorce. They'll ask questions and help you dig through things you may need to consider, both emotional and practical. On the practical side, are you financially okay? Do you need to put the house up for sale? Do you still need to clean out that storage room? Do you need to find a permanent place to live? Find a job? Go back to school? On the emotional side, they may just keep an eye on you. Although I said you need to feel what you feel, I don't advise that you wallow or stay incapacitated for any significant length of time. It's understandable to want to do that for a day or two but then get up and go do something else. That is symbolic of yes, you are in pain, but you are moving forward, too.

And of course, processing the meaning of it all is always a journey worth taking. Humans are meaning-making animals. We all need to answer the questions of how and why this happened. What was your part in it? What was their part in it? Every marriage that ends has takeaways to learn and grow from. If you're like I was, you'll uncover regrets and mistakes made, and you'll begin to see your former mate through more realistic eyes—which helps with a wounded person's healing process tremendously.

Divorce is agonizingly painful, but with pain comes wisdom and compassion. You show me someone who has compassion, and I'll show you someone who has suffered. For example, the reason I reach out to my divorcing friends is because I know how they feel and how isolating it can be. I know they need someone because I've been there. What are the lessons and takeaways you are learning in this process, things that will make you wiser as a human being?

Just in this moment, where you are right now, I'd like you to be still for a moment or two and reflect on the following questions:

1. What have I learned about myself so far in this marriage crisis process?

2. What have I realized about my former partner that I never saw before?

3. If I could do one thing over and differently, what would it be?
4. If lemonade can be made from lemons in a divorce, my lemonade will be . . .

Mine would look like this:

1. I learned that I can function well and enjoy being on my own. I also learned that the process should have been slowed down instead of rushed.
2. I always thought he thought he was better than everyone else, but I see now that he had the opposite problem. I wish I'd seen that when we were married because I would have had more compassion for him as opposed to judgment.
3. Try with all of my being to work things out and not divorce him so our children would not have experienced the negative effects of our decisions.
4. I found myself. My identity was as so-and-so's daughter or wife. Becoming single allowed me to create me and who I was and learn to put myself first.

Divorce Therapy

The divorce process and recovery from it will require mental health assistance, and I urge you to find a therapist to guide you through and help you process these things. They will make certain that you are processing everything in the healthiest possible way. Trust me when I say do not do this alone without professional help. I know you want to stop hurting, and the quickest way is to process it with someone who knows what they're doing, who isn't close to the situation, and who has no skin in the game other than to be helpful and compassionate. A note about the cost of these things: I tell clients with limited finances to see me every few weeks, once a month, every six weeks, whatever fits their budget. Over time, we will get you where you need to be, but the important thing is to keep coming and be consistent.

Divorce therapy, with or without your ex, is not the same as run-of-the-mill therapy. Divorce therapists are specialists in helping people get through divorce, much as you would choose a cardiologist for your heart issues over your family doctor. They are an invaluable tool to be using during this time, as I described in the last chapter. Not only will your feelings be normalized, but the divorce therapist will keep a couple rational while working through the logistics and details of how to split the two lives apart. The best part of it is that the divorce therapist will make sure that a blame mentality is avoided and that each person is able to look within at their part in the marriage not making it. Those who think they didn't play a part in the destruction of the marriage are either in denial, are naïve, or are ignorant. Trust me when I say it takes two to take down a marriage.

Another advantage is that a divorce therapist will steer you through the process in a way that will least damage your children. How well you cooperate and coparent peacefully with each other will determine how well your children cope with it. This is a time when you absolutely must do what's right for the sake of the children.

Fear of Being Alone

For those of you afraid to be on your own, once again, I urge you to step into it. I used to be afraid of being alone, too. But after being forced to be alone after my divorce, I got used to it, and that is the way to get past it. Besides, not being able to be alone is a red flag for not being ready for a relationship because when we are unable to be on our own physically and emotionally, we make foolish and desperate relationship decisions just so there will be a warm body around—and that's self-sabotage. If you can be alone, you can be fine until you can fill your life with a relationship or relationships that are based on compatibility and similar values.

Not only did I get used to being alone, but I came to cherish the times I was single and could do whatever I wanted. No one was holding me accountable; no one griped when I didn't want to cook or if I bought a nice dress. When my children were younger, this would be during the times they were with their dad. When they got older and went off to school, it was all the time. I had to think long and hard before remarrying after almost ten years on my own because I so closely guarded and cherished my alone time. When and if the time comes, you'll want a partner who can give you all the space you need so you can find the balance between relationship and individuality. That's what healthy people do.

I've Never Felt So Terrible

It is super important for you to understand that feeling crummy, crazy, angry, sad, and sometimes glad are all normal feelings following a marriage crisis and divorce. You may feel you are losing your mind, but I assure you that you are not. Breaking an attachment to someone makes all of us feel crazy. It's part of it. This emotional upheaval stage is unavoidable and very necessary.

The Value of Divorce Therapy

I went to a divorce therapist on my own during my last divorce, and we got down and dirty about my part in the disaster that was that marriage. I knew I was marrying a volatile, emotionally immature man, but he was fun and funny, and I thought he'd behave once married. I never should have told myself that lie. I loved the man, sure, but was also so attracted to his public prominence as a politician and the life we could have that I sold myself out to have the experience of a high-profile man's wife. Once again, I was getting my identity through someone else. I learned through divorce therapy that my shallow ego, which craved heady experiences, was causing me to make terrible relationship decisions. If I didn't get that part of myself under control, the pattern would repeat, and the idea of that was abhorrent. My ego hasn't been involved in my relationship decisions since the day I understood that.

Looking back through the history of the relationship, making sense of it, and finding takeaways to heal and grow from is called a *marital autopsy* (Pino, 1980) by some divorce therapists. I personally would have loved the opportunity to do this with my former spouse, but I know that some estranged spouses just want to look forward instead of backward even though there may have been a lot of helpful gold to be mined in such a process of retrospection. No matter: this is definitely something you can do on your own with a therapist.

The five phases of a marriage autopsy involve an interview and investigation of the following:

1. **Premarriage.** Why did you choose each other? Who were you when you entered this relationship? How did you decide to marry?

2. **Course of the marriage.** The patterns and trajectory in the relationship. For example, "When she went back to school,

everything changed."

3. **Dissolution stage of the marriage.** How the disillusionment in the marriage reached a breaking point.

4. **Preterminal stage of the marriage.** Marriage crisis, separation.

5. **Postmarriage.** Where we are now.

The advantages of this process are:

- Getting closure, which so many have told me they want but have never gotten;
- Gaining an understanding of the things that set them up for a future divorce that they may not have been aware of;
- Gaining a clear understanding of their relationship dynamic that took them down; and
- Getting clear on why a separation was necessary.

With an emphasis on themes from the marriage rather than blaming or rehashing, this process helps individuals or couples move on emotionally and psychologically. With that in mind, let's see where you are in this process today.

Ask yourself:

1. Why did I choose my former spouse as my mate?
2. Why did our relationship not work?
3. What is my part in it?
4. What are my takeaways?

As I said before, one indicator that you are healing is when you begin to have a more realistic view of your former spouse. Most of us experience a phenomenon of idealizing our partner when we fall in love. During the initial seduction stage of a dating relationship, our brain tends to filter out negative things or red flags and focuses on our lover's positive attributes. Under a blinding love trance, when dopamine is surging, we can even talk ourselves into believing that negative things are actually positive things, like that lack of a job shows his unwillingness to settle.

In the typical marital scenario, you marry Person A, a person you likely idealize like a favorite movie or music star, and after the trance has worn off, you begin to see Person B, a less-perfect, even flawed person with far less talent than you thought. As the stock drops in the relationship, your brain now focuses on your partner's negative attributes over the positive. After divorce and with more time passing, I believe that Person B is replaced by Person C, a yet-again updated and hopefully more accurate perception of the person you married.

Some of the postdivorce things I've heard involve rewriting history, which is a common phenomenon for people looking back at past relationships. We shouldn't be surprised, as studies of memory have long shown that human recall is very inaccurate, and humans tend to meld several different memories into one big one and take bits and pieces from here, there, and everywhere. One that always makes me cringe is "I realize now that I never loved them." A distant relative said this to his wife at the end of their marriage, and when I was told this, I was aghast. About twenty years before, I was there and saw firsthand when they fell in love. He was obsessed and goo-goo eyed over her, jumping around and hugging and touching her constantly, but this is the nature of rewriting marital history. If you find that your former spouse does something like that, remember this paragraph. What they say about your relationship now may have no resemblance to what was going on then.

Realizing that our partner never should have been put on a pedestal or viewed through rose-colored glasses in the first place and now seeing their many flaws—as we all have plenty—it is much easier to move forward into the healing process than if we stayed in a false state of having found and lost the perfect person. A good divorce therapist will discuss your premarital fantasies with you and help you see your life and marriage through more accurate eyes.

In the beginning, a Leaning-In partner is likely to see divorce as the worst thing in the world. With good divorce therapy, you will begin to see that not only is divorce not that, but it can offer hope for positive changes and growth moving forward. You may even end up better off than ever before; I know I did.

The Divorce Story

My ex is going around telling everyone who will listen
that I cheated on him and that is not true!
How can I get him to stop?

—A Disgruntled Ex

How many times have I heard someone complain about things their former spouse is saying about them to fellow friends and family members? Too many, and I can remember many times I was guilty of that myself. What I've since learned is that we all tell our own divorce stories in a way so that we are the hero, our ex is the villain, and that is that. In all the thousands of divorce stories I have heard over the years, a couple of people blamed themselves entirely, but that is exceedingly rare.

Although the stories are not told fairly or accurately in most cases, it is human nature to present the story of the wronged partner to the world. I encourage my clients who complain about this that it is something that happens in divorce, and we can't control it, so why expend a ton of energy worrying about it?

When a person contemplates divorce and worries about this happening, I tell them it probably will happen, but that's no reason not to leave someone when you're miserable and have lost hope. The problem really is that we don't want to be talked about negatively, but most people, if not all, do it. We can't control anyone but ourselves, so why be surprised? Remember, if you two were big fans of each other, you wouldn't have divorced.

I once met an old beau named Wayne for drinks in a nice restaurant. One of his friends came up and asked to join us. Even though Wayne was in his sixties, was divorced a couple of times, and had grown children and grandchildren, he still had a reputation as a lady's man and a player, and this is exactly why our very short dating episode had drifted into friendship only. His friend began telling stories about conquests and dastardly things Wayne had done over the years, and we all laughed. What was Wayne's response?

"Yes, all of it's true and probably then some, and the stuff I don't remember is probably true, too." This got a huge belly laugh, but I respected him so much for just admitting it.

For most people, it is painful to own up to flaws, mistakes, breeches of morality, or just doing something we wanted to do despite it being the wrong thing to do. Understanding that we all do things like that now and again because we are human and taking full ownership of it rather than putting up a defense or deflecting by pointing out other people's mistakes is a sign of being a healthy adult with a solid sense of self. When you can accept yourself—mistakes, flaws, and all—it'll be a great day. Beating yourself up or acting like a situation didn't happen is to step into toxic shame and self-abuse. I think it's a much better use of time and energy to examine yourself and see the areas where you want to be different while also sending love and compassion to the part of you that screwed up.

Restructuring of Roles

Divorce changes a family and friend system, and this often means there will be differences in these relationships moving forward (Rice & Rice, 1986, p. 192). My own siblings sided with my children's dad in the beginning and shut me out of activities they were doing together. I was shocked and dismayed at the time, but now I understand it. They didn't want to lose my generous and prominent ex for themselves, thought I should cope with his neglect and workaholism by having affairs, and felt strongly I should have stayed with him at all costs. This gave me new insight into how they thought and what was important to them, and our friendship was never the same. It's also a good example of how relationships can become restructured in the divorce process.

Common patterns of restructuring may include:

1. **Parents, siblings, and grandparents** may take on a more nurturing role for their divorcing child. Family members may step in and help with the children more than before.
2. **Loss of in-laws.** Though I've seen many in-laws stand by their daughter-in-law or son-in-law in a divorce, this almost always drifts into a distancing process that may result eventually in no contact at all.
3. **Friends.** Friends may take sides or want to stay away from negative emotions or may be uncomfortable with the "third wheel" concept. Some friends may see you as a threat to their own marriage as a newly single person.

4. **Children.** The parent-child relationship may alter for a variety of reasons. If a parent had an affair, accepting the betrayal and new relationship can be difficult for a child. If the parents can't get along or the children are put in the middle, a child's relationship with one or both parents may turn sour. Parents may overcompensate for the guilt they feel from the divorce or time spent apart, which will affect the relationship.

5. **New friends.** Most divorced individuals feel it is necessary to expand their network of friends to compensate for the losses they have suffered in the divorce process. Divorced people may feel more comfortable around other divorced people, who are likely to be more supportive of the change process you are experiencing.

6. **New romantic relationships.** A newly single person may shock themselves by having a period of promiscuity, sexual exploration, or numerous dates, which is completely normal postdivorce. Humans are sexual animals, and if done responsibly, they can do whatever they choose in this department. I urge newly single people to not be harsh with themselves for whatever path they choose during their adjustment period or at any other time.

7. **Ex-spouse.** The loss of the spouse role but not the parent role means loss of power and influence when it comes to your ex, and this can be a difficult adjustment. For a while, you may continue doing family activities together, but this may change drastically, especially when new romantic partners enter the scene. Rarely are divorced couples able to remain friends. Also, the person who treated you relatively well

while married may withdraw their warmth and positive regard, and this is especially true with Leaning-In partners who are hurt, distrustful, and find interactions painful (Rice & Rice, 1986, pp. 192–193).

Some People Do Better Than Others

It may seem like common sense that some people will fare better than others in a divorce. Someone once asked me why so many celebrities seem to divorce, and my answer was "Because they can." What did I mean?

Finances

If a wealthy or famous person divorces, most likely they will come out the other side and still have plenty of money, their living situation will probably stay the same or be of the same caliber as before, their support system will probably stay intact as people don't often dump rich and powerful friends, and their life of privilege, positive attention, and power will continue. I imagine that if a study were done, these types would be shown to recover from divorce faster than anyone because the loss and change experienced are less than for most people.

Of course, divorce then is hardest on those who lose the most. Status, power, money, the ability to support themselves, companionship, friends, reputation, and lifestyle will all be processed by a person's brain as huge losses. Many a person have told me they would divorce their spouse in a nanosecond if they knew they'd be financially okay, not lose friends, or be negatively judged. It's sad that these are common reasons why people are reluctant to disrupt an unhappy marriage. It is my hope that whatever energy you may have about the loss of your marriage, you will use it now to get yourself to a place where you'll be able to support yourself comfortably and thrive. If you are married now and contemplating divorce, start on your ability to support yourself today. I strongly believe all married folk should be prepared with a strong Plan B in case their marriage doesn't survive. It just isn't wise to put all your eggs in the marriage basket.

Education

Each of us who goes through divorce needs to figure out the best ways to course correct moving forward and find what support is available. When clients tell me they would like to go back to school but can't afford it, I'll ask them to check available grants and scholarships. I've worked for nonprofits and know there is a lot of grant money to be had to help people in need if you just look for it, especially when it involves bettering yourself. Even taking one class at a time at a community college will get you to where you want to be at some point, and your brain will process it as a positive move as you have a plan that ensures survival and brings less suffering. Your brain needs to know these things because if it is experiencing suffering without a plan to come out of it, it's going to adjust itself in way that will weigh you down even further. The amazing brain tries very hard to get your attention when you're moving in a direction that threatens survival. Becoming industrious and finding solutions to your own problems would be a superb first postdivorce hobby to take on.

Self-Confidence

Those who are severely introverted or must raise children mostly on their own with not enough money will not do as well as those who don't have those issues. Still, all of us can seek out what can be done rather than slink away in defeat. There are postdivorce groups and communities in person or on social media in which resources, emotional support, and great advice abound. Confidence can be gained by sticking out your neck, taking smart risks, and having positive gains. Time and again, I have seen newly divorced clients who started at the bottom and were terrified to reenter the working world soar in their new jobs and careers and quickly gain confidence. It's so important to get back out there and make things happen for yourself. It's part of being an adult.

Dysfunctional Plan B: Quick Replacements

When I have divorcing clients who are emotionally dependent, have little or no money, and have no post–high school education, training, or confidence, I can almost always guess what their postdivorce strategy will be: Find someone else quickly to rescue and support them so all their problems will go away. This is a terrible coping and life strategy in every aspect.

If a relationship hasn't been fully mourned, the person with undealt-with and lingering emotions will be a poor bet as a long-term romantic partner, but that won't stop the many fixers and rescuers out there who get their sense of self-worth from saving people. I coach people who meet a newly divorced person they're interested in to be their friend, stand by, let them get through it, and consider taking the relationship into the romantic realm after the emotional coast is clear. I liken a newly divorced person to a skittish and frightened horse. You might be able to ride it, but you are taking a high-risk chance with your heart and well-being. Newly divorced people need friends, but they are not good romantic relationship material and won't be for quite some time.

A divorce therapist will encourage a freshly divorced Leaning-In partner to recognize the loss of a very important role—the one that their spouse was in—and to look for and find healthy and fulfilling ways to fill that space other than new romances. Still, just because a therapist may give you the best advice doesn't mean you'll take it, and we know this. In a book like this that is guiding men and women to be their healthiest selves during one of life's most difficult experiences, it still has to be said.

We've all heard the term *rebound relationship*. When I was newly divorced, men I knew would call and say, "I don't want to become a rebound relationship, but how about joining me for dinner Saturday night?" No thanks.

Rebound relationships happen when a newly divorced person enters a relationship before completing the new developmental stage they just entered. In the immediate postdivorce recovery, a person needs to question, rework, redefine, analyze, and feel the feelings of what just happened (Rice & Rice, 1986, p. 199). This is a period of growth that is necessary and will not take place if a Band-Aid in the form of a new relationship is brought in too soon.

I have heard a wide variety of reasons why someone has chosen the replacement path, and it often involves the concept of loneliness. Also, some people have no sense of identity on their own and feel they must get it through their significant other. This is another reason why it is so important to learn to be comfortable living on your own. Learn to be independent, figure out who you are, what you're about, and live true to that. Also, take the new freedom you now have to learn how to educate and entertain yourself. Take workshops, read books, study what healthy relationships are. Do your own relationship autopsy. Figure out what just happened to you. This will all be time well spent in the postdivorce period. At the end of this book, I've included a list of books and other recommendations for ways to be healthy and recover postdivorce.

Thanks to learning how to be alone, when my husband is gone for a day or two, I spend time doing the things he wishes I wouldn't do when he's home, like talk on the phone with a girlfriend for hours, catch up on TV shows he doesn't like, skip meals, and leave the kitchen a mess because there's no pressure to worry about another person's preferences. I love not having to think of someone else now and again. Learn to enjoy this time while you have it. Most of us get into a new serious relationship within three years of a divorce, so learn to enjoy every minute you have to yourself while also considering the possibility of staying single and enjoying the freedom that comes with that.

When Are You Ready to Date?

Although many initially can't fathom the idea of dating, sooner or later you will probably begin to feel the pangs of romantic longing, but this does not mean you are ready to give it a whirl. Understandably, new relationships can be helpful to the Leaning-In partner as a way to heal their narcissistic injury of being rejected and get used to the idea of dating and being a single and available adult. It also fills the void where the other person used to be. The problem that often occurs, and why it makes divorce therapists so nervous, is that the emotionally injured Leaning-In partner can get prematurely attached and create a false image of who they want this new person to be rather than who they really are. I remember becoming aware of being attracted to men who looked like my ex. My brain thought, *Wouldn't it be nice to find a clone of your ex who treats you the way you deserve?* As soon as I realized what I was doing, I snapped out of it.

What I experienced isn't unusual. The new potential mate may likely have the opposite qualities of your ex, which may seem refreshing at first, but later these qualities are likely to drive you up the wall. Just like I pleaded with you to do during the separation and divorce process, take your time. Let things unfold. Don't jump into anything.

Marian is fifty-seven and has been married three times. She had affairs in the first two marriages, and her teenage children are disgusted with her for being so love obsessed. After leaving her children's stepdad, husband number two, whom they adored, she quickly married husband number three. She contacted me because her children recently moved back in with their biological dad, still visit their ex-stepdad regularly, and want very little to do with her. "What have I done to my family?" she cried.

Now Marian finds that her new husband is verbally and emotionally abusive and controlling. "I shouldn't have married so fast," she says. "I knew better. Now my kids hate me. I can't get divorced a third time, I just can't!"

Learn from Marian. If someone wants to rush you into marriage, something is wrong. Marian knew this when she chose to go ahead and marry her new husband, but she went for it anyway. "I told myself he's wealthy, he's funny, he loves to travel, and I never got to travel much. Blah, blah, blah." But now she knows he acts like a jerk, and she feels trapped. And guess what? He's jealous and suspicious.

Why? Because she shared with him that she had affairs while married to each of her previous husbands. Abusive people listen to all your revelations during the initial seduction period of a relationship and mentally file them away with an intent to use them against you later. It is the worst kind of getting zinged. For Marian, it was out of one mess and straight into another. Don't let this happen to you.

There is no rational reason to rush remarriage unless you or your mate are on their deathbed. If someone is in a hurry to seal the deal, I can make an intelligent and informed guess that (1) they are needy, (2) they are dependent, (3) they are controlling, or (4) they are nuts. A person rushing marriage can be all four, and the reason they want to rush things is they're highly motivated to get you locked in before you notice their extremely dysfunctional behaviors. Take this advice: don't fall for it.

I'm Now with the Person I Had an Affair With

All bets are off for the person who divorced because of an affair and is now planning a life with their new partner with no downtime to be alone, heal, and go through the developmental growth that is needed. The odds are so stacked against these relationships that it's difficult to know where to start.

I have done hundreds of sessions with couples who met while married to other people. The one common denominator all these couples have is lack of trust. Why wouldn't that be true? You both already know that when things aren't grooving in your marriage, the other person is likely to cheat. You also know that your new love will lie, gaslight, and withhold information from the person they're married to. Not a great foundation to start a marriage on. Also, if you had children in your previous marriages, they are likely to reject your new relationship, as will your ex. Older children feel disloyal to their biological mom or dad when they act friendly with the Decider's new amour, so get ready for the pushback if you choose this path.

I'm Doing Better Since the Divorce, but My Kids? Not So Much.

There is a common postdivorce dynamic in which a parent moves forward and ends up doing at least fairly well while the children tend to do less well. This does not mean we need to stay in unhealthy marriages for the sake of the children; there are children who find their parents' split a relief. It simply means that overall, the adults and children are likely to have diverging interests when it comes to divorce, and it pays for parents to be aware of this (Wallerstein et al., 2000, p. 105).

Older kids will push back against a new girlfriend or boyfriend who they feel had a large part in their parents' divorce. If you are taking my words to heart and remember that we need you to put your kids' needs first and get along with your ex so you can be great coparents, then please understand that if you bring the partner who betrayed their parent into your children's lives, achieving both of those important goals will most likely not be achieved. Having obstacles such as these will work against the Decider's new romance having any chance of being successful. Then add blending families to the mix, which almost all children do not want (see Chapter 6), and the impossible and frustrating job of being a stepparent, what could go right? Indeed, the divorce rate for second marriages with blended families is between 60 and 75 percent.

Speaking of being a stepparent, if your spouse's children are nine years old or younger, you can probably get away with parenting the children without pushback from the kids, but older kids will not tolerate it at all. In any event, leave the major parenting decisions to their biological parent no matter how old your children are, and adopt the role of a loving and kind mentor or coach who turns the other cheek in the face of rejection and pushback. For it to work, you will have to play the role of a saint. Going toe to toe with an older stepchild will put their mom or dad in the middle, and most moms and dads will choose their children over you, as they should. I always beg my clients who are considering becoming a stepparent of teens not to do it because there are so many ways in which it can go south, and stepparenting is one of the most thankless family roles there is.

Reconciliation

There are usually two types of reconciliation scenarios: those that happen almost immediately after separation or divorce and the ones that happen after all the ink has dried, residences have been sold, and the two are well into the postdivorce recovery period.

In the first-case scenario, couples part, and very soon into the process, the Decider concludes they don't like being on their own and want to return. This is one reason why I ask people contemplating divorce to try separating first and then take each step slowly. We never know how we're going to feel when we split because it's a totally new experience.

This type of reconciliation is built on the thinnest of foundations and not likely to succeed. In these situations, Deciders leave their spouse and find that life away from the marriage is dismal. If they were in a new relationship, they may start seeing their lover's flaws, or, if they started dating others, they may say to themselves, "I'm not able to attract a mate better than the one I had." The Decider may experience loneliness, loss of friends or family esteem, financial issues, and other new and negative life experiences that cause them to wonder, *Did I make a mistake?* Also, for men, some of you don't do very well without a female helpmate. I'm sorry, but it's true. Why?

More men remarry than women, and part of it has to do with survival instinct; men stay healthier and live longer when they are married (Pam & Pearson, 1998, p. 348). Also, since time immemorial, a majority of women have taken on more of the tasks and responsibilities around the home, even though many work and have lives of their own. The lack of balance in the home is the most complained about thing I hear when doing individual therapy with women. They say, "Why doesn't he notice and help me with what needs to be done? I hate nagging him to help me out," and "He doesn't appreciate all I do to keep the house running." This conversation is something I hear several times a week.

Well, imagine what happens when these unaware and unappreciative men decide to leave women who made their lives so much easier. If a replacement isn't soon found, the man is likely to feel lost and overwhelmed, and that can make him think about the possibility of returning. If he doesn't return or is spurned when and if he does, statistics show 50 percent of men will find someone else and remarry within five years, whereas 45 percent of women will (Kreider, 2005).

The problem in this type of reconciliation is that there hasn't been significant growth and change with either spouse, which would be necessary for a successful reunion, and the Decider's main reason to return is that they "badly underestimated the problems of separation" (Pam & Pearson, 1998, p. 349).

Most Leaning-In partners will be turned off by the Decider's realization that returning home might be the "least bad" option for them. This does not mean the Leaning-In partner won't agree to let the Decider come back because their ego has been beaten up; if attachment remains, it is a rare Leaning-In partner who will refuse the offer of a reconciliation. However, with few or no changes and no divorce therapy or marital autopsy, the same issues that caused the separation and divorce in the first place will likely return after an initial honeymoon period, and the marriage probably won't make it.

Research shows that if the Decider's separation and divorce experience goes well for them personally, they will not return no matter what dire circumstances their family may be experiencing because of the divorce (Wolfe, 1975). The sad reality is that most reconciliations that take place immediately following divorce involve the Decider's realization that their life is not better off without the Leaning-In partner but not because of the Leaning-In partner's personal characteristics and the warm feelings the Decider has for them. They miss the situation.

The type of reconciliation I typically see happens much later, usually a year or so after a divorce. Take, for example, Marcus and Trina, who left the marriage with determination. She was so certain she wanted out that there was nothing he could do or I could say that would persuade her otherwise. With three young children to consider, she convinced herself that they'd do fine once everything settled down after the divorce.

Almost one year to the day their marriage ended, Trina called. "I want to reconcile with Marcus, but he isn't interested. Can you help?"

When I called Marcus to see what he was thinking, he described suffering during the year of their divorce process and hoping she'd change her mind, followed by a year of recovery and self-reflection.

"Becky, I'm worn out with her emotionally," he said. "The kids are coming out of all the changes, and I just got over the hump of denial and am well into acceptance and feeling so much better. I just don't want to step back into it, especially knowing she could turn back around and do it to us [the family] again. I no longer trust her."

And so it often is in divorce with the second type of reconciliation. Just about the moment the Leaning-In partner has completely moved on emotionally and is feeling like themselves again, the Decider may call and feel them out about the possibility of giving things another shot. The percentage of Deciders who do this is low, but if it's going to happen, it usually occurs after the Leaning-In partner has broken their attachment.

I once met a person who had just bought my house and was about to move in. She said she and her husband had divorced. She was certain she wanted out of the marriage, she said. They split everything up, shared custody of the kids, and went on with their lives. Then he brought a new girlfriend to one of the children's soccer games.

"I said to myself, 'Oh no you don't, he's mine,'" she recalled. "I called him almost immediately and told him to get rid of the girl because we were going to reconcile." In her case, he came back, they bought my house, and they were planning to move back in with their kids. I don't know if they are still together today or not, but I wouldn't be surprised if they weren't. Why?

The way I heard this woman's story is that her ego wanted the challenge of getting her husband back. It wasn't a story of "I missed him, realized I love him so much, and I made a huge mistake." Her description reminded me of how a child never plays with the toy in the corner, but when another child comes in and grabs it, suddenly the ignored toy becomes a hot commodity. It sounded like a shallow reason to reconcile, and if neither of them had done serious work on themselves and their marriage, then I'd bet almost everything I have that the reconciliation would fail.

It's not uncommon for people to have mixed feelings about their divorce, perhaps still loving the ex-spouse but not able to see a path to change. If the stirrings of reconciliation come your way, you may have a legitimate chance of it being successful if you base your decision on wanting to return to the marriage because of who your spouse is and what they offer but not if you base it on how poorly you fared as a newly divorced person.

There are predictors of whether a postdivorce reconciliation can be successful, and as you can imagine, they have been studied. The characteristics of successful reconciliations are:

1. Making reconciliation and strengthening the marriage a priority
2. Outlining an actionable plan for what you are willing to do to make this a priority
3. Having the support of family and friends
4. Ability to remember the good times
5. Approaching reconciliation with a long-term perspective.
6. Having the abilities to endure and persevere in the face of problems, view the relationship as a source of happiness, communicate and resolve differences, emotionally support one another, and commitment to children

In a study by the University of Minnesota and Brigham Young University (Hawkins et al., 2012), correlating the reasons for divorce with an interest in reconciliation, lack of attention and trouble with in-laws seemed to be things Deciders could get over, especially if the promise of quality time and setting boundaries with family were part of the reconciliation plan.

The authors lamented that some of the common reasons cited for divorce were things that could have been overcome had a couple tried professional intervention to help them while still married, like infidelity, inattention, inability to communicate, division of household labor, and more.

Reconciliations that are put together willy-nilly, without rhyme or reason, are probably doomed to fail, and when a Leaning-In partner justifies allowing the Decider back by telling themselves lies like "They must have learned their lesson," they are making a huge mistake (Pam & Pearson, 1998, p. 354).

In my practice, one couple I saw divorced after an affair on her part was discovered. She got engaged to the new man, and about a year and a half later, she came back wanting to reconcile. They had younger children, and I cautioned them about getting back together too soon only to have their marriage fail and the children be destroyed all over again. They had to earn their reconciliation, I said, and if they did it, there was no going back. I told them, "You have to stay together and work things out as they come up because of your children and what you have already put them through."

They agreed, followed my plan, and went through the process of a marital autopsy—including the affair she'd had—and we did extensive healing and repair work. We created a detailed plan for a new relationship and how it would work. After one year of hard work and doing everything I asked, they told me they wanted to remarry, this time in a covenant marriage, which in our state is a voluntary license that makes it much harder to divorce. I agreed that they were ready, and a few weeks later, I married them myself under a gazebo in their small Arkansas town. It was a very moving scene, indeed, but this couple is rare.

One of the things that was amazing to watch about them was the wife's ability to get real about why she did what she did, taking full ownership of every part of it. Her husband had worked with me individually after the divorce and had completely changed his perspective. He knew he wasn't ready for a new relationship while he worked on himself, so he spent his time reading books about how to heal and be a better man. Having been one who fretted over every last detail, he had become flexible and "go with the flow," and his wife jokingly called him her new "Zen man." She joined one of my childhood trauma classes and came to every meeting to make sure she understood and practiced what it is to be a healthy, functioning adult. They did everything I could ever hope a couple could do to have a successful reconciliation.

Unfortunately, most couples will not dedicate the time, money, and effort to plan a reconciliation that will be erected on a solid foundation. If you think you might want to do this, do it right. If a Decider does want to return, they will likely find a formerly rejected partner who now views them with a skeptic's eye (Pam & Pearson, 1998), and who wouldn't? If you dumped me once, why wouldn't you do it again? Understand that there will be a lot of rebuilding to do within yourself and as a couple. A Decider will have to be humble and patient as they may not be welcomed back with streamers and a fireworks show but more of an attitude of "Okay, let's see how you've changed and what lessons you've learned."

Marrying Again to Someone Else

This is a subject near and dear to my heart because I've done it the right way and the wrong way, and I've learned a lot from my mistakes and successes. One of the reasons I have become passionate about marriage crisis, separation, divorce, and the aftermath is because I want others to learn from my experience and perhaps avoid the dead ends, roadblocks, and collisions. Why? Because mistakes like these hurt people and forever change their lives, not just the lives of two people, and no one more than yourself.

Of my three failed marriages, only one had the possibility for success, and whether I would have admitted it then or not, I knew it at the time. If I could boil it all down to one lesson learned, it was this: Don't marry anyone unless you can look at yourself in the mirror and say, "This person is so fantastic and will enhance my life so much that I am a damn fool if I don't marry them." Anything less than that is a no-go. Marriage is hard; it is long; it will go up; it will go down. The person you are choosing needs to have substantiveness, perseverance, depth, responsibility, stability, flexibility, and a history of sticking with things. The wise decisions you make now can prevent much suffering later.

The worst criteria for choosing a mate are potential, financial support, rescuing and rehabbing, fear of being alone, everyone else is doing it, because you think you're aging out, or you can't do any better. I recently had a client tell me he chose his wife because she is beautiful and a belly dancer. That may sound ridiculous, but I've heard worse, and it's not that unusual to select a mate for reasons that won't serve you in the long term. I've often said people spend more time selecting a car than they do a mate. If you knew you would only get to drive one car your entire life, wouldn't you spend even more time choosing one for yourself that would most likely fit your life as you pass through all the stages people experience in a lifetime? I certainly wouldn't get a two-seat convertible as a lifetime choice when I might have kids later in life and develop an interest in camping.

One factor influences the success or failure of a marriage so much that I can't emphasize it enough: Do not marry anyone who cannot support themselves. Those who plan to be stay-at-home moms or dads, that's fine, but don't marry until you can support yourself if need be. You owe it to yourself to have a solid Plan B so you'll be okay whatever happens. Healthy marriages can't be created when one person is dependent on the other for survival with no other options.

Just because you may want to remarry, perhaps as a symbol of life returning to normal, doesn't mean you are ready to or should. I am calling for newly divorced people to go for broke individually when it comes to introspection, personal growth, being alone, dealing with loneliness, and healing before hanging a shingle out again as available to date. To end the madness of disastrous remarriages that happen too soon, you must do this for yourself.

This postdivorce period is an important developmental stage that can only be skipped at your peril. Those who ignore this wise advice will likely find themselves remarried to the wrong person and feeling trapped yet again. A person may be ready to marry again when they have mostly healed from their major life change, grown, matured, have worked on and understand the negative things about themselves that contributed to the last marriage failing, and have learned a thing or two about selecting healthy partners. When you no longer feel like the walking wounded and you understand why your last marriage didn't work because of things you did or didn't do, we might be getting somewhere. If your postdivorce story is all about what the other person did wrong, then you're not ready.

We will change our culture when it comes to marriage, divorce, and working through problems that come up through thoughtfulness, self-discipline, and a mindset that refuses to go low in family interactions. We should teach our children that one is not ready for marriage because they have reached a certain age or station in life but when one is mentally and emotionally prepared to be fully relational in a give-and-take interdependent union between two people. I have never met anyone who has had this conversation with their children.

What it means to be relational and in an interdependent union should be taught in schools and religious organizations and talked about in families. We should teach what it is to be a healthy, functioning adult and what the dynamics are of healthy families. How to effectively communicate and set boundaries should be common knowledge, not things someone like me has to teach every adult she sees in her private practice. If we did all this, we could save families from the pain and suffering marital crisis and divorce bring. And that is my hope for our future.

Epilogue

Marriage crisis and divorce are some of life's most difficult experiences and gathering knowledge and awareness of what's happening and how to best navigate it, is how to manage it in as sane a way as possible. It is my hope that you can use what I've learned through personal and professional experience to get an outcome that is for the higher good of yourself and your family.

We can make the world a better, kinder place, and we must if we want to stop the madness and trauma that family strife brings. I know we can be better when it comes to interacting with others.

Having a healthy relationship with another is a learned skill, yet few if any people learn about it while growing up. Most of us have poor to horrific role models, and the things we learn in basic communication classes don't cut it. It is imperative for our culture that we do more to help people understand what it is and how it's done. We could change the world if it became a reality.

In this book, I have shared with you the bulk of what I have learned about marriage crisis, separation, the divorce decision, and its aftermath. It is knowledge born of pain, a need to understand, and the desire to be better. There is still a lot more to share about how to be healthy and to have better relationships, and at the end of this book are suggested resources for you to use on your journey.

We all need to be able to tell ourselves we did all we could to try to save our marriage, and if the answer was still to part, you can know you made the decision wisely.

You learned how to dismantle a marriage in the most humane way while remembering that couples with children will always remain a family. It is my fondest desire that something you read in this book helped you and your family. Please let me know if it has.

I wish you the best in your future.

Becky Whetstone
Heber Springs, Arkansas
May 2024

Appendix I: Resources

Exercise: Understanding Your Problems

The following has been adapted from *Mind over Mood: Change How You Feel by Changing the Way You Think* by clinical psychologists Dennis Greenberger and Christine A. Pedesky and *The Clinicians Guide to CBT Using Mind over Mood* by Christine Pedesky with Dennis Greenberger.

Cognitive behavior therapy (CBT) is a research-based method for helping people sort through their thoughts and feelings to get to the heart of what's going on and to help people learn how to process their thoughts so their feelings will improve.

A crucial part of a marriage crisis is working on yourself and repairing the things that caused either partner to not be as good a mate as they'd hoped. There are five areas from CBT we will want you to be monitoring and working on throughout this process, and hopefully, these will help you keep moving forward. Keep in mind that what you think and tell yourself have everything to do with the other four, especially what your mood and feelings are. This is why it is very important to become aware of your thoughts and make certain they aren't unhealthy for you. For example, any time you are beating yourself up in your thoughts, it is not healthy for you.

In addition to those, I have added feelings as a fifth piece to monitor, as well as an opportunity to practice more positive thinking. Therapists know that one idea can be approached in numerous different ways, from the most negative to the most hopeful themes. I am for people steering themselves in a more positive direction. Try it!

1. **What is your current life situation or changes in environment?**
   Example: My spouse may want to leave the marriage.

2. **What are your physical reactions? That is, do you feel tired, achy? Where in your body do you feel out of sorts?**
   Example: I feel tightness in my chest. My head hurts. I'm emotionally exhausted.

3. **What moods and feelings are you experiencing?**
   Example: I am anxious (fearful) and depressed.

4. **What behaviors have you been engaging in?**
   Example: I have been lying around the house, eating and drinking too much. I'm spending too much time on the Internet looking for solutions to our marriage problems.

5. **Thoughts: When my feelings and moods are intense, what are my thoughts?**
   Example: Why didn't I do anything (or enough) when my spouse was asking me to? What am I going to do if my spouse leaves for good? How will I cope? My lifestyle will change completely. I can't believe they are doing this.

6. **Positive reframe:** Look on the bright side of what can come from this crisis. Explore belief in yourself, that you are a survivor, for example.

   Example: I trust myself to make intelligent decisions during this crisis. I know I can grow and learn from this, and no matter what happens, I'll be okay and will be a better person for it.

Exercise: Feelings

When working with people and trying to help them heal, Pia Mellody, author of *Facing Codependence*, realized that many were not in touch with their feelings and emotions. How do you teach someone what an emotion is? She listened as people described their feelings and also tracked where each person felt the emotions in the body. This allowed her to create a chart that helped people figure out what they were feeling. During this time in your life, it is imperative that you learn to identify and feel your emotions. In the beginning of this exercise, you may want to work on feelings from your past that have nothing to do with your marriage crisis.

I often tell clients that feelings are how our souls communicate with us. I visualize my soul tapping on my shoulder, trying to get my attention. It gives me a feeling, and it is telling me, "Hey, look at this, this may be important. What's going on?"

The important things are to be aware of feelings and where you feel them in your body. Learn to identify what is going on and what you may need. Humans need to tweak their lives constantly to maintain inner peace. By paying attention to your feelings, you can learn what needs to be dealt with.

To me, one of the clearest feelings our soul sends our way is dread. I once was visiting an old and dear friend who had hurt me deeply a couple of years before. She had wanted to reconcile and began to invite me to go out or come to her house and visit. Never when we met did she mention what had happened nor offer any apology. It was all swept under the rug as if it had never happened.

I found myself dreading our get-togethers. My mind sent me clear messages: "Beware, don't let your guard down, she's not safe, she will gossip about you, you can't trust your heart with her." The feeling my soul sent me was dread.

Finally, she was set to come to my house one evening, and thirty minutes before arriving, she said something had come up and she wouldn't be able to come. I felt completely relieved.

I had heard my soul's message loud and clear and went into my office and wrote her an e-mail that said, "I can't plan for us to visit anymore. This has nothing to do with you canceling tonight. It has to do with my feelings and what's going on with me. I hope you will understand, and I wish you all the best in life." There was no need to tell her I didn't trust her or how angry I was about how she had treated me when we had our bad moment. If I had told her that, she would have gossiped about it in a negative away; I heard her do it to others numerous times. I just needed to end the friendship once and for all. This is a good example of how the soul speaks to us through our feelings and how, if we listen, we can bring ourselves to peace.

The eight core feelings are anger, fear, pain, joy, passion, love, shame, and guilt. Some of the words you might use to describe these feelings are:

- **Anger:** resentment, irritation, frustration. You may feel this emotion all over your body.
- **Fear:** apprehensive, overwhelmed, threatened, dread. You may feel this emotion in your stomach and upper chest.
- **Pain:** hurt, pity, sad, lonely. You may feel this emotion in your lower chest and heart.
- **Joy:** happy, elated, hopeful. You may feel this emotion all over your body.
- **Passion:** enthusiasm, desire, zest. You may feel this emotion all over your body.
- **Love:** affection, tenderness, compassion, warmth. You may feel this emotion in your heart.
- **Shame:** embarrassed, humble. You may feel this emotion in your face, neck, and/or upper chest.
- **Guilt:** regretful, contrite, remorseful. You may feel this feeling in your gut.

Now, create a chart for yourself. Recall a time you felt each feeling and write it down. After that, try to recall what you told yourself, and finally, if you could relive it, what you might you have done instead—wild fantasies are perfectly fine here. After imagining your fantasy, note how you feel now.

If anything else comes to mind, or you want to write down numerous times you felt a feeling and do this exercise, go right ahead. Here's an example:

Feeling: Anger.

Where I felt it: All over.

When did it happen: The coach chose his son to be quarterback for the team even though I was better qualified.

What I told myself: Life isn't fair, there's no use working hard to get what you want.

What I might (or wished to) have done instead: Said something by telling the coach exactly what was going on from my viewpoint and asked him to explain to me why that was okay.

My fantasy, if any: I punched him out, then he wiped his face, started crying, and admitted he was wrong. He asked if I would allow him to make it right.

Feeling now: A bit relieved, vindicated. Satisfaction. Peace.

Exercise: Track Your Shame and Intense Emotional Feelings

I talk about the enormous role our autonomic nervous system plays in our relationships. A person says or does something, or fails to say or do something, and it triggers something inside you, activating extreme emotions. Once your sympathetic nervous system is activated, you go into the fight-flight-freeze survival threat mode, where damage to the relationship takes place. Damage occurs because when your nervous system is activated, your cognitive abilities fall offline, and you act on primal instinct. Unfortunately, the part of the personality that responds to fight, flight, or freeze is not very mature and reacts much like an irreverent teenager or bully.

When your nervous system gets activated like this, it shows that one of your very old trauma wounds has been rewounded. Whatever is happening now mirrors an old theme from your past, like a string or bind from now back to long ago. The good news is that by asking yourself a few questions, you can often become aware of this bind and snap the cord between the two, which means you likely won't get activated again the next time that theme shows up. The more work you do on this, the less often you will become activated, and the easier it will be for you to communicate peacefully and thoughtfully, no matter what the other person is saying or doing.

In addition to healing the old wound, you can also learn to control the bully part of your personality that responds to sympathetic nervous system activations.

Toxic Shame

We first experience toxic shame in our childhood. Later, a shame bind is triggered when something in the present triggers our old feelings of not being good enough, being defective, or not fitting in or belonging. The feeling of toxic shame we feel in the moment is directly related to similar themes from our childhood. A toxic shame, fear, or pain bind is the thread that exists from what happened between the past situation and the present, making it intensely painful.

Exercise: The Painful Four: Toxic Shame, Panic/Fear, Rage, and Pain Attacks

The first way to free yourself from intense negative emotions is to become aware of them, locate and feel them, define what happened to you that caused the current attack, and trace it to a similar occurrence much earlier in your life. There, you find the shame-bind theme. The intense feelings are called *carried emotions* because they literally are carried from your childhood into the present moment. Once you figure out which of the four negative emotions it is hitting you in, you can affirm yourself out of the bind.

Here is a look at these intense, trauma-related feelings:

- Toxic shame: The feeling of not being good enough, less than, defective, not fitting in
- Fear: Terror of impending harm
- Rage: Overwhelming anger
- Pain: The feeling of emotional injury, hurt, wounding

Problem: I was triggered by something that happened or what someone did or said. I know because I felt it all over my body, and I became extremely distressed.

1. **What happened:** Example: "My family member made a negative comment about me."

2. **How I felt and where I felt it:** Describe body sensations and the emotions felt, and identify where in your body you felt the emotional pain.
   Example: "When my family member said they can't count on me because I am always late, I felt flush all over my body, my heart raced, my chest felt compressed. I felt fear and panic, shame, and rage."

3. **Which of the four intense negative emotions did I feel?**
   Example: "Toxic shame. I felt they were saying something is wrong with me, that I'm not good enough."

4. **What is the toxic shame bind, the reoccurring theme over which I have not yet healed myself?**
   Example: "I was verbally bullied in my childhood by my family and kids at school. They would all tell me I was no good or worthless. This caused me to fill up with shame and feel bad about who I was. Now, when my family member (or anyone) says something negative about me, I feel the same toxic shame I felt as a child."

5. **Recognizing the connection between the past and present**
   will go a long way in helping you remain calm in the future
   and healing this bind. The next time, you will realize that
   person hit one of your old wounds as opposed to it being
   tucked away in your subconscious mind, but you also need
   to create a positive affirmation to yourself about that theme.
   This will kill the power that bind has over you. Do that here.
   Example: "I have a right to be who I am, mistakes and all,
   and I esteem and value myself no matter what others think of
   me."

Pia Mellody's chart is designed to help people understand their
feelings and track where they feel them in their body. I mentioned
these feelings before, but this chart shows you how to recognize
when your feelings come from old childhood wounds, wounds Mellody calls "carried" because they have been carried from your past
into this moment. Your feelings from your current experiences are
less intense than the ones that are from your past.

Basic, Owned, and Carried Emotions

BASIC EMOTIONS		OWN	CARRIED
ANGER	Resentment Irritation Frustration	ALL OVER BODY Power Energy	GUT Pressure Rage
FEAR	Apprehension Overwhelmed Threatened	TINGLING IN UPPER STOMACH TIGHTNESS IN UPPER CHEST	EXTREMITIES Numbing and/or tingling Panic
PAIN	Sad Lonely Hurt Pity	LOWER CHEST AND HEART Hurting	GUT Pressure Hopeless
JOY	Hopeful Elated Happy Excitement	ALL OVER BODY Lightness	ALL OVER BODY Lightness
PASSION	Enthusiasm Desire	SEXUAL AROUSAL Excitement	SEXUAL PASSION Icky, slimy, dirty feeling Nausea Fanaticism
LOVE	Affection Tenderness Compassion Warmth	WARMTH AND SWELLING IN CHEST AREA	WARMTH AND SWELLING IN CHEST AREA
SHAME	Embarrassment Humble Exposed	FACE, NECK, AND/OR UPPER CHEST Hot/red	GUT Worthless
GUILT	Regretful Contrite Remorseful	GUT Gnawing sensation	BOTTOM OF FEET Sensation of being stuck to the ground

Source: Meadows Behavioral Health Center

Exercise: Nervous System Activations

Now, learn to track when your nervous system gets activated; think of it as a diary of each time you get triggered and feel the super-intense feelings that old trauma wounds bring. You can use the same questions on the facing page for yourself. Here is how one person went through the process successfully:

Q: When did the triggering happen?

A: Yesterday.

Q: What happened right before you got activated that served to trigger your nervous system?

A: My older brother said something ugly and critical about my grown daughter.

Q: What did you feel when that happened?

A: I immediately felt rage.

Q: Where did you feel it in your body?

A: All over.

Q: What was your first thought?

A: Get the hell out of here, you don't have to put up with that.

Becky's note: In this example, the person heard the voice of their inner bully, the immature part of their personality, try to take over the situation, but this client knew not to allow this part of her to actually respond to her brother. She slowed herself down and worked to access her best self, the part we call the functional adult.

Q: Were you able to slow yourself down and access your functional adult?

A: Yes, she came in and coached me down from doing something I'd regret, telling me that I didn't want to act immature or like an idiot, and I also didn't want to freeze and say nothing, so I came up with something to say to my brother from my best self.

Q: What did you say?

A: I said, "You haven't been around my daughter in fifteen years, and not since she was a rebellious and obnoxious teenager. She is grown now and not the same as then. Maybe it'd be good if next time she is in town you spend some time with her to see who she is now."

Q: How did you feel after that?

A: Like I had done the right thing. All the intense feelings I had before immediately left my body because I had said something helpful and in an adult way. I realized my nervous system needed me to do that, and it immediately released all that negative energy.

Q: Did you figure out which rage bind set you off like that?

A: Yes. When I got home, I asked myself when this theme that upset me presented itself at another time in my life, and it immediately came to me as if my subconscious mind spoon-fed it to me. It said, "Your family scapegoats people at an early age, and once they decide you are a certain way, which is usually negative, you can't wriggle free from it, and you will always be labeled that way. Your family scapegoated you in a negative way, and you felt rage when your brother scapegoated your daughter based on one or two incidents long ago. It was an old theme that presented itself again."

The beauty of this process is that the next time this person experiences the scapegoating theme, they will be aware, and it won't trigger their nervous system again, sending them into the intense carried rage emotion.

Right now, you may be able to track what triggered you and recognize the theme from your past but are not currently able to control the obnoxious bully that responds. The ability to do that comes with awareness, slowing yourself down, and consciously working to access the functional adult part of you that waits in the wings to help. It takes practice, and you likely will never be 100 percent successful, but you'll get better at it, and the positive results, identified with the relief it brings, will encourage you.

Being successful at controlling that nasty and immature responder and instead responding as a functional adult is the difference between acting immaturely or acting like an adult. Adults control themselves so they can have healthy relationships with others.

Exercise: Where Is the Evidence?

Something that has amazed me since learning about relationship dynamics, communication, and the many ways they can all go wrong is how terrible people are in understanding one another in general. Many times, a couple's marriage went downhill, leading them to the marriage crisis they are now in because of misunderstandings, things assumed, and miscommunications. Making certain we understand what another person is trying to get us to understand when they speak is vital.

Instead, what I see is the listener jumping to conclusions (often negative ones), making up meanings that aren't even close to accurate, and unnecessarily making themselves miserable or driving themselves crazy. I teach couples how to check their perception and reality because it is so common for people to misread situations.

In the book *The Clinician's Guide to CBT Using Mind over Mood,* clinical psychologists Dennis Greenberger and Christine Pedesky show clients how to stop this dysfunctional habit that tears up relationships needlessly (1995, p. 78).

Here is how dysfunctional thinking goes:

Situation: Sue complains to the therapist that her husband doesn't care about her because he refuses to call her twice a day from work to check in. He says he doesn't because he is super focused and busy while there. He loves her dearly but finds her demands unreasonable. He says he will call when he can.

Sue's initial thoughts about this: her husband doesn't care.

Sue's feelings about that: Sue is hurt and angry.

Evidence that supports Sue's initial thoughts about her husband is true: her husband refused to do what she asks.

Evidence that does not support her initial thoughts: Her husband says he loves her dearly, that he is simply focused while at work and wants to stay focused. He also says he will call when he can. When asked by the therapist if she really believes what she is saying, that her husband doesn't care, she responds quietly, "No, I know he does care."

Alternative/balanced thought: My husband does care; he is focused on work and wants to stay focused. This has nothing to do with his feelings about me. I know he cares about me no matter what he is doing.

After running through this exercise, Sue is able to find her way back to rational, evidence-based thinking and processing. The result is she feels better and is able to reassure herself that her husband cares, which is the truth. The last thing I want you to do is to waste time and energy thinking and believing things that are inaccurate and have no evidence to back them up.

Now it's your turn to check your own beliefs about your relationship to see if you have the evidence to back up any of your negative assumptions.

Situation:

Initial thought that caused your negative opinion:

_____

_____

Your feelings after initial thoughts:

_____

_____

Evidence that supports your initial thoughts:

_____

_____

Evidence that does not support your initial thoughts:

_____

_____

Alternative/balanced, more positive, and accurate thought:

_____

_____

Working on your relationship with yourself during this process is important because people who think they are not good enough often make negative assumptions about themselves and about how others think about them. In my early twenties, I was full of self-loathing and assumed everyone hated me! Of course, I eventually got therapy and learned that I was literally telling myself two lies: that I wasn't good enough to be anyone's friend and that everyone hated me on sight. I made myself needlessly miserable with this thinking, and once I learned to stop doing it, my life and relationships vastly improved.

In marriage, having this self-esteem disability will likely cause you to make incorrect, negative assumptions about your spouse and others you have relationships with. I urge you to turn this sad situation around, come to terms with it, and accept and learn to value yourself.

Custody Calendar Examples

Traditional Custody Calendar (not 50-50)

SUN	MON	TUES	WEDS	THURS	FRI	SAT
					1	2
3	4	5	6	7	8	9
10	11	12	13	14	15	16
17	18	19	20	21	22	23
24	25	26	27	28	29	30
31						

Enhanced Custody Calendar (about 50-50)

SUN	MON	TUES	WEDS	THURS	FRI	SAT
					1	2
3	4	5	6	7	8	9
10	11	12	13	14	15	16
17	18	19	20	21	22	23
24	25	26	27	28	29	30
31						

7 Days on/7 Days off Custody Calendar

SUN	MON	TUES	WEDS	THURS	FRI	SAT
					1	2
3	4	5	6	7	8	9
10	11	12	13	14	15	16
17	18	19	20	21	22	23
24	25	26	27	28	29	30
31						

Appendix II: Recommendations

Recommended Books

These are the books I recommend to my clients regularly for healing from trauma. I always tell them there is no pressure to read them; I don't give pop quizzes, but you will get out of the process what you put into it. The people who do read them come back with insight and questions. They begin to remember things they had long forgotten. That's when I know the wheels of healing are starting to turn.

Books by Pia Mellody

Childhood developmental trauma causes us to have emotional disabilities in certain areas of our lives. Yes, you have it; we all have it. Once you understand it, you can begin recovering from it. Pia Mellody created the model for treating trauma back in the 1970s and wrote her first book about it in the 1980s. *Facing*

Codependence explains what happened to us when we were young. It's eye-opening, to say the least. Forget the word *codependence* here; she is talking about trauma. Read it to understand how childhood trauma is related to and informs your current life. This is the way to get to the root of your issues and heal them once and for all.

Please do yourself the favor of reading Mellody's books to learn about childhood developmental trauma, or complex trauma as it is also known. You'll learn how the emotional disabilities from our trauma affect our relationships today. I was trained by Mellody in Scottsdale, Arizona, over three years between 2010 and 2013.

Facing Codependence: What It Is, Where It Comes from, How It Sabotages Our Lives by Pia Mellody with Andrea Wells Miller and J. Keith Miller:

This book is the one I use as the basic textbook for almost all the clients I work with. The first step in healing trauma is educational, and this book describes what childhood trauma is, how it happens, the emotional disabilities we take on as a result, and how they trickle down into our relationships. I've seen hundreds of clients become slack-jawed after starting the book and realizing what happened to them. It's life-changing and a fantastic first step in dealing with childhood wounds.

The Intimacy Factor: The Ground Rules to Overcoming the Obstacles to Truth, Respect, and Lasting Love by Pia Mellody and Lawrence Freundlich:

The disabilities we attain while children affect us in our relationships moving forward. This book explains that and also begins the conversation about what to do about it.

Breaking Free: A Recovery Workbook for Facing Codependence by Pia Mellody with Andrea Wells Miller:

A wonderful workbook based on the same expensive techniques used at the Meadows Behavioral Health Center in Wickenburg, Arizona. This is the healing part.

Books by John Bradshaw

After my training with Pia Mellody, I became fascinated with the subject of toxic shame and how crucial understanding it is to unlocking most of the issues people present with. As I studied it more, I discovered the work of the late John Bradshaw, who was a pioneer in the self-help and trauma field. Reading his books took me on a deep dive of understanding presented so tenderly that I felt I had a gentle hand on my shoulder, leading me to healing.

Healing the Shame That Binds You by John Bradshaw:

Bradshaw is influenced by Pia Mellody, but in his book not only does he explain the trauma dynamic in great detail, and differently from Mellody, he offers practical tools for healing and dealing with it. He clearly feels great tenderness toward those of us with childhood trauma, and that is healing in itself.

Homecoming: Reclaiming and Championing Your Inner Child by John Bradshaw:

Like it or not, we all have a wounded little girl or boy that sits beside us at all times. It is vital to identify this part of ourselves and learn how to take care of them when they need our assistance and care, such as when they feel a threat or feel wounded or hurt. This sounds silly to some, but I have never had a client who didn't feel more settled and calmer after learning this skill. I use it all the time.

Bradshaw On: The Family: A New Way of Creating Solid Self-Esteem by John Bradshaw:

Self-esteem is vital to healthy relationships, and here Bradshaw shows us the patterns that families engage in, whether to intentionally harm us or not, and the destructive effects that impair our ability to esteem ourselves in a healthy way. His message is to heal yourself to heal the world.

Book on Healing Your Wounded Child

Healing the Child Within: Discovery and Recovery for Adult Children of Dysfunctional Families by Charles Whitfield:

I found Dr. Charles Whitfield's work long before becoming a therapist. Today, this book, which teaches us how to nurture the lost child within, remains a classic in trauma recovery.

Book on Love Addiction

You may or may not be working on this issue in your therapy. If you suspect that you will or are told you may have this issue, this is the book I recommend.

Facing Love Addiction: Giving Yourself the Power to Change the Way You Love by Pia Mellody with Andrea Wells Miller and J. Keith Miller:

This book is eye-opening to my clients who are locked in the most common pattern of love addiction, which is when a love addict is anxious-attached and their partner is avoidant-attached. The love addict pursues the avoidant, finally gives up, and only then does the avoidant return to the love addict to woo and seduce them back into the relationship, only to become avoidant again. Mellody explains the different patterns and tells us how to break the pattern and learn healthy relating.

Books on Somatic Experiencing Therapy

I am a somatic experiencing practitioner (SEP). This means I was trained extensively over three years to learn an extremely powerful method for releasing trauma. Every one of us has stored-up trauma—thousands of wounds, some we remember, many we don't. If you see an SEP, they may use touch—among other things—to help you release trauma. There is a lot to know, but the following workbook has an enormous amount of information about becoming emotionally healthy with yourself by becoming self-aware and doing various forms of healing therapy on yourself. I use almost all the techniques discussed in this book myself and highly recommend it.

The Somatic Therapy Handbook: Self-Soothing Techniques for Healing Trauma, Enhancing the Mind-Body Connection, and Stress Relief by Cher Hampton:

We all know babies use various things to soothe themselves—blankies, pacifiers, dolls, stuffed animals, and more. Did it ever occur to anyone that adults need to learn how to self-soothe, too, when their inner child is feeling vulnerable or lost? This is never truer than in a marriage crisis. This workbook shows readers how their thoughts manifest in their body and how to manage this and soothe themselves through easy but powerful exercises.

The Somatic Experiencing Workbook: Your Companion with Tools and Exercises for Self-Discovery, Trauma Recovery, and Mastering the Mind-Body Connection by Cher Hampton:

I frequently implore clients to become more self-aware or tuned into themselves. How else can a person practice self-care and do the daily tweaking we all need to stay calm and content? This workbook teaches us self-discovery, trauma recovery, and mastering the mind-body connection.

Books on Getting Healthy at Your Core

The Power of Now: A Guide to Spiritual Enlightenment by Eckhart Tolle:

This book helped me rid myself of my ego that led me to terrible decisions and the nasty negative voice in my head. If you want relief from this, I can't recommend any book more highly.

The Four Agreements: A Practical Guide to Personal Freedom by Don Miguel Ruiz:

I often tell clients that if they read Ruiz's books and follow what he says, their lives will change so much in a good way that in therapy we will only need to tie up some loose ends. I sincerely mean that. His books are short, beautifully written, and power packed with rich, profound concepts.

Books on Marriage and Relationships

Fierce Intimacy by Terry Real (audiobook only):

I am also Terry Real–trained. Terry Real and I have something in common, too: We are both Pia Mellody–trained. Real developed a model of therapy for couples and relationships based on Mellody's model. This is the best way for couples to springboard themselves into awareness about how individuals should conduct themselves in relationships. I highly, highly recommend that every couple listen to this book.

The New Rules of Marriage: What You Need to Know to Make Love Work by Terry Real:

After studying trauma under Mellody, Real then created a theory of helping marriages using her guidelines—genius. This book contains his guidelines and shows couples how healthy relationships work. He tells it like it is. I love it.

Us: Getting Past You and Me to Build a More Loving Relationship by Terry Real:

A lot of people don't realize that childhood trauma creates emotional disabilities that will ultimately show up in our relationships. In this book, Real talks about being relational and what that means.

Mastery of Love: A Practical Guide to the Art of Relationship: A Toltec Wisdom Book by Don Miguel Ruiz:

More of his amazing work but addressing relationships.

Hold Me Tight: Seven Conversations for a Lifetime of Love by Susan Johnson:

The late Susan Johnson was a respected marriage and family therapist who developed the concept of emotionally focused therapy, which is built around the idea that most relationship issues center around attachment issues. She may well be correct. Her work is powerful and worth learning about.

The 5 Love Languages: The Secret to Love That Lasts by Gary Chapman:

A classic must-read for all couples.

Books for the Leaning-In Partner

Divorce Remedy: The Proven 7-Step Program for Saving Your Marriage by Michelle Weiner Davis:

I recommend this book for Leaning-In partners as it reiterates the points I underline about how a Leaning-In partner should conduct themselves that will give them the best shot at saving their marriage.

The Somatic Therapy Handbook: Self-Soothing Techniques for Healing Trauma, Enhancing the Mind-Body Connection, and Stress Relief by Cher Hampton: (Listed previously.)

Book on Postdivorce

Crazy Time: Surviving Divorce and Building a New Life by Abigail Trafford:

This book is a classic and must-read for anyone licking their wounds after a divorce. Trafford shows us how to analyze what happened and why, an essential part of the postmortem understanding that leads to healing, and hopefully not repeating mistakes.

Books on Divorce and Children

Helping Your Kids Cope with Divorce the Sandcastles Way by M. Gary Neuman and Patricia Romanowski:

Written by two people who have years of experience helping families who divorced. They offer great, age-appropriate advice and therapeutic activities that parents can do with their children.

Helping Children Cope with Divorce by Edward Teyber:

It is not new, but it is a classic, and its advice still holds true. I have been recommending it for years.

Book for Women Wanting to Better Understand Men

It's a Guy Thing: An Owner's Manual for Women by David Deida:

Deida explains men to women. I love it.

Books on Infidelity

Here are some classics on the subject of infidelity that I recommend to my clients.

After the Affair, Third Edition: Healing the Pain and Rebuilding Trust When a Partner Has Been Unfaithful by Janis Abrams Spring:

Spring is a marriage and family therapist and became especially interested in this subject after her husband cheated on her.

How Can I Forgive You? The Courage to Forgive, the Freedom Not To by Janis Abrams Spring:

After an affair, the question becomes how to forgive, and what is forgiveness anyway? Spring delves into this intelligently and with the eye of a marriage and family therapist.

Not "Just Friends": Rebuilding Trust and Recovering Your Sanity After Infidelity by Shirley P. Glass:

Glass provides a step-by-step guide through the infidelity process. She discusses how to prevent it and how to recover and heal.

The State of Affairs: Rethinking Infidelity by Esther Perel:

Perel, a marriage therapist, presents a whole new perspective on how to process infidelity. Her ideas really got my attention and caused me to think deeply about the complicated phenomenon of cheating.

Books on Stepfamilies

If you are in or plan to be in a blended family, you must read these books.

Surviving and Thriving in Stepfamily Relationships: What Works and What Doesn't by Patricia L. Papernow:

I work with couples experiencing stepfamily issues all the time. To this day I have not met one of these families that has read or looked into how to do it in the healthiest possible way. Papernow has researched this subject for many years and presents great insight into what happens when two complete groups come together and form a family. This is a must-read for stepfamilies and those considering being part of a stepfamily.

The Stepfamily Handbook: From Dating, to Getting Serious, to Forming a Blended Family by Patricia Papernow and Karen Bonnell:

More from the great researcher Patricia Papernow. Provides essential guidance to parents who are dating and to those who are dating a parent.

Book on Communication Dynamics

Love More, Fight Less: A Relationship Workbook for Couples by Gina Senarighi, PhD:

They say relationships are work, and if you do the exercises in this book you will be doing some of that work. Couples complain about communication all the time. Whether you do this alone or with your partner, it will improve your communication if you apply it. Virtually everyone needs it.

Book on Cognitive Behavioral Therapy

CBT is a research-based, proven form of therapy based on changing your thinking, which leads to changes in your feelings. It's powerful and effective.

Retrain Your Brain: Cognitive Behavioral Therapy in 7 Weeks: A Workbook for Managing Depression and Anxiety by Seth J. Gillihan, PhD:

The way most think of and process information is inaccurate, and CBT is a fantastic way to correct that. Everyone can benefit from learning the basic tenets of CBT.

Recommendations for Men

Book on Depression

I Don't Want to Talk about It: Overcoming the Secret Legacy of Male Depression by Terry Real:

The best book I have read for male depression. So many of my male clients have benefited from this.

Books for Nice Guy Men and Male Pleasers

No More Mr. Nice Guy: A Proven Plan for Getting What You Want in Love, Sex, and Life by Robert Glover:

A must-read for male pleasers. My male clients often tell me it was like they were reading a book written especially for them. If you are a pleaser and you know it, read this.

The Integrated Man: A Handbook for the Recovering Nice Guy by Sidharth Agarwal:

A companion workbook for Glover's book.

The Way of the Superior Man: A Spiritual Guide to Mastering the Challenges of Women, Work, and Sexual Desire by David Deida:

This is a must-read for every man, and I think women benefit from reading it, too.

Hold On to Your N.U.T.S.: The Relationship Manual for Men by Wayne M. Levine:

Men often say they don't understand women, while most women believe they are easy to understand. (What about treating us like you love, adore, and value us on a regular basis do you not understand, guys?) Anyway, Levine talks about this and about how women appreciate men who are strong as opposed to wimps and underlines that there is a way to give a woman what she needs while also maintaining yourself.

Recomendations for Women

Book for Female Pleasers

The Disease to Please: Curing the People-Pleasing Syndrome by Harriet B. Braiker, PhD:

Some clients brag to me that they are pleasers, showing that they have no awareness about how toxic this dynamic is. Pleasing is a persona we hide behind to win approval, it is exhausting, and it doesn't work. Learn how to end this madness once and for all. Braiker explains the dynamic and shows you how to recover from it.

Book for Female Love Addicts and Those with an Insatiable Need for Sex and Love

Mother Hunger: How Adult Daughters Can Understand and Heal from Lost Nurturance, Protection, and Guidance by Kelly McDaniel:

Written by my former neighbor and classmate, it's a must-read for anxious-attached and love-addicted women. So tenderly presented.

Other Personal Improvement Recommendations

Healing at Your Core—Workshops, Health Centers, and Books

Part of becoming relational, which means being healthy in a give-and-take relationship, is peeling away old layers of dysfunctional beliefs and behaviors and becoming your authentic self.

A few years ago, I attended a Meet the Masters workshop in New York City hosted by the Meadows Behavioral Health Center, where Pia Mellody created her trauma treatment model decades ago. The "masters" were some of the world's top trauma experts, all of them published authors. One of the speakers, psychiatrist Shelley Uram, author of *Essential Living: A Guide to Having Happiness and Peace by Reclaiming Your Essential Self*, gave a quiet but powerful talk about the importance of becoming your authentic self. I bought her book, read it, and was pleased to find numerous resources and a framework to help people heal their trauma and become their essential selves, so I checked them out. Uram says she has benefited from them herself, and I highly recommend her path, though I have edited the list:

1. Learn Pia Mellody's model for childhood developmental trauma. (See Mellody's books listed previously.)

2. Do "the work." I am grateful I found the work of Byron Katie, all thanks to Uram. I highly recommend you check out her work, specifically *Loving What Is: Four Questions That Can Change Your Life; The Revolutionary Process Called "The Work."*

3. Explore *The Sedona Method: Your Key to Lasting Happiness, Success, Peace and Emotional Well-Being* by Hale Dwoskin. Described as a simple, easy-to-learn method for letting go of unwanted and limiting thoughts and emotions in the moment.

4. Attend twelve-step programs. For all of us who have been living hidden behind a false persona, as I did for many years as a pleaser, this is not about substance abuse, though it applies to that, too. Many of us cope with addictions such as overachieving, perfectionism, work, shopping, television, tobacco, the Internet, obsessing, and more.

I have two more to add to Mellody's list. If every person could afford to go through the Meadows Behavioral Health Center's program, it would be a great thing, but it is very expensive, and the stay is more than thirty days. There are other ways to overhaul your mental and emotional health, some sponsored by the Meadows, such as their Survivor's Workshops and Couple's Repair and Reset Workshops, which are attended in one-week bites. Still, last I checked, they were in the range of $4,000 for an individual and $6,000 for a couple.

Thankfully, there is also a more affordable option: the Green Shoe Foundation in Guthrie, Oklahoma, founded in 2015 by Chad Richison. Based on Mellody's work, this is a five-day intensive focusing on childhood developmental trauma.

The Green Shoe Foundation requires a small deposit to make a reservation and refunds it when you complete the program.

The Omega Institute for Holistic Studies

The Omega Institute offers cutting-edge workshops in person and online, presenting many subjects including emotional healing, meditation, sparking creativity, and more. It's not unusual to find world authorities presenting the workshops. I highly recommend it.

Bibliography

Ahrons, C. R. (1994). *The good divorce: Keeping your family together when your marriage comes apart.* HarperCollins.

Al-Anon Family Groups. (n.d.) *Al-Anon's three Cs—I didn't cause it, I can't control it, and I can't cure it—removed the blame.* Al-Anon Family Groups. https://al-anon.org/blog/al-anons-three-cs/

American Association for Marriage and Family Therapy. (n.d.). *Infidelity.* AAMFT. https://aamft.org/Consumer_Updates/Infidelity.aspx?WebsiteKey=8e8c9bd6-0b71-4cd1-a5ab-013b5f855b01

American Bar Association. (2018, July). *Judges love collaborative law here's why.* https://www.americanbar.org/news/abanews/publications/youraba/2018/july-2018/neither-mediators-nor-negotiators—collaborative-lawyers-emphasi/

American Psychiatric Association. (2022). *Diagnostic and statistical manual of mental disorders (DSM-5-TR).* American Psychiatric Association.

Bancroft, L. (2003). *Why does he do that? Inside the minds of angry and controlling men.* Berkley Books.

Bieber, C. (2024, January 8). *Revealing divorce statistics in 2024.* Forbes Advisor. https://www.forbes.com/advisor/legal/divorce/divorce-statistics/

Bonnell, K., & Papernow, P. (2020). *The stepfamily handbook: From dating, to getting serious, to forming a "blended family."* CreateSpace Independent Publishing Platform.

Bowlby, J. (1969). *Attachment and loss,* Vol. 1: *Attachment.* Basic Books.

Bretherton, I. (n.d.). *The origins of attachment theory: John Bowlby and Mary Ainsworth.* http://www.psychology.sunysb.edu/attachment/online/inge_origins.pdf

Casablanca, S. S. (2021, February 11). *What is a personality disorder? Symptom, clusters, and types.* PsychCentral. Retrieved February 26, 2024, from http://psychcentral.com/personality/

Centers for Disease Control and Prevention. (2020, October 19). *Brain health.* Centers for Disease Control and Prevention. Retrieved March 29, 2024, from https://www.cdc.gov/marijuana/health-effects /brain-health.html

Chapman, G. D. (2010). *The five love languages: How to express heartfelt commitment to your mate.* Walker Large Print Books. Christian Large Print.

Cleveland Clinic. (n.d.). *Obsessive-compulsive personality disorder* (OCPD). Cleveland Clinic. https://my.clevelandclinic.org/health/diseases/24526-obsessive-compulsive-personality-disorder-ocpd

Doherty, W., & Harris, S. M. (2017). *Helping couples on the brink of divorce: Discernment counseling for troubled relationships.* American Psychological Association.

Duluth Abuse Intervention Programs. (n.d.). *What is the Duluth model?* https://www.theduluthmodel.org/

Fife, S. T., Gossner, J. D., Theobald, A., Allen, E., Rivero, A., & Koehl, H. (2023). Couple healing from infidelity: A grounded theory study. *Journal of Social and Personal Relationships,40*(12), 3882–3905. https://doi .org/10.1177/02654075231177874

Glass, S. P. (2004). *Not "just friends": Rebuilding trust and recovering your sanity after infidelity.* Free Press.

Gottman, J. M. (1994). *What predicts divorce? The relationship between marital processes and marital outcomes.* Lawrence Erlbaum Associates.

Gottman, J., & Silver. N. (1999). *The seven principles for making marriage work.* Crown Publishing.

Gravotta, L. (2013, February 12). Be mine forever: Oxytocin may help build long-lasting love. *Scientific American.* https://www.scientificamerican.com /article/be-mine-forever-oxytocin/

Greenberger, D., & Pedesky, C. A. (1995). *Mind over mood: Change how you feel by changing the way you think.* Guilford Press.

Hawkins, A. J., Fackrell, T. A., & Harris, S. M. (2013). *Should I try to work it out? A guidebook for individuals and couples at the crossroads of divorce.* CreateSpace.

Holmes, T. H., & Rahe, T. H. (1967). The social readjustment rating scale. *Journal of Psychosomatic Research, 11*(2), 213–218. https://doi.org/10.1016/0022-3999(67)90010-4

hooks, bell. (2004). *The will to change: Men, masculinity, and love.* Washington Square Press.

Hooper, J. (1999, April 29). Infidelity comes out of the closet. *New York Times.* Retrieved March 31, 2024, from https://www.nytimes.com/1999/04/29/garden/infidelity-comes-out-of-the-closet.html

Johnson, S. (2008). *Hold me tight: Seven conversations for a lifetime.* Little, Brown, Spark.

Kitson, G. (1992). *Portrait of divorce: Adjustment to marital breakdown.* Guilford Press.

Kreider, R. M. (2005, August). *Remarriage in the United States.* U.S. Census Bureau. https://www.census.gov/content/dam/Census/library/working-papers/2006/demo/us-remarriage-poster.pdf

Lee, R. (2017). Mistrustful and misunderstood: A review of paranoid personality disorder. *Current Behavioral Neuroscience Reports, 4*(2), 151–165. https://doi.org/10.1007/s40473-017-0116-7

Lenzenweger, M. F., Lane, M. C., Loranger, A. W., & Kessler, R. C. (2007). DSM-IV personality disorders in the National Comorbidity Survey Replication. *Biological Psychiatry, 62*(6), 553–564. https://doi.org/10.1016/j.biopsych.2006.09.019

Levine, A., & Heller, R. (2012). *Attached: The new science of adult attachment and how it can help you find—and keep—love.* TarcherPerigee.

Lindner, J. (December 23, 2023). *Marriage after infidelity statistics [fresh research].* Gitnux. https://gitnux.org/marriage-after-infidelity-statistics/

Looti, M. (n.d.). *Narcissistic personality disorder.* Psychological Scales.

Lyne, A. (Director). (1987). *Fatal attraction.* [Film]. Stanley Jaffe & Sherry Lansing.

Marín, R. A., Christensen, A., & Atkins, D. C. (2014). Infidelity and behavioral couple therapy: Relationship outcomes over 5 years following therapy. *Couple and Family Psychology: Research and Practice, 1*(3), 1–12. chrome-extension://efaidnbmnnnibpcajpcglclefindmkaj/https:/www.apa.org/pubs/journals/features/cfp-0000012.pdf

Mason, P. T. T., & Kreger, R. (2010). *Stop walking on eggshells: Taking your life back when someone you care about has borderline personality disorder.* New Harbinger.

Mellody, P. (2003). *Facing love addiction: Giving yourself the power to change the way you love.* HarperSanFrancisco.

Mellody, P., Miller, A. W., & Miller, K. (1989). *Facing codependence: What it is, where it comes from, how it sabotages our lives.* HarperSanFrancisco.

Murphy, H. (2019, May 28). Kanye West gets candid about his bipolar diagnosis, says at one point he had to be handcuffed. *People.* https://people.com/music/kanye-west-opens-up-about-bipolar-diagnosis-episode-handcuffed/

National Academies of Sciences, Engineering, and Medicine, Health and Medicine Division, Board on Population Health and Public Health Practice, & Committee on the Health Effects of Marijuana: An Evidence Review and Research Agenda. (2017). *The health effects of cannabis and cannabinoids: The current state of evidence and recommendations for research.* National Academies Press (US).

National Domestic Violence Hotline. (n.d.). *Is change possible in an abuser?* National Domestic Violence Hotline. Retrieved March 29, 2024, from https://www.thehotline.org/resources/is-change-possible-in-an-abuser/

National Institute on Drug Abuse. (2019, May 21). *Cannabis dependence is associated with changes in neural circuitry that may contribute to psychopathology.* Retrieved July 12, 2022, from https://nida.nih.gov/news-events/nida-notes/2019/05/cannabis-dependence-associated-changes-in-neural-circuitry-may-contribute-to-psychopathology

National Institute of Mental Health. (2007, October 18). *National survey tracks prevalence of personality disorders in U.S. population.* U.S. Department of Health and Human Services, National Institutes of Health. https://www.nimh.nih.gov/news/science-news/2007/national-survey-tracks-prevalence-of-personality-disorders-in-us-population

Neuman, G. M., & Romanowski, P. (1999). *Helping your kids cope with divorce the sandcastles way: Based on the program mandated in family courts nationwide.* Random House.

Padesky, C. A., & Greenberger, D. (1995). *Clinician's guide to "mind over mood."* Guilford Press.

Pam, A., & Pearson, P. (1998). *Splitting up: Enmeshment and estrangement in the process of divorce.* Guilford Press.

Papernow, P. L. (2013). *Surviving and thriving in stepfamily relationships: What works and what doesn't.* Routledge/Taylor & Francis.

Papernow, P. L. (2018). Clinical guidelines for working with stepfamilies: What family, couple, individual, and child therapists need to know. *Family Process, 57*(1), 12–68. https://doi.org/10.1111/famp.12321

Paul, M. (2012, September 19). Your memory is like the telephone game. *Northwestern*. Retrieved April 11, 2024, from https://news.northwestern.edu/stories/2012/09/your-memory-is-like-the-telephone-game/

Pearce, K. (2022, October 1). Understanding brain waves: Beta, alpha, theta, delta + gamma. *DIY Genius*. Retrieved March 29, 2024, from https://www.diygenius.com/the-5-types-of-brain-waves/

Peck, M. S. (1978). *The road less traveled: A new psychology of love, traditional values, and spiritual growth*. Simon & Schuster.

Perel, E. (2017). *The state of affairs: Rethinking infidelity*. Kindle. https://www.amazon.com/State-Affairs-Rethinking-Infidelity-ebook/dp/B01N5PY4ZN/

Perry, F. (Director). (1981). *Mommie dearest* [Film]. Paramount Pictures.

Phelan, P. (1986). The process of incest: Biological father and stepfather families. *Child Abuse & Neglect, 10*(4), 531–539. https://doi.org/10.1016/0145-2134(86)90058-X

Pino, C. J. (1980). Research and clinical application of marital autopsy in divorce counseling. *Journal of Divorce, 1*(4), 31–48.

Powell, A. (2018, February 13). When love and science double date. *Harvard Gazette*. https://news.harvard.edu/gazette/story/2018/02/scientists-find-a-few-surprises-in-their-study-of-love/

Raffel, L. (1999). *Should I stay or go? How controlled separation (CS) can save your marriage*. Contemporary Books.

Real, T. (1998). *I don't want to talk about it: Overcoming the secret legacy of male depression*. Scribner.

Recovery Connection. (n.d.). Explaining the cycle of addiction. *Recover Connection*. http://www.recoveryconnection.org/cycle-of-addiction/

Rice, J., & Rice, D. (1986). *Living through divorce: A developmental approach to divorce therapy*. Guilford Press.

Salam, M. (2019, January 22). What is toxic masculinity? *New York Times*. https://www.nytimes.com/2019/01/22/us/toxic-masculinity.html

Sansone, R. A., & Sansone, L. A. (2011). Personality disorders: A nation-based perspective on prevalence. *Innovations in Clinical Neuroscience, 8*(4), 13–18.

Schneiderman, I., Zagoory-Sharon, O., Leckman, J. F., & Feldman, R. (2012). Oxytocin during the initial stages of romantic attachment: Relations to couples' interactive reciprocity. *Psychoneuroendocrinology, 37*(8), 1277–1285.

Soloman, S. D., & Teagno, L. J. (2018, August 17). Frequently asked questions about infidelity. *DivorceMag.* Retrieved March 31, 2024, from https://www.divorcemag.com/articles/frequently-asked-questions-about-infidelity

Somatic Experiencing International. (n.d.). *Somatic Experiencing (Landing Page).* Retrieved June 1, 2024, from https://traumahealing.org/

Spring, J. A. (2020). *After the affair: Healing the pain and rebuilding trust when a partner has been unfaithful.* (3rd ed.). Harper Paperbacks.

Squires, S. (1985, June 14). Effects of divorce last indefinitely: Study shows how family members fare 10 years later. *Los Angeles Times.* Retrieved May 5, 2024, from https://www.latimes.com/archives/la-xpm-1985-06-14-vw-2440-story.html

Tennov, D. (1984). *Love and limerence: The experience of being in love.* Stein and Day.

Teyber, E. (1992). *Helping Children Cope with Divorce.* Lexington Books.

Wallerstein, J. S., Lewis, J., & Blakeslee, S. (2000). *The unexpected legacy of divorce: A 25-year landmark study* (1st edition.). Hyperion.

Wanck, B. (2019). *Mind Easing: The three-layered healing plan for anxiety.* HCI Books.

Watson, P. C. (1960). On the failure to eliminate hypotheses in a conceptual task. *The Quarterly Journal of Experimental Psychology,* 12, 129–140.

Weiss, R. (1975). *Marital separation.* Basic Books.

Wolfe, L. (1975). *Playing around: Women and extramarital sex.* New York: Signet.

Woo, E. (2013). Judith Wallerstein dies at 90; psychologist was described by Time magazine as the "godmother of the backlash against divorce" *Los Angeles Times.* Retrieved May 5, 2024, from https://www.latimes.com/local/obituaries/la-xpm-2012-jul-04-la-me-judith-wallerstein-20120703-story.html

Wyns, A., Hendrix, J., Lahousse, A., De Bruyne, E., Nijs, J., Godderis, L., & Polli, A. (2023). The biology of stress intolerance in patients with chronic pain—state of the art and future directions. *Journal of Clinical Medicine,* 12(6), 2245. https://doi.org/10.3390/jcm12062245.

Yellen, J. L. (2020). The history of women's work and wages and how it has created success for us all. Retrieved June 1, 2024, from https://www.brookings.edu/articles/the-history-of-womens-work-and-wages-and-how-it-has-created-success-for-us-all/

Acknowledgments

The seeds of this book began during my marriage crisis back in 1992 when I was lost, confused, and felt completely unsupported by the marriage therapist we went to for help. My gut told me there was something that could be done beyond what we'd tried, but he said if I wasn't motivated to work on the marriage at the time, there was nothing else he could do. We walked away, managed our marriage crisis ourselves, and ended up divorced too soon, changing multiple lives.

I still don't know if our marriage could have been saved, but I think there were endless possibilities with the right help. What haunts me is we weren't informed of the possibilities. I want to acknowledge that situation for igniting my interest in finding answers, and it's my hope that something good will come from it.

Our children paid for our ignorance, and I want to share with them that I know we could have done better, and I am so sorry for our many bad decisions. I dedicate this book to you, Benjamin and Casey, not just because of the price you paid but because when I went back to school and left you several evenings a week and spent weekends studying or disappearing to the library for years, you always supported me and encouraged me to keep going.

My husband, John, has sacrificed the quality time he cherishes so I could write content for my blog and so I could research and write this book. He has never complained and has rooted for me all the way, believing that the dream of seeing this book published really would come true. Thank you, Johnny, for being solid and accepting; for your patience, love, and support; and for showing me that what I learned in my studies about how to have a healthy relationship is true, that I could have a wonderful, life-lasting marriage if I could be healthy with myself and choose the right person for me, and that person is you.

The work in this book is sitting on the shoulders of numerous researchers and scholars over many decades who have studied mental and emotional health, marriage, separation, divorce, postdivorce, children of divorce, remarriage, and stepfamilies, and I thank them for the knowledge and information we have gained from that. Here's to hoping that there is even more research coming on the dynamic so we can better understand how to help people.

A lot of people tell me they'd like to write a nonfiction book, and when they do, I wonder if they have any idea about what it takes. Knowing about that now, it's a wonder any book gets published. To that end, there is so much to know and navigate from start to finish, and I had a person who was an invaluable tour guide; I can safely say this project would not exist without the help of my editor, Candace Johnson. She hasn't just guided me to organize this work and make it all it could be but has provided insight, encouragement, emotional support, and enthusiasm for the subject and how we were presenting it. In the end, she is the one who pushed it over the finish line and got it to HCI Books, our publisher. I am forever grateful for the huge role you've played in my life, Candace.

Divorce, marital bad times, and separation are subjects that agents and publishers tend to run from, which is why it is so difficult to find good information on the subject. I have wanted to right that wrong for a long time. HCI Books has stepped up to the plate, and it is my hope that together, we will change the culture of marriage crisis, separation, divorce, and postdivorce behavior around the world. I am grateful that they are willing to put this work out there. I would like to thank everyone at HCI Books, and especially my editor, Darcie Abbene, who sees things and makes them better.

Finally, thanks also to my brave and wonderful clients who have trusted in me as I helped them through their individual and family issues, and who have taught me so much about people and relationships.

About the Author

Becky Whetstone, PhD, is a licensed professional counselor and licensed marriage and family therapist (LMFT) in Arkansas, an LMFT in Texas, and a marriage crisis expert. Becky earned a PhD in marriage and family therapy from St. Mary's University in San Antonio, Texas. She has trained with Pia Mellody, author of *Facing Codependence*; with Terry Real, author of *Us* and the *New Rules of Marriage*; and is a certified hypnotherapist and somatic experiencing practitioner.

When a story hits the news cycle about anything related to a rocky marriage, Becky is often the go-to source for comments. She has written for the Huffington Post online, *Newsweek* and *Family Therapy* magazines and writes a regular blog, which she posts on Medium.com with links on Facebook, Twitter, Reddit, Pinterest, and LinkedIn. She creates and posts occasional videos about marriage and relationships on YouTube and TikTok.

A native of Arkansas, Becky graduated in 1980 from George Washington University in Washington, DC, with a BA in journalism.

In 1984, she moved to San Antonio, Texas, and after a period of being a stay-at-home mom and later a journalist for the *San Antonio Express-News*, she entered St. Mary's doctoral program in 2001 and graduated with a PhD in 2006. Her dissertation research was an investigation of how individuals in long-term marriages (ten years or longer) decide to divorce. The information she learned during this extensive research project changed how Becky viewed courtship, marriage, and divorce and made her even more passionate about helping people create and maintain healthy relationships. In the spring of 2006, she opened her private practice in San Antonio, where she worked with individuals, couples, and families. In December 2011, Becky returned to Arkansas to be near family, and she opened her Little Rock practice in January 2012. Today, Becky has a private telehealth practice and is a sought-after marriage and family therapist and life coach for clients around the United States, Canada, and other parts of the world.

In the early 1990s, Becky plunged into journalism when she interned at the San Antonio CBS-TV affiliate KENS as a medical reporter. Soon after, she began freelancing for the San Antonio Express-News. She was hired there in 1994 as a features writer, and in 1996 she began writing about relationships in a column that ran in the SA Life section. Interested in relationships and psychological issues for as long as she could remember, Becky's dream since childhood had been to replace famed advice columnist Ann Landers when the writer eventually retired.

While writing the column, Becky created an area-wide phenomenon called the Singles Revolution, dedicated to professional singles who were seeking healthy relationships. She convened get-togethers that backed up traffic in San Antonio's Quarry Market and facilitated

a singles volunteer force that cleaned up and remodeled a deteriorating playground at a local San Antonio elementary school. While
Becky spoke to singles about how to have a better life, she also wrote
about her own life as a single mother and about the lives of many
South Texans—married, gay, families, stepfamilies, and seniors—
who wanted to have better relationships with themselves and others.
Only now, looking back, Becky believes her column was the first of
the *Sex and the City* genre that became so popular almost ten years
later.

Becky's areas of interest are personal growth, trauma, how humans select mates, the courtship process, the agony of the divorce
decision, grief, and divorce recovery.